BAPTISTS AT

The Theology of the Lord's Supper
amongst English Baptists
in the Nineteenth Century

Michael J. Walker

BAPTIST HISTORICAL SOCIETY
1992

ISBN 0 903166 16 X

© 1992 (in this version) The Baptist Historical Society

All rights reserved. No part of this publication may be reproduced, stored in a retrieval system, or transmitted in any form or by any means, electronic, mechanical, photo-copying, recording or otherwise, without the prior permission of the Baptist Historical Society.

Registered address:

Baptist Historical Society, Baptist House,
PO Box 44, Didcot, OX11 8RT

Cover design by Jo Small
Printed by Tyndale Press, Lowestoft, Ltd

CONTENTS

Michael John Walker - An Appreciation by Dr David S. Russell   vii

Acknowledgements   xi

Chapter One   The Doctrine of the Lord's Supper   1

A. The Zwinglian Norm   3
B. Sacramental Explorations   8
C. The Lord's Supper in Nineteenth Century
Baptist Hymnody   17

Chapter Two   The Communion Controversy   32

A. Background of the Dispute   32
B. The Hall-Kinghorn Debate   42
C. The Unity of the Church: Robert Hall   45
    i. The Lord's Supper as a sign of the church's unity   45
    ii. The precedence of faith over symbol   55
    iii. The historical factor in the communion debate   62
D. The Integrity of the Church: Joseph Kinghorn   65
    i. Only those properly baptized may be Admitted to the Lord's Supper   65
    ii. The church is weakened by mixed communion   69
E. Baptists and Unity   70
F. Baptists and Schism   76
G. Summary   78

Chapter Three   Baptists and the Catholic Revival   84

A. The Baptist Response to the Catholic Revival   85
B. The Lord's Supper   91
    i. The presence of Christ in the eucharist   91
    ii. The exegesis of the eucharistic texts   97
        a) The eucharistic narratives in the Gospels   98
        b) The Corinthian eucharistic passages   100
        c) The eucharistic teaching of John 6   100
    iii. The place of Christian tradition   105
    iv. The Lord's Supper as a means of grace   110
    v. The conflict between 'spiritual' and 'ceremonial' religion   115

Chapter Four	**Order and Discipline at the Lord's Table**	121

A. The Presidency of the Lord's Table 121
   i. A question of right order 123
   ii. The laying on of hands 126
   iii. Ordination by ordained ministers 130
   iv. The presidency of the Lord's table 131
   v. Conclusion 136
B. The Lord's Supper in Sundry Times and Places 138
   i. The Lord's Supper and the sick 138
   ii. The Lord's Supper and Association and
      Assembly Meetings 141
   iii. Conclusion 143
C. Weekly Celebration of the Lord's Supper 143
D. The Use of Unfermented Wine in the Lord's Supper 147
E. The Lord's Supper and Church Discipline 157

Chapter Five	**The Lord's Supper and Two Baptist Preachers**	164

A. The Lord's Supper in the Preaching of
Charles Haddon Spurgeon 165
   i. The case against catholicism 167
   ii. The centrality of the atonement 170
   iii. The presence of Christ 174
   iv. The relationship of the material and
      the spiritual 180
B. The Lord's Supper in the Thought of John Clifford 182
C. Spurgeon and Clifford: Heirs of Two Traditions 192

Chapter Six	**A Baptist Theology of the Lord's Supper?**	197

Books mentioned in text 206
Journals mentioned in text; Biblical references 207
Index 208

MICHAEL JOHN WALKER

Born in 1932 of English and Welsh parents, Michael Walker spent his early years in London where he came to faith in Christ at Camrose Baptist Church, Edgware. Following national service with the Royal Air Force, he entered Rawdon College, Leeds, in 1954 and four years later gained an external Honours BD degree of London University, to which he subsequently added the degrees of MTh (1963) and PhD (1986).

On leaving College he served as minister of Baptist churches in Grove Road, Southgate (1958-64), Dublin Street, Edinburgh (1964-67), Highams Park, Walthamstow (1967-71) and Elm Road, Beckenham (1971-81). Thereafter he was appointed lecturer in Christian Doctrine in the Cardiff Collegiate Faculty of Theology in the University of Wales and the South Wales Baptist College and served in this capacity until his untimely death from cancer in 1989.

MICHAEL JOHN WALKER

An Appreciation

The young student who entered Rawdon College in 1954 was shy and retiring, diffident and unpretentious. He wore a gloomy air and spoke with a slight stammer that concealed a remarkable eloquence of speech. His student days were precious to him, as he would often testify. There, in a new way, he learned to laugh and think and pray - a great trilogy! He owed much to his fellow-students who, without their knowing it, helped to cultivate in him those qualities of humanity and spirituality that were to characterize his life-long ministry. He owed much too to his tutors: one, an iconoclast, a breaker-down of false images, who could not bear the sight or smell of 'sacred cows', especially when their lumbering gait impeded the traffic of truth; another, whose scholarly insights and ecumenical vision made an indelible impression on him; and yet another, whose careful scholarship and fine preaching had their desired effect. I myself was privileged also to have a share in his teaching and readily acknowledge that in later years 'the teacher' became 'the taught'.

Both then and throughout his ministry he showed himself to be a complex individual. At times he seemed to be rather unsure of himself; and yet he had about him an air of unpretentious authority that confirmed others in their faith. There was something of the mystic about him and something of the monk; and yet he was a realist through and through. He was rational and objective in theological debate; and yet in personal relationships he could become emotionally involved to the point of mental anguish and tears. His head was often in the clouds; but his feet were planted firmly on the ground. His ministry was marked by sensitivity and spirituality; but his concern for others was unmistakably earthly - and even earthy - in its expression. He stood in awe before the greatness and the grace of God; but he was passionately concerned about a broken humanity - the homeless teenager, the bereaved parent, the cancer victim, the prostitute who walked the street. His mood was sober and sombre; but his guffaws of laughter filled the room. Words, written as well as spoken, were his tools, finely honed and deftly used; but he was himself a man of few words, preferring to sit in prayerful silence beside the bed of suffering or death.

Small wonder that his people remember him with affection as a faithful and sensitive pastor. No stranger himself to suffering and grief, he seemed somehow to absorb the pain and sorrow of others, making them his own, and then offering them as praise and prayer to God.

Most will remember him, however, for his preaching and his conduct of worship. Here is how the secretary of the church in Beckenham graphically described Michael's first visit there: 'I well remember his appearance in the pulpit - a dark, hunched, saturnine figure, gazing gloomily down the church. Yet when he rose to read the scriptures, the word was with fresh meaning and the voice had the clarity of a bell. The prayers were with power, were related to our needs and situation and commanded attention.' His sermons were brief and to the point and, almost invariably, memorable. His Bible studies and expositions of scripture were in great demand throughout the country and abroad and right across denominational boundaries. His impressive Bible studies delivered at the Baptist Assembly in Bradford in 1987 led to a much wider use of his gifts, not least through the Baptist Union Retreat Group movement which has enriched the whole denomination.

There can be no doubt that he was an eloquent preacher and gifted expositor. But his preaching was no easy oratory, no glib or facile speech, but born out of much thought and prayer. The preacher in the pulpit had been first the pastor in the home. He had the gift of getting alongside people and sitting where they sat. He did not set himself up as some kind of 'plaster saint', free from depression and doubt. In sharing the gospel he shared himself.

He approached his pulpit ministry with the utmost respect; he refused to indulge in 'pulpit trifling', but preached on big themes, going deep down into the very heart of the gospel. In both his preaching and his spoken and published prayers he recognized with wonder not only that God had become man, but also that man was created in God's own image and was destined to be changed into his glory.

In his conduct of worship Michael was deeply influenced by the liturgical renewal felt by Baptists and others in the 1960s and perhaps most markedly in the 1980s. It showed itself, *inter alia*, in a greater measure of participation by the congregation in worship and by the more central place given to the observance of the Lord's Supper which, in not a few churches, ceased to be 'tagged on' at the end of public worship, as had been the custom, but was now seen as integral to it. He took great care over the preparation of worship, bringing to it thought and imagination, variety and colour, word and symbol. He laid emphasis on observance of the Christian Year and used the gifts of others to help him plan special services such as the Three Hours Meditation on Good Friday and the midnight Communion Service to welcome Christmas and Easter Days. In such services he gloried in God's creation and in Christ's incarnation - his death, his resurrection and his ascension to God's right hand.

In all of this he stood for a form of Baptist 'high churchmanship' which disavowed sectarianism on the one hand, with its tendency to non-sacramental worship, and on the other hand looked to 'the coming Great Church' in which the sacraments, so often the cause of the Church's fragmentation, would become instead the symbol of its unity. To him baptism and the Lord's Supper were not simply 'ordinances', but sacraments in the observance of which, he would have argued, what we do is of much less significance than what God does.

As his doctoral thesis makes plain, he deeply regretted those influences in the nineteenth and early twentieth centuries which diverted Baptists from that 'high churchmanship' which, at an earlier date, had characterized their life and worship. Such devaluation of the sacraments represented a theological tradition that could claim neither the support of the Lutheran or Reformed Churches nor the consent of historical catholicism and could claim, only questionably, biblical justification. The object of the dissertation is an honest and able attempt to investigate the nature of that theology of the Lord's Supper held among English Baptists in the nineteenth century and the way in which it influenced Baptist thinking and practice in the century that followed.

Michael was an able theologian. But he was fully aware of the warning uttered by Søren Kierkegaard that 'to be a professor of theology is to have crucified Christ'. To claim to 'explain' God is a sign of overweening presumption. Conscious of this danger, Michael kept reminding himself that 'theology and prayer are inseparable'. God must be approached with a humble and contrite heart. He was a man of prayer whose 'spirituality' (a word not often used among Baptists) was obvious to all. This quality is clearly demonstrated in both his spoken and his written words and in his very bearing. It is demonstrated perhaps most clearly in his two books of prayers, *Hear me, Lord* and *For Everything a Season*, which illustrate, sometimes quite dramatically, that 'mystical realism' to which reference has been made, and in the last book he wrote, published just before he died, *The God of Our Journey*. For me, the reading of this book was a profoundly moving experience, disclosing as it did not only Michael's own heart but also the very heart of God himself.

But Michael would have been the first to say that any 'spirituality' he may have shown owed much, not just to the Baptist tradition in which he had grown up, but also to other Christian traditions, some of them altogether different from his own. But he was no ecclesiastical magpie, picking up at random attractive morsels from here and there, no mere dilettante, toying with different expressions of the faith. Just as he saw truth to be one, so he saw the Church to be one also. To a remarkable degree he was able to enter into the spiritual heritage of the Great Church without betraying that tradition to which he himself belonged.

That having been said, it has to be confessed that he was far from being a typical Baptist (if indeed such a being ever existed!). In his later years in particular he was deeply influenced by the Anglo-Catholic and the Roman Catholic traditions. He has pointed out that, in the eyes of some Baptists of the nineteenth century, to see the sacraments as in any way 'a means of grace' was 'to flirt dangerously with Catholicism'. There were no doubt some staunch Welsh Baptists who thought this way about Michael himself. He made no secret of his love of ritual and the expression of worship he found in churches of that ilk. Indeed, though faithfully preaching the gospel in Baptist chapels throughout the valleys of South Wales and a member of Llandaff Road Baptist Church, he was occasionally to be found on a 'free' Sunday worshipping in the nearby St Luke's Anglo-Catholic church where his presence and preaching was welcomed. His funeral service was held in St Luke's and in the crowded congregation there were no fewer than thirty priests, standing cheek-byjowl with Baptist worshippers. In the lectures he gave at the University, Roman Catholics, Anglicans, Presbyterians and Baptists rubbed shoulders with one another and listened together with rapt attention to his words of spiritual insight. His was no mere 'tolerance' of fellow-Christians within traditions different from his own. It was an honest and open attempt to seek, together with them, 'the unity of the Spirit in the bond of peace'. It must have been for him in some ways a painful experience as he pursued his spiritual pilgrimage along paths unfamiliar to many of his companions and friends.

Michael was a rare spirit for whom the search for truth and unity was one, for it grew out of his love for his Saviour and a devotion to that one Church which is Christ's Body for which he died.

David S. Russell

ACKNOWLEDGEMENTS

The text of the author's PhD dissertation, accepted by the University of London in 1986, is published by the Baptist Historical Society.

The Society is grateful to Mrs Alison Walker for making the text available for publication, to Dr David Russell, the author's principal at theological college, for writing the appreciation, to Dr David Bebbington of the University of Stirling for final editing, to the Revd Douglas Sparkes and Mrs Doris Sparkes for checking the quotations and references, and to Mrs Faith Bowers for preparing the script and producing the index.

Chapter One

THE DOCTRINE OF THE LORD'S SUPPER

The path followed by any theological journey is determined by the place from which it begins. Baptists did not begin with the Lord's Supper. Unlike Roman Catholics and many Anglicans they did not make it central either to their understanding of salvation or to their religious experience. They came to neither font nor table believing that there God's grace was channelled to them in the setting of a sacramental church served by a sacerdotal ministry. They did not believe that the bread and wine of the communion was a real feeding upon the ubiquitous body and blood of a Christ in whose nature true humanity shared in the attributes of divinity and divinity had surrendered itself to a true humanity, as did the Lutherans. They did not see themselves as a church both reformed and faithful to the ancient and catholic tradition of the church, as did the Anglicans. Their starting point was neither a sacramentally mediated grace, nor a sacramentally embodied word, nor an unbroken Christian tradition spanning the centuries. Lest one should be misled by the name by which they were happy to be known, they did not even begin with baptism. They began with the men and women whom, they believed, Christ had called to be his church on earth.

The early Baptists, who broke away first from the Church of England and then from the rest of the Puritan separatist movement, believed that they were establishing a church that was faithful to the teaching of the New Testament. Fundamental to that conviction was their belief that the church should consist of those only who had in the freely chosen, conscious assent of faith, surrendered their lives to the lordship of Jesus Christ. This led them to reject infant baptism which they held to be responsible for what they saw as the corrupt state of the church. A baptism administered, as they thought, indiscriminately to infants who were unable to distinguish their right hand from their left, let alone make a conscious and responsible assent of faith, created a 'mixed' community, composed of some who had regenerating faith and of others who did not. For Baptists faith was crucial. They had no argument with the great reformers on the central Protestant principle of justification by faith. They differed in the primacy they accorded to it and its consequences for their beliefs about the church and sacraments. If faith was central then the church should consist only of those who were capable of confessing faith. It followed that these and these alone were the proper recipients of the initiating ordinance of baptism. The rite was a recognition of what already existed, not a means of bringing it into being. Thus their view of faith, church and baptism formed a sequence, each step deriving from the one that preceded it. It was at the point of baptism and admission to the church that this single theological track began to divide and different emphases to compete for order of importance. At this stage the Lord's Supper was one competitor amongst others. It took its place amongst the calls to a devout and holy life, the struggle to reach a theocratic goal by democratic means in the newly emerged Church Meeting, and the problems that faced 'regenerate' Christians, separated from society by clearly defined ecclesial boundaries, but compelled to live in and come to terms with an 'unregenerate' and open world.

The derivative nature of the Lord's Supper in Baptist doctrine accounts for the absence of any major work by a Baptist on the subject, in either the nineteenth century or either of the two that preceded it. It did not share the place of honour that baptism held in Baptist thinking, being at a further remove from the heart-lands of faith. Baptists saw no reason to invest it with a theology in its own right, providing it with secure ground upon which it could stand amid the competing claims to priority of faith, church, baptism, holiness and life in the world. It was surrounded by beliefs that had the consistency of clay, capable of being moulded and shaped by the needs of successive decades and imprinted clearly with the enthusiasms or faintly with the uncertainties of any given generation of Baptists. The equivalent of only a fraction of the intellectual energy expended on baptism was devoted to it, except when Baptists felt compelled to defend what they said and did at the Lord's table in the light of what other Christians practised.

Their own practices were the cause of various debates amongst themselves. Questions of order were to recur throughout the nineteenth century, beginning with the anguished debate on open and closed communion, followed at different periods by disagreements on matters such as the presidency of the Lord's table, the frequency of communion and the use of unfermented wine. The chief challenge from beyond their own denominational boundaries came from the Catholic revival in the middle of the century. The Tractarian movement, followed by the Ritualist movement, combined with a national growth in the numbers of the Roman Catholic section of the population, brought about mainly by the immigration of Irish Catholic workers, and an aggressively pursued reassertion of Catholic dogma, particularly before and after the First Vatican Council, seemed to pose a threat to all Evangelicals, Anglican and Nonconformist alike. Along with the others, Baptists took up the challenge posed by resurgent Catholicism.

These debates were conducted in part through published work and, to a greater extent, in the newspapers and journals of the denomination of which, fortunately, there were many, compared with the pauper's rations of the twentieth century. In articles and editorials and, of especial significance, in letters written to the editors of the various journals, a picture of Baptist belief and practice emerges. If it be argued that the sort of people who write letters to editors are hardly representative of their fellows, it can be rejoined that they are at least as representative of grass-root attitudes as avant-garde theologians whose words are pored over in the belief that they represent the convictions of others than the writers themselves. From the outraged conservatives who felt that the Lord's Supper was being tampered with by the introduction of 'raisin water', to the bewildered country deacons dismayed by the rifts caused through the closed communion debate, to the bright, forward-looking people who failed to see what the fuss was about, given the relative unimportance of sacraments, we can glean a picture of a denomination struggling to find a theology of communion.

In addition to these sources, something of what Baptists believed may be gained from the hymns they sang at communion. For Baptists, as for other Nonconformists, the sermon was the central act of public worship and hymn-singing the chief corporate act of the congregation. Given the absence of credal affirmations, hymns often acted as statements of faith, lodged in the memory and subconscious long after a sermon or even a passage of scripture had been forgotten.

From this environment of debate and piety Zwinglianism emerges as the chief contender for a blanket description of Baptist attitudes to the Lord's Supper. This is the controlling line, as it were, that runs through Baptist thinking in the nineteenth century. It is, however, no more than that. Baptists veered to either side of that line. Some were influenced more by their roots in Calvinism than the prevailing Zwinglianism of the Nonconformist churches. Unwillingness to be limited to memorialist language and ideas recurred throughout the century, beginning with Robert Hall at its outset and ending with Charles Haddon Spurgeon at its close. Others defended the middle ground of Zwinglianism, finding in the Lord's Supper an effective reminder of those doctrines of salvation that were central to their belief and experience. Yet others were more at home with the legacy of radical Anabaptism with its separating of spirit and matter and its suspicion of anything that smacked of 'ceremony'. None of these views emerged as the result of systematic thinking about the Supper but nevertheless provide impressive testimony to the constant place of the sacrament in the affections of Baptist people, in spite of the many combative gauntlets it had to run.

A) THE ZWINGLIAN NORM

The eucharistic theology that Baptists shared with other Nonconformists and probably the majority of Evangelical Anglicans in the nineteenth century can be described as Zwinglian only in the loosest sense. It did not result from a close study of the 'third man of the Reformation', nor from sympathy with his broader Reformation ideals. Indeed, between Zwingli and the Anabaptists of his time an animosity existed that Zwingli, who had the support of the civic authorities, was able to channel into positive victimisation. In so far, however, as Evangelicals valued their roots in the historic Reformation, it was with the eucharistic theology of Zwingli that they were most easily able to identify. It accorded well with their emphasis on the centrality of faith in the work of Christ, the sole mediator between man and God. Zwinglianism seemed to offer a view of the sacrament that in no way intruded into the direct and personal relationship between God and the believer that was brought about by faith born of the active working of grace in the human heart. The aspect of Zwinglianism on which they fastened was its memorialism, not always catching the nuances in Zwingli's own thought which served to prevent a total decline into a subjectivism that placed the inner spiritual experience of the communicant at the centre of the sacrament's significance.

A rounded Zwinglianism is found in Joseph Kinghorn's *Baptism a Term of Communion at the Lord's Supper*.[1] Kinghorn, as we shall see, was Robert Hall's chief antagonist in the communion debate. His definition of the Lord's Supper comes in the course of his argument on the terms of communion, in which he finds the purpose of the sacrament intimated at the last supper in the upper room, but its full significance made possible only by the subsequent passion and ascension of our Lord:

> ... the Lord's Supper was to be celebrated in remembrance of Christ, although he was then present with his disciples; and it was intended to be a memorial of that love, the great display of which was not then completed ... Both [ordinances] were enriched and rendered more significant and impressive, by the additional light and glory with which they were invested.[2]

The memorialism of Kinghorn's position is in no doubt: he linked the Last Supper, however, with the subsequent story of the crucified and risen Lord. The Lord's Supper was not to be seen simply as a re-enactment of the events in the upper room. Indeed, there could be no Lord's Supper, no sacrament of the church, until the cross, resurrection and ascension had taken place. It was from these that the sacrament derived its meaning. Where Christians gather in the presence of the risen Lord, the sacrament directs them again to that atoning death upon the cross by which, through faith, they have been forgiven and restored to a living relationship with God, through Christ.

This rounded Zwinglianism became more qualified as the constraints of the Catholic revival and the need that Baptists felt to distance themselves from sacramentalism became more urgent. Writing in 1852, W. Walters deals with a series of scenes from the public life of our Lord, amongst them the institution of the Supper. He traces five ends which the Supper is meant to serve, the first of which he couches in memorialist language:

> Brethren, what an appropriate memorial it is! how well it has served its end! How often, amid the thick of worldly cares and the enticement of vanities, has it collected the wandering affections of the soul and centered them on Jesus! How often has the sight of it stirred up the dying embers of our love and kindled them to an ardent flame!ered[3]

The second, third and fourth points emphasise the teaching function of the Lord's Supper, its purpose in pointing the hope of believers towards the second coming of Christ, and its benefit for Christian fellowship, drawing together as it does Christians of different persuasions. The fifth point recognizes that the Lord's Supper is a means of good to the receiver but does so by treading a careful path between attributing either too much or too little to it:

> While we disclaim everything like sacramental efficacy, yet we deem it possible to go too far in another direction. We believe that in the Lord's Supper, as in baptism, or any other act of divine service or worship, there is an adaptation to promote the spiritual good of the receiver; the good, however, depending not on the person who administers it, nor on the ordinance itself, but on the state of mind of the receiver at the time.[4]

Walters demonstrates how a perfectly respectable Zwinglianism was in danger of veering off into ambivalence. It is not clear whether he regards the sacrament as having any distinctive feature compared with any other act of worship in which Christians are gathered together. Further, whilst rejecting both the role of the celebrant and the efficacy of the sacrament itself, he finds no alternative ground upon which to base the good which is given to the communicant other than his state of mind at the time. It is all too easy for Zwinglianism to end here. Memorialism can be construed either as a re-presentation of the passion of our Lord, moving the communicant to renewed love and faith in Christ, or as an exercise of the faculty of memory. If the former, the Lord's Supper forms part of the church's proclamation of the gospel; if the latter, it is an event whose chief significance resides in the psychological dispositions of its recipients.

Compared to Walters, others were even more guarded in endeavouring to describe what a Zwinglian view actually meant for Baptists. Writing five years later, T. Pottenger sees the Baptist view of the sacrament almost entirely in terms of protest and reaction, the Baptist observance being designed to defend it 'from mistakes and perversions'. Pausing briefly in his anti-Catholic crusade, Pottenger in two sentences sums up the Baptist view of the sacraments which he so strenuously claims to be defending:

> The Lord's Supper is a memorial of [our Lord's] sacrifice for our sins, and a standing pledge of His coming again in the end of the world. Both ordinances were appointed for believers only; and they require from all who keep them worthily, repentance and faith, the renunciation of sin, and union with our Lord.[5]

There was much there to develop and explore, but Pottenger was too impatient to be about the business of resisting priest-craft to see to it.

A similar defensiveness is evidenced in Charles Williams' book, *Principles and Practices of the Baptists*,[6] which he wrote to introduce Baptist beliefs to non-Baptists. Williams had a distinguished ministry at

Cannon Street in Accrington, one of the outstanding churches in the north of England. His chapter on the Lord's Supper begins its exposition:

> All Baptists agree in declaring that the Lord's Supper is not a sacrament in the ecclesiastical sense of the word. They hold that it is neither the cause nor the vehicle of grace.[7]

Much of what Williams initially has to say is in repudiation of Catholic doctrine. His memorialism is expressed briefly. In contrast to Catholics who locate Christ in the bread and wine, Baptists locate him in the gathered congregation. It is the members of the congregation who

> ... observe it as a commemoration by a company of believers of the love of their dying Saviour, a memorial of His sacrificial sufferings and atoning death ... In thus thinking of what the Lord Jesus did and suffered for them, and opening their minds and hearts to the influence of His all-conquering love, Baptists strive to eat and drink worthily, 'discerning the Lord's body' ...[8]

The remainder of what Williams has to say, forming as it does the bulk of the chapter, deals with the 'social aspect' of the Lord's Supper and an explanation of the debate about open and closed communion in which Baptists had so long engaged. The former point he sums up:

> ...Baptists who do not restrict communion at the Lord's table to the baptized ... admit ... those who see in Jesus the Lamb of God, their Saviour, but all who ask permission to commemorate the love of their Lord and Redeemer.[9]

Williams' emphasis has marked similarities with that of John Clifford, as we shall see.[10] Despite his testimony to the presence of Christ in the congregation, the focal point of remembrance in the sacrament itself was the death of Christ. The reader, however, is frustrated by the dominance of polemics even in what is avowedly an exposition of Baptist beliefs.

One of those outstanding amongst Baptists of the nineteenth century was Alexander Maclaren (1826-1910). In 1858 he became minister of Union Chapel in Manchester where he remained until 1903. He was a gifted expository preacher, his published work having an influence comparable to that of Spurgeon. His sermons were gathered in successive volumes to form a continuous exposition of the whole of Holy Scripture which remained a source of enlightenment and inspiration long after his death. In his sermon on the eucharistic words in 1 Cor.11.24 he avows his memorialism:

> ... I, for my part, am contented to be told that I believe in a poor, bald Zwinglianism when I say with my Master, that the purpose of the Lord's Supper is simply the commemoration, and therein the proclamation of His death. There is no magic, no mystery, no 'sacrament' about it. It

blesses us when it makes us remember Him. It does the same thing for us which any other means of bringing Him to mind does. It does that through a different vehicle. A sermon does it by words, the Communion does it by symbols.[11]

Maclaren clearly has the unnamed enemy of Catholicism in his sights. The equation of sacrament and mystery with 'magic' indicates a repudiation not only of transubstantiation but of any eucharistic doctrine that would accept the mystery of Christ's presence in the Lord's Supper. It also betrays the influence of eighteenth-century rationalism in general, and Socinian suspicion of the religious and mysterious in particular. Maclaren wished to portray the Supper as in no way unique. However, the analogy he draws between the communion and the sermon suggests that he believed that the former played a key role in the experience of Christian men and women. For it could be said of nineteenth-century preaching that it was neither poor, bald, lacking in mystery or anything other than a means of grace. The pulpit was a place of nurture, of fire and light, from which words gave wings to the religious aspirations of the hearers, bringing them, they felt, to the gates of heaven. The thousands who beat footpaths to the leading pulpits of nineteenth-century Nonconformity, Catholicism and Anglicism alike, came not to learn but to encounter the living God. The pulpit was the burning bush, alight with unconsuming flame.

Whatever the angry denunciations of the sacramental principle in the life of the church, the pulpit was a means of grace to at least three generations. Thus Maclaren's analogy of the Lord's Supper with preaching, if pressed, accorded the former a content that was neither adequately or justly described as a 'bald' Zwinglianism. This becomes apparent in the remainder of the exposition where he describes the Supper as a symbol of the believer's present relationship with Jesus Christ and a prophecy of the Messianic feast in which one day all will share. His treatment of the Christian's union with Christ, despite his insistent rejection of the mystical, is movingly eloquent. It illustrates the power of the sermon to evoke that experience which for others was embodied in the sacrament as well as in the word:

> We are to live upon Him. He is to be incorporated within us by our own act. There is no mysticism, it is a piece of simple reality. There is not Christian life without it. The true life of the believer is just the feeding of our souls upon Him - our minds accepting, meditating upon, digesting the truths which are incarnated in Jesus; our hearts feeding upon the love which is so tender, warm, stooping and close; our wills feeding upon and nourished by the utterances of His will in commandments which to know is joy and to keep is liberty; our hopes feeding upon Him who is our hope . . . the whole nature thus finding its nourishment in Jesus Christ.[12]

Of all this the Lord's Supper is a symbol. Maclaren's Zwinglianism is clear in the separation of sign and that which is signified. Yet that which was signified was absent from neither word nor sacrament; the ineffable grace of God was in the Supper even as it was present in the words with which Maclaren described it with all the eloquence at his command.

From the testimony of one of the denomination's outstanding preachers we turn to its foremost historian. W. T. Whitley made an enormous contribution to Baptists' understanding of their own origins and to cataloguing the material from which they might learn about their history. In 1896, in a series of articles in the *Baptist Magazine* he ventured into the field of doctrinal reflection in which he tried to demonstrate that the wider history of the church bore its own, albeit sometimes unconscious, testimony to Baptist principles. He identified sacerdotalism and sacramentalism as the two great evils that had dogged the church throughout its long history.[13] Their emergence in the early church he attributed to heathen, pagan and heretical influences within the church, quoting Ignatius' reference to the eucharist as 'the medicine of immortality' as an example of a development that contained 'the germ of errors'.[14] Coming to the Reformation period, he accused Luther of inability to shake himself free from a sacramentalism carried over from his Catholic past. By contrast Zwingli was far more radical, and went to the core of the matter by flatly denying both errors (i.e. sacerdotalism and sacramentalism).[15]

To sum up his own approach, Whitley was content to quote with approval the words of Dr James Grant of Toronto:

> The teaching of Baptists concerning the ordinances has ever been that they have no efficacy, either in themselves or as channels of communication from God or as the condition of anything saving, and that they are means of grace only as they teach and enforce truth.[16]

Even a scholar like Whitley ended up espousing Zwinglianism not so much for what it affirmed in the doctrine of the Lord's Supper as for what it denied. Zwinglianism kept Baptists in the Protestant mainstream whilst furnishing them with the clearest rejection of Catholic eucharistic beliefs held by any of the leading reformers. Central to their thinking was a memorialist approach to the Lord's Supper that kept sign and thing signified at a safe and 'unsacramental' distance from each other.

B) SACRAMENTAL EXPLORATIONS

Whereas some Baptists allowed their Zwinglianism to veer off into an extreme subjectivism, there were others who were less than content with the memorialist limits imposed by the denominational norm. In the early years of the century, particularly, traces remained of a Calvinist emphasis that continued to mark the Baptist approach to other doctrinal matters well into the nineteenth century. The outstanding exponent of this approach was Robert Hall who, in the course of his advocacy of open communion, claimed that paedobaptists should be admitted to the Lord's table since it was a federal rite. By this Hall was concerned to emphasise the corporate participation of those who had been reconciled to God through Christ. It also echoed the covenant theology, derived from Calvinism, that had so markedly characterised the early separatist movements of which Baptists had been a part. Hall specifically rejected a bare memorialism and stressed the nature of the sacrament as a participation in the sacrifice offered by Christ:

> To consider the Lord's supper . . . as a mere commemoration of [our Lord's death and passion] is to entertain a very inadequate view of it. If we credit St Paul, it is also a *federal rite* in which, in token of our reconciliation with God, we eat and drink in his presence: it is a feast upon a sacrifice, by which we become partakers at the altar, not less really, though in a manner more elevated and spiritual, than those who under the ancient economy presented their offerings in the temple. In this ordinance, the cup is a spiritual participation of the blood, the bread of the body, of the crucified Saviour . . . [17]

There is here an uncompromising claim that to share in the Lord's Supper represents a real participation in the body and blood of the risen Lord. The Calvinism of Hall's position is seen in this and in his reference to a 'feast upon a sacrifice'. Calvin, differing from Luther in his Christological emphases, was unable to accept the former's view of an ubiquitously present Christ upon the altars of the church. Whereas Luther emphasised the descent of Jesus into humanity, a descent which, in touching the profound depths of Calvary, most surely revealed God (*revelatus*) where he was most hidden (*absconditus*), Calvin stressed Christ's ascension to the right hand of God the Father. It followed that he could not be both in heaven and on earth. A Christ who had ascended into heaven could not be everywhere present in the sacrament. The presence of the Holy Spirit in the sacrament, however, raised the believer into the presence of Christ where he fed upon him by sharing in his risen and glorified life. It was the active agency of the Holy Spirit in the Lord's Supper that made possible a participation in the body and blood of the ascended Christ. It was of this 'spiritual participation' that Hall was speaking. His reference too, to a 'feast upon a sacrifice' has its roots in Calvin. Calvin himself had written of the Lord's Supper:

> We see then, for what end this mystical benediction is designed; namely, to assure us that the body of the Lord was once offered as a sacrifice for us, so that we may now feed upon it, and feeding on it, may experience within us the efficacy of that one sacrifice . . . [18]

Ironically, it was Hall's belief in the value of the Lord's Supper that was to set him upon a road that was to lead others to value it far less highly than did he. He argued that a rite with such implications for the Christian life should be kept from none on the grounds of baptismal 'irregularity'. Admission to the Lord's table was of more importance than whether the communicant was a Baptist or a paedobaptist. This led him, however, to relegate baptism to the status of 'ceremonial', one to which others were to assign the Lord's Supper itself later in the century.

The phrase 'feast upon a sacrifice' appears again in a small book which one of Hall's contemporaries, William Newman, President of Stepney College, wrote for the members of his church. In addition, Newman claimed that the Lord's Supper presented 'a memorial of the stupendous love of him who gave himself for us'; it was also a pledge of devotion to Christ and a token of the special union and mutual love of a particular church.[19]

Another contemporary of Hall's, William Button, who was to take the opposite view in the debate about closed and open communion, is nevertheless one with him in his belief that the Lord's Supper is a participation in Christ. The bread

> ... is a sign, symbol and token of fellowship with Christ in his death, and is a means of having communion with him, and of enjoying the blessings of grace which come through his death.[20]

The presence of a Calvinist theology of the eucharist in the writings of Hall, Newman and Button, all of whom were Particular Baptists, should excite little surprise. As Particulars they were all agreed in the Calvinist view of a limited atonement. Traces of a similar approach from a General Baptist, committed to an Arminian soteriology, would, at first sight, seem less likely. It has to be remembered, however, that the General Baptists came from the same roots in the Puritan and Calvinist tradition of Dissent and separatism. Differences in understanding of the atonement did not preclude agreement on matters of church polity and the interpretation of the sacraments. Addressing his fellow Baptists of the New Connexion of General Baptists in 1836, J. Jarrom sees the Lord's Supper as serving two purposes. The first is broadly Zwinglian: Jarrom in his preference for the term 'represents' to 'commemorates' is probably closer to Zwingli himself than were the later thorough-going memorialists.[21] The second purpose of the sacrament was 'to show the benefits which [Christians] derive from [Christ]'.[22] Of these, he says:

> ... the eating of the bread, and drinking of the wine, represent believing in him as our sacrifice, and participating spiritually of his body as meat indeed, and of his blood as drink indeed; and the nourishment derived to the corporeal frame from the bread and wine when eaten and drunk, is illustrative of the spiritual life and nourishment derived to the soul from his body and blood when received and fed upon by faith.[23]

The realism of Jarrom's language is underlined by his rebuke of those who claim that any other sign, such as 'plucking a leaf or flower' would have done equally well. The bread and wine, he says, more than anything represent 'our participation of the blessings procured by [Christ's] sufferings and the shedding of his blood'.[24]

All these writers represent a theology that had not yet shifted the centre of balance under the constraints of the Catholic revival. Apart from Hall's clear rejection of stark memorialism, they incorporated a Zwinglian stress on the 'representative' aspect of the Supper. They were also aware, however, of the Calvinist bequest of which they were heirs and boldly appropriated its language to emphasise the participatory aspect of the sacrament. Their words provide a sharp contrast with those later writers for whom every positive statement about the benefits accruing to believers by their participation in the sacrament had to be accompanied by a string of denials, qualification and reservations. They possessed a freedom to delight in the blessings of the Lord's table that seemed to be denied to most of those who followed them. Not least of the adverse effects of the Catholic revival upon many Baptists was their apparent inability to give priority to what they did believe about the Lord's Supper over what they did not believe.

An exception to this tendency is found in a remarkable series of articles published in the *Baptist Magazine* in 1857 when hostility to Catholicism was riding high. The six articles were meant to provide a basis for reflection on the celebration of the Lord's Supper on the 'Communion Sabbath'. They bravely carried the title 'Sacramental Meditations'. They were completely anonymous and to name Samuel Manning, the then editor of the magazine, as their author, is to do no more than hazard a guess.

The articles begin by endeavouring to allay suspicion of the word sacrament. In spite of the abuse to which it had been subjected yet 'its true and original meaning, in its application to the Lord's Supper, is full of beauty'.[25] The author, like Zwingli, traces the original meaning of the word to the soldier's pledge, seeing in it 'the oath of fidelity and allegiance taken by the Christian soldier'.[26] The word also meant a pledge deposited by the parties to a covenant or in a law suit. The two sides of such a covenant are seen in baptism in which, for their part, believers commit themselves to the grace of Christ, whilst, for his part, God provides evidence of his commitment to his people in the succeeding generations who have 'passed away from the world of type and symbol, of sacrament and earnest, into the full fruition, the perfect enjoyment, of all that they hoped for here'.[27] As well as being a pledge of our love to Christ, the Lord's Supper is a pledge of his love to us. It is also a family festival. The Passover celebrations of the Jews took place within the setting of the family. When our Lord instituted the sacrament, it was in the setting of that new family which he himself had brought into existence and to which successive generations of Christians would belong:

> Let us endeavour to bear in mind, as often as we meet for the celebration of this ordinance, that Christ is as surely with us, and does as really acknowledge us to be members of his family, as when he met the twelve in the upper room in Jerusalem, that he might eat the passover with them rather than with Mary, his mother, and his brethren and sisters.[28]

This was not because he was unmindful of earthly ties, an assumption nullified by his deliverance of Mary his mother into the care of John the apostle, but because his love embraced all who were, like the disciples, to be his kinsfolk in generations to come. We, numbered amongst them, gather around him in the sacrament:

> At the table he calls us around himself, that we may meet with him and partake of the symbol which commemorates both his love to us and our relationship to him.[29]

The Zwinglian language of remembrance appears again in the next article, but the author puts commemoration in the setting of celebration:

> He did not build a tomb by which to be remembered, but he appointed a feast of remembrance ... it was by no sad ceremonial, by no gloomy and funereal rites, that we were to attest our remembrance of his obedience unto death, but by a festival.[30]

The writer wrestles with the paradox of death and festival. There cannot be an absence of grief and sadness as the death of the redeemer is remembered and as his followers rehearse the events of Calvary. Yet the cross is also the source of all the believer's hope:

> This appointment is in perfect harmony with the whole system of the gospel. To his cross we owe the crown, from his suffering flows all our joy, by his death we receive everlasting life. Those blessings which come to us so freely and so gratuitously cost him dear. We receive them without money and without price, but he shed his heart's blood to secure them for us.[31]

The Lord's table is thus a place of mingled feelings, of sorrowing remembrance and of joyous thanksgiving. The cross, rather than the cross and the resurrection, stands central to the writer's understanding of the sacrament, but he has avoided the melancholy heaviness that could so easily cover the Lord's table like a pall. It is a place of celebration since from the cross of Christ flows all the good in the believer's experience.

In the fourth meditation, the writer deals with Christ's choice of bread and wine as the symbols of his sacrifice. In the Jewish Passover, he claims, it is the lamb that is central to the meal. It was the lamb that was divinely instituted at the inauguration of the feast, the bread and wine being later additions. The lamb, however, represents the sacrificial part of the feast. With Christ's offering of himself upon the cross, once for all, that which was represented by the lamb, under the type and symbol of the old covenant, has been fulfilled. The sacrifice is no longer a shadow of things to come. The sacrifice has been offered and is complete. The bread and the wine were chosen because of their simplicity. If the Lord's Supper was to be an abiding ordinance of commemoration, then the materials with which it was to be celebrated should be 'of the most common and widely diffused of the earth'.[32] The very simplicity of the bread and wine emphasises two important truths. The first is that outward appearances are of no account. The sacrament is no place for 'pomp and grandeur', but a place to which people come in their broken, human need and, here, in the simplicities of bread and wine, find that for which they are seeking:

> Christ can communicate the greatest blessings by the meanest instruments. A piece of bread shall convey a whole Christ with all his benefits; but then it must be to hungry souls. It is Christ's blessing which gives it all its virtue.[33]

The second truth bread and wine signify is that it is in the ordinary matters of life we are to glorify Christ. In words that could as easily have come from the pen of St Thérèse of Lisieux a few years later, the writer perceives the true arena of Christian spirituality and obedience to Christ:

> ... we do not need to wait or turn out of our way for opportunities of heroic service. He who consecrated elements so common as water, bread and wine, to the holiest uses, and employed them as instruments of the most sacred rites in his church, would have us similarly consecrate to him the commonest duties of our daily life.[34]

The fifth meditation deals with the believer's appropriation of Christ. The author emphasises that the believer takes the bread and wine, and his taking is part of that faith, central to the Christian life, by which we receive all that Christ gives to us. He rejects the notion of transubstantiation, whilst insisting that the dominical words, 'Take, eat; this is my body - drink, this is my blood', are full of meaning. There is a true participation in Christ at the table:

> What ... is the true force and meaning of this language? Did he not teach us, under this emblem, that he does give to each one of us his flesh, his blood, himself? Not in the bread, but with it - not in the wine, but with it, is faith to receive the body and blood of Christ. The human administrator gives but bread and wine - the Lord of the assembly gives to believing souls, himself.[35]

There is no timid restraint upon the writer's eloquence as he describes the soul's appropriation of Christ in the ordinance. The entry of the bread and wine into our bodies is like the entry of Christ into our souls:

> The bread and the wine are to enter into our system; to become assimilated with and incorporated into our very being. It is not enough that we touch the elements or gaze upon them, they are to be eaten and drank. Just so, we are not simply to lay our hands upon the head of the great Sacrifice, not merely to gaze upon him with adoration and gratitude, but actually to receive him into our spirits . . . Let us each seek, as we take the bread and wine of the supper, to take and eat the flesh and drink the blood which were so freely given for us on the cross, and which are given to us to feed and strengthen our fainting souls.[36]

The sixth, and final, meditation covers familiar ground. The Lord's Supper is commemorative, declaratory and anticipative. The writer deals finely with the commemorative aspect, refusing to let Zwinglianism, as so many of his fellow Baptists understood it, drain the sacrament of objectivity:

> . . . loving and remembering us, he desires to be loved and remembered by us . . . But far more for our own sakes than for his does he desire that we should remember him. The loving grateful remembrance of Christ is the source at once of the life and strength of our religious character. In partial forgetfulness of him we grow weak, in total forgetfulness we die.[37]

The Lord's Supper 'recalls our vagrant hearts to the cross, to bring us back to that great event whence are derived all our strength and joy'.[38] As a declaratory rite, the sacrament proclaims the gospel. It proclaims it both to those who already know and have received its truth and to those who have still to do so. Yet none is free of the scrutiny with which it searches the hearts and minds of those who witness it. In setting forth the crucified Christ and confessing him in the Supper, the church is called to examine again its confession of him in the life of its members in order that the sacrament may be free of all hypocrisy. The common life of the church should 'illustrate, and not disparage, the testimony we thus bear to our crucified Lord'.[39] As an anticipatory rite, the sacrament looks forward to the coming of Christ. It is celebrated till he come. It connects the first and the second coming of the Lord, it unites faith with hope. No matter how long the ages, the sacrament will continue to testify to the faith and hope of the church:

> Through the ages that have already elapsed, and may yet elapse between his first and his second coming, his church will continue to connect the two by this ordinance; 'for as

often as ye eat this bread and drink this cup ye do proclaim the Lord's death till he come.'[40]

This series of magazine articles from an anonymous hand is one of the finest pieces of Baptist writing on the Lord's Supper to be found in the mid-nineteenth century. Its strength lies in the fact that its prime purpose was instructive and devotional. There are occasional glances over the writer's shoulder as, aware of the Catholic challenge, he shapes what he has to say in the light of it. The challenge, however, is kept firmly in the wings and never allowed to take central stage where its presence would have brought confusion and distortion to the drama being enacted there. With this writer it was the worship of the church and the devotional life of Christian men and women, not confrontation and polemic, that preoccupied his mind, with the result that the Baptist tradition was able to yield its own rich contribution to an understanding of the sacrament. Another source of the articles' strength was their alignment with the ministry of the word. The writer's intention was that they should provide material for others to use in their own preaching ministry at the Lord's table. As Spurgeon was to show, great preaching did not set the pulpit in opposition to the table or overshadow and diminish its role in the life of the church. Preaching, when turning all its energy and its eloquence to the benefits made available by Christ through his table, was able to create a mood of expectancy that turned commemoration into participation and celebration.

Towards the end of the century, two more writers took up the theme of the sacrament in the pages of the *Baptist Magazine*. Edward C. Alden, writing on 'Baptism and the Lord's Supper' in 1891,[41] frames much of what he has to say in terms of anti-Catholic polemic. He makes space, however, to say positive things about the sacraments and their significance for the believer. Baptism sets forth Christ's work in the remission of sins and the gift of eternal life. The Lord's Supper, he says, is given for the perpetual sustenance of that life. On the divine side, it exhibits what God gives us, on the human side

> . . . it exhibits the . . . perpetual need of the soul - the need of sustenance in the new life - a need only to be supplied by the continual feeding of our faith on the Bread of Life.[42]

He emphasises that the bread and wine are only symbols of the body and blood of Christ. To claim for them more than that is to 'overthrow the nature of a sacrament'.[43] The sacraments are of value as a means of grace only in so far as they represent a truthful setting forth of facts in the spiritual life. In saying this, he warns Catholics that a sacrament cannot bring into being what is not already there. A Christian is made by faith and grace, not by the *opus operatum* of the sacraments. Yet he was aware also that a warning had to be given to his fellow-Baptists, for they too were capable of separating the sacrament from the inner disposition of those who observed it:

> If we come to the Lord's Supper in a perfunctory spirit, as to a duty which we do not like to neglect, or because it is expected of us as members once a month or so; and not as the spontaneous act of glowing love, the natural and harmonious outcome of the soul's inner life; we come to His Table as a mere form, and so 'eat and drink condemnation to ourselves', 'not discerning the Lord's body'.[44]

The second writer, J. Hunt Cooke, wrote on 'The Lord's Supper' in the same magazine in 1899.[45] Here too, there is a string of repudiations of Catholic beliefs, this time in a brief historical survey of the early Fathers and the medieval church. Perusing the great Reformation teachers, he concludes that the truth of the matter lies with Zwingli:

> Surely the simple commemorative idea is the fundamental one, and covers all that is taught in Holy Scripture in relation to this ordinance.[46]

His Zwinglianism, however, does not prevent him stating that the Lord's Supper is a means by which spiritual discernment is quickened. Neither would he have been content with Maclaren's 'bald' Zwinglianism:

> We do not regard the elements as altogether *inania symbola*, for they are incandescent with spiritual associations. The monument is not of cold marble. The question has been asked: Would not another form of rite do as well? and a two-fold denial reveals the truth. For, first, discipleship is shown in implicit obedience, and, secondly, none other would have the same significant associations.[47]

It was a tragedy for Baptists that they allowed controversy and polemic so to determine a great deal of what they wrote during the nineteenth century. When those concerns could occasionally be put to one side, there is sufficient evidence to show that their experience of the Lord at his table was one that created hope, love and expectancy in their hearts. At its best, their language echoes the authentic testimony of the Christian church that has found, from generation to generation, the table to be a place of sustenance and participation in the life of the risen Lord, beyond the arena of public debate, in the loyal offering of worship Sunday by Sunday, There were many for whom this was true. The testimony of one of the Baptists' greatest sons, H. Wheeler Robinson, to the power of the Lord's Supper in his early life, is recorded by E. A. Payne:

> Wheeler Robinson often paid tribute to the influence on him of College Street and its young assistant minister [Frank Ward Pollard]; but he spoke at least as often of the aged J. T. Brown and in particular of the Communion Service, which from 1849 to 1896 was the sole service on the first Sunday evening of each month. Those not partaking of the elements

sat in the galleries. The simple service proved by itself one of the most effective of evangelistic agencies.[48]

Robinson's students at Regent's Park College, Oxford, were later to testify to the power of that abiding legacy in the way that he himself presided at the Lord's table throughout his ministry.

C) THE LORD'S SUPPER IN NINETEENTH-CENTURY BAPTIST HYMNODY

A further source of learning what Baptists believed about the Lord's Supper, and one inevitably confessional and experiential in its emphasis, is found in the hymns they sang in their communion services. Hymns have played a leading, if at times controversial, part in the life of Baptists. From their beginnings in the seventeenth century until the formation of Dan Taylor's New Connexion in the eighteenth, the General Baptists forbade the singing of hymns in their churches. Hymns were viewed as a first step towards a formalism in worship that they so strenuously sought to avoid. They were also seen as a threat to the solemnity that the General Baptists believed to be appropriate to the act of public worship. Further, they smudged the dividing line between the church and the world, being 'man-made inventions' and thus a Trojan horse that brought the world into the sanctuary beneath the cover of pious religious exercises. Dan Taylor challenged this negative view of hymns. Deeply influenced as he had been by the Wesleyan revival, it was inevitable that he would be affected by the hymns in which the Wesley brothers set their great Evangelical themes to music. Soon after their formation in 1770, the New Connexion Baptists published their own hymn book entitled a *Collection of Hymns*. Others were to follow as, in the nineteenth century, opposition to hymn-singing was abandoned and it became common practice in General Baptist churches. In 1791 the General Baptist association sanctioned the preparation of a hymn book that was published in 1793 under the title of the *General Baptist Hymn Book*. It was followed in 1851 by *The New Hymn Book*, edited by J. B. and J. Carey Pike and, in 1879, by the *Baptist Hymnal*, edited by W. R. Stevenson.

The Particular Baptists offered some early resistance to hymn-singing, but had recognized its value by the end of the seventeenth century. Benjamin Keach (1640-1704), minister of the Horsley Down church in London, was an enthusiastic advocate of hymn-singing and himself the author of a prodigious number of hymns, none of which survived in general use. In 1697, another London minister, Joseph Stennett, published a collection of hymns under the title *Hymns in Commemoration of the Sufferings of our Blessed Saviour Jesus Christ, Compos'd for the Celebration of his Holy Supper*, a work that appeared in a second edition in 1703 under the title *Hymns for the Lord's Supper*. During the eighteenth century there appeared other gifted writers of hymns. Amongst them were Anne Steele (1716-1778), the daughter of William

Steele, lay-pastor of the Baptist church in Broughton, Hampshire, 144 of whose hymns were published, 47 of them appearing in Rippon's *Selection*[49] in 1787; Benjamin Beddome (1717-1795), pastor of the Baptist church in Bourton-on-the-Water for fifty-five years, regularly wrote hymns for his congregation, thirty-six of which appeared in Rippon's *Selection*; Samuel Stennett (1727-1795), the grandson of Joseph, had thirty-eight of his hymns included in Rippon's *Selection*. In addition to these were Benjamin Jones, Robert Robinson, John Fawcett and Dr John Ryland, together with a number of lesser known writers.

The wealth of eighteenth-century Baptist hymn-writing was carried into the nineteenth century through Dr John Rippon's *Selection*, published in 1787 whilst he was minister of Carter Lane, later New Park Street, in London. The full title of the work was *Selection of hymns from the best authors, intended to be an Appendix to Dr. Watts' Psalms and Hymns*. As the title implies, the hymnal was largely based upon the superlative hymnody of Isaac Watts (1647-1748), supplemented by other writers, a large number of them Baptists. This was to go through more than thirty editions and became the standard hymn book amongst the Particular Baptists until well into the nineteenth century. In 1828 *A New Selection* was published under the editorship of John Haddon, revised in 1871 under the title *Praise Waiteth*. The major book to appear in the middle of the century was *Psalms and Hymns* (1858) which held first place amongst the Particular Baptists and, increasingly, the General Baptists. In 1900 the *Baptist Church Hymnal* was published and this proved to be the staple diet in hymnody for Baptists, most of whom, both General and Particular, were now united within the Baptist Union. One other book of interest was *Our Own Hymn Book*, published in 1886 by C. H. Spurgeon and used by him in the Metropolitan Tabernacle and in many of those churches where men from his Pastors' College had settled as ministers.

A representative sample from this wealth of hymnody will provide some indication of what Baptists wrote about the Lord's Supper in their hymns and what they were prepared to sing about the Lord's Supper in their worship. Rippon's *Selection* will provide evidence both of the eighteenth-century legacy of Baptist hymns and of what was sung in the first part of the nineteenth century. The *Baptist Hymnal* reveals those communion hymns that found greatest acceptance amongst the General Baptists. *Psalms and Hymns* is to be valued both for the evidence it provides of communion hymns in the middle of the century and as a comparison with the *Baptist Church Hymnal* by which development in the latter part of the century may be traced. Attention will also be given to *Our Own Hymn Book* which, like his sermons, provides evidence of Spurgeon's own unique approach to an understanding of the Lord's Supper.

A noticeable feature of nineteenth-century hymnody among Baptists is that they stopped writing communion hymns and, further, allowed those that they had inherited from the eighteenth century to fall into disuse. Stennett's 1709 edition of *Hymns for the Lord's Supper* had contained fifty hymns. Of these two appeared in Rippon's *Selection*. In addition to these, Rippon included nine hymns by other Baptists, three from Stennett's grandson Samuel, four from the pen of Anne Steele and two from Benjamin Beddome, making eleven Baptist hymns in all out of a selection of eighteen hymns in the 'Lord's Supper' section of the book. Of these only three survived into the later books, one of them, 'Lord, at Thy table I behold', by Joseph Stennett appearing later in the *Baptist Hymnal, Psalms and Hymns* and *Our Own Hymn Book*.[50] The latter book, compiled by Spurgeon, included also two hymns by Joseph Stennett and one by Spurgeon himself. None of these hymns was used in the *Baptist Church Hymnal* of 1900, thus effectively bringing to an end their own understanding of the Lord's Supper as Baptists had expressed it through their hymnody in previous generations.

If the Baptist hymns were not marked by their enduring poetry, they did nevertheless possess a robustness that deserved a longer life than was allowed to them. They set the Lord's table within the context of the death, resurrection and coming glory of Christ; they presented the sacrament as a place where faith and love were quickened by the remembrance of Christ's sufferings on behalf of his people; and they invited men and women to share in Christ and in his healing grace through participation in the communion. All these elements are found in Samuel Stennett's most popular hymn:

> Lord, at Thy table I behold
> The wonders of Thy grace . . .
> Eat, O my friends, the Saviour cries
> The Feast was made for you:
> For you I groan'd, and bled, and died,
> And rose, and triumph'd too.[51]

Stennett also emphasised the context of resurrection and future glory in 'Come, every pious heart'[52]:

> From the dark grave he rose . . .
> From thence he'll quickly come,
> His chariot will not stay,
> And bear our spirits home
> To realms of endless day:
> There shall we see his lovely face
> And ever be in his embrace.

The same remembrance that the sacrament is to be celebrated 'until he come' is found in Stennett's 'Thus we commemorate the day'[53]:

> Come, King of Kings! with thy bright train,
> Cherubs and seraphs, heavenly hosts!

Assume thy right, enlarge thy reign
As far as earth extends her coasts.

The Joseph Stennett hymn included by Spurgeon in his collection[54] but not found in Rippon's *Selection* affirms that remembrance of our Lord's passion prompts praise to the risen Lord and a reaffirmation of the believer's future hope:

We'll praise our risen Lord,
While at His feast we sit,
His griefs a hallow'd theme afford
For sweetest music fit . . .

Stretch'd on the cruel tree,
He bled, and groan'd, and cried;
And in a mortal agony,
Languish'd awhile and died.

Then up to heaven He rose,
That we might thither go,
Where love and praises have no end,
Where joys no changes know.

These Baptist hymns also display their understanding of the table as a place where love and faith are quickened by meditation upon the physical sufferings of Christ. This aspect of the Lord's Supper particularly characterised the hymns which Rippon selected from the many written by Benjamin Beddome and from those of Anne Steele.

Beddome encouraged the worshippers to gaze upon the figure of Christ in his passion:

So fair a face bedew'd with tears!
What beauty, e'en in grief, appears!
He wept, he bled, he died for you;
What more, ye saints, could Jesus do?[55]

In the hymns of Anne Steele there is an almost Abelardian emphasis upon the power of the love shown upon the cross to awaken love in the hearts of those who see it. The table becomes the place where the worshippers are brought face to face again with the sufferings of Christ and the terrible costliness of divine love. In her hymn, 'To Jesus our exalted Lord',[56] she links the gift set forth in the Supper with the responding love of the communicants:

But while around his board we meet,
And humbly worship at his feet;
O let our warm affections move
In glad returns of grateful love!

A similar response is provided in her hymn, 'To our Redeemer's glorious name'[57]:

> Dear Lord! while we adoring pay
> Our humble thanks to thee;
> May every heart with rapture say,
> 'The Saviour died for me.'

The miracle of divine love that spans the yawning gulf between God and his creation in the atoning gift of Christ is recalled in her hymn, 'And did the holy and the just'[58]:

> And did the holy and the just,
> The Sovereign of the skies,
> Stoop down to wretchedness and dust,
> That guilty worms might rise? . . .
>
> Dear Lord! what heavenly wonders dwell
> In thy atoning Blood!
> By this are sinners snatched from hell,
> And rebels brought to God . . .
>
> What glad return can I impart
> For favours so divine?
> O take my all - this worthless heart,
> And make it only thine.

This emphasis upon the power of the love recalled in the Supper to awaken love in the hearts of the worshippers could have been a form of memorialism and nothing more, were it not balanced on the one hand by the wider kerygmatic setting in Stennett's hymns and, on the other, by the belief of the other writers that the Lord's Supper was a place where the gifts of God's grace might be both sought and found. The Joseph Stennett hymn revived by Spurgeon in his collection[59] recalls the healing that flows from the cross, preceded by amazement at the extent of divine love and followed with the anticipation of a day when faith will be turned to sight:

> Gracious Redeemer, how divine,
> How wondrous is Thy love,
> The subject of th' eternal songs,
> Of blood-wash'd hosts above.
>
> Behold how every wound of His
> A precious balm distils,
> Which heals the scars that sin has made
> And cures all mortal ills . . .
>
> We see Thee at Thy table, Lord,
> By faith with great delight;

O how refined those joys will be
When faith is turn'd to sight!

In language far bolder, his grandson Samuel celebrates the gift of body and blood given in the bread and wine of the Lord's Supper:

Here at thy table, Lord! we meet
To feed on food divine:
Thy body is the bread we eat,
Thy precious blood the wine . . .

His body torn with rudest hands,
Becomes the finest bread;
And with the blessing he commands,
Our noblest hopes are fed.

His blood, that from each opening vein,
In purple torrents ran,
Hath filled this cup with generous wine,
That cheers both God and man.[60]

Beddome, too, in his hymn 'Jesus! when faith with fixed eyes' writes of the healing power of the cross experienced at the Lord's table:

Hence, O my soul, a balsam flows,
To heal thy wounds, and cure thy woes;
Immortal joys come streaming down,
Joys, like his griefs, immense, unknown.[61]

It was hymns such as these, with their emphases on the wider kerygmatic setting of the cross, the power of the love revealed there to awaken love in the hearts of the worshippers, and the gifts distributed by Christ to his people at his table, hymns written by Baptists, that were sung by Baptist congregations in the early part of the nineteenth century and until the appearance of the later books that superseded Rippon's *Selection* in popularity. The decline of Rippon's hymn book leaves two mysteries surrounding the Baptist repertoire of communion hymns. The first is why, as we have seen, they largely fell into disuse, and the second, why the repertoire was not added to. There is no clear reason for supposing a theological rejection. Stennett's longest surviving hymn, 'Lord, at Thy table I behold', contains elements of kerygma, amazement and invitation that had characterised so many of the others. Given a growing memorialist interpretation of the sacrament, the hymns of Anne Steele with their touching and ardent recollection of the passion of Christ would have sat at ease with the most committed of memorialist interpretations. It was, perhaps, style rather than theology that led to their exclusion from the later hymn books. For nineteenth-century tastes, the language of their predecessors had grown dated and lacked the poetic power of Isaac Watts or the Wesley brothers, whilst lines such as,

THE DOCTRINE OF THE LORD'S SUPPER

His blood that from each opening vein,
In purple torrents ran,

may have seemed too brutally realist for congregations coming to expect a greater degree of sophistication. To Spurgeon the old Baptist hymns continued to speak powerfully and to express those truths that he himself associated with the Lord's table, but for the majority they deployed a vocabulary that was no longer readily accessible. It was Spurgeon, too, who provided a rare exception to the dearth of Baptist hymn-writing on communion themes. The one hymn from his own pen which he included in his selection had all the emphases of earlier writers, except for the wider kerygmatic setting:

Amidst us our Beloved stands,
And bids us view His pierced hands;
Points to His wounded feet and side,
Blest emblems of the Crucified.

What food luxurious loads the board,
When at His table sits the Lord!
The wine how rich, the bread how sweet,
When Jesus deigns the guests to meet!

If now with eyes defiled and dim,
We see the signs but see not Him,
Oh may His love the scales displace,
And bid us see Him face to face![62]

Neither his own hymn, however, nor, despite his advocacy, the two Stennett compositions, secured a place in the communion hymnody of Baptists as they entered the twentieth century. Why had they stopped writing communion hymns? One can only speculate that an area of Christian devotion so fraught with the arguments and disclaimers of the nineteenth-century controversies was discouraging soil in which to plant poetic invention. Hymns are, after all, affirmations of a people's faith. In a denomination that had so vigorously Yes,eschewed credal statements, that delegated to its ministers, in the act of Christian worship, the task of being sole spokesmen in prayer, reading of the scriptures and preaching, in all, in fact, save the singing of the hymns, those hymns became both the corporate utterance of what the people believed, their words long remembered, and the corporate expression of their ardour and love for Christ. It was a daunting task for any hymn-writer to gather up all this in an area so fraught with contention as was the Lord's Supper. Thus, Baptists turned to others to provide them with their communion hymns.

An examination of the sections providing communion hymns in each of the four remaining hymn books under review reveals a choice of hymns from a wide denominational background. The *Baptist Hymnal* of 1879 contained nineteen communion hymns. These included five by

Anglican writers, two Moravian hymns, one Free Church of Scotland, one Plymouth Brethren, two by Isaac Watts, two by Philip Doddridge, one by another Congregationalist, four by the Wesleys, and Joseph Stennett's sole surviving Baptist contribution. *Psalms and Hymns* contained a selection of twenty-eight communion hymns. Of these four were from Anglican writers, two Moravian, one Free Church of Scotland, one Plymouth Brethren, six by Isaac Watts, five by other Congregationalists, four by the Wesleys, one by James Allen (who, in the course of his life-time, was an Anglican, a Sandemanian and finally ministered in a chapel he built himself), the incomparable 'O Sacred Head, once wounded', attributed to Bernard of Clairvaux and designated a communion hymn, and Stennett's 'Lord, at Thy table I behold'. Spurgeon's *Our Own Hymn Book* included fourteen communion hymns which, in addition to his own hymn and the three hymns by the Stennetts, comprised two from Anglican pens, one Moravian, six by Isaac Watts, one by another Congregationalist and one by the Wesleys. The *Baptist Church Hymnal* of 1900 contained twenty-five communion hymns, thirteen from *Psalms and Hymns* and, in addition, six by Anglican writers, one Plymouth Brethren, one Free Church of Scotland, one by Isaac Watts, one by Philip Doddridge, and one by another Congregationalist.

The relative popularity of various hymns may be gauged by the number of times that they make their appearance. Only two hymns appeared in all four hymn books. They were Isaac Watts' 'How sweet and sacred [aweful] is the place'[63] and 'According to Thy gracious word' by the Moravian author, James Montgomery.[64] Seven appeared in three of the hymns books. They were 'Bread of the world, in mercy broken' by Bishop Reginald Heber,[65] 'By Christ redeemed'[66] by George Rawson, a Congregationalist, 'For ever here my rest shall be'[67] and 'Jesus, we thus obey'[68] both by Charles Wesley, 'If human kindness meets return'[69] by G. T. Noel, an Anglican and brother of the Hon. Baptist Wriothesley Noel who forsook the Anglican allegiance of his family and became a Baptist, Joseph Stennett's 'Lord, at Thy table I behold',[70] and 'How condescending and how kind'[71] by Isaac Watts. Of the remaining hymns eleven appear twice.

A comparison of these hymns with the earlier *Selection* by John Rippon points to changes of emphasis in some themes and continuity in others. The memorialist interpretation of the Lord's Supper is more explicitly stated in the later hymns than in any of those in Rippon's *Selection*. Further, the wider kerygmatic setting of the cross receives less emphasis. On the other hand, there continue to be hymns that foster a spirit of devotion to Christ at the Lord's table and those which speak of his presence in the celebration of the supper.

Memorialism is the insistent theme of the widely used hymn by James Montgomery, 'According to Thy gracious word'.[72] Each of the four-lined verses ends with a reference to remembrance:

THE DOCTRINE OF THE LORD'S SUPPER

> According to Thy gracious word,
> In meek humility,
> This will I do, my dying Lord –
> I will remember Thee . . .
>
> Remember Thee, and all Thy pains,
> And all Thy love to me;
> Yes, while a breath, a pulse remains,
> Will I remember Thee.

Another popular hymn, by the Congregationalist, George Rawson,[73] emphasises the memorialist theme:

> By Christ redeemed, in Christ restored,
> We keep the memory adored,
> And show the death of our dear Lord
> Until He come.

The last line, repeated at the end of each verse, whilst not lessening the memorialist emphasis, does place the sacrament in the setting of the final return of Christ, a theme explicitly developed in the fourth verse:

> And thus that dark betrayal night
> With the last advent we unite,
> By one blest chain of loving rite,
> Until He come.

The memorialism of Charles Wesley's 'Jesus, we thus obey'[74], is similarly balanced by a recognition of the presence of the risen Lord amongst his people now. The one, expressed in the third verse,

> Thus we remember Thee.
> And take this bread and wine
> As Thine own dying legacy,
> And our redemption's sign.

is followed by the other,

> Thy presence makes the feast;
> Now let our spirits feel
> The glory not to be expressed,
> The joy unspeakable.

The theme of the second advent again provides the setting for Bishop Edward Bickersteth's memorialism in 'Till He come: O let the words'[75]:

> See, the feast of love is spread,
> Drink the wine and break the bread:
> Sweet memorials, – till the Lord
> Call us round His heavenly board;
> Some from earth, from glory some,
> Severed only, *'Till He come'*.

Language from such an impeccably Anglican source reveals that a Zwinglian emphasis was by no means peculiar to Baptists but something they shared with Evangelicals of other persuasions.

If memorialist hymns were amongst the most popular, so also were those that continued the earlier tradition of hymns expressing devotion to Christ, such as those composed by Anne Steele. Isaac Watts' 'How sweet and aweful is the place', used in all four books,[76] takes the theme of amazement at Christ's love to those who have gathered around the table:

> While every heart and every tongue
> Join to admire the feast,
> We each exclaim with grateful song,
> Lord, why was I a guest? . . .
>
> 'Twas the same love that spread the feast,
> That sweetly forced us in;
> Else we had still refused to taste,
> And perished in our sin.

Another hymn of Watts, 'How condescending and how kind',[77] takes the same theme:

> How condescending and how kind
> Was God's eternal Son;
> Our misery reached His heavenly mind,
> And pity brought Him down . . .
>
> Here let our hearts begin to melt,
> While we His death record;
> And, with our joy for pardoned guilt,
> Mourn that we pierced the Lord.

Whilst appearing in the sections of the hymn books designated for use at the Lord's Supper, this hymn, and others like it, could equally well have been used on other occasions. Whilst the cross is central to them, they do not draw on the imagery of the sacrament itself. For instance, in Charles Wesley's hymn,

> For ever here my rest shall be,
> Close to Thy bleeding side;
> This all my hope and all my plea,
> For me the Saviour died . . .
>
> Wash me, and make me thus Thine own;
> Wash me, and mine Thou art;
> Wash me, but not my feet alone,
> My hands, my head, my heart.[78]

The connection is only obliquely seen in its poetic use of Peter's protestations in the Johannine account of the foot-washing at the last supper. Similarly, the hymn by James Allen and Walter Shirley 'Sweet the moments rich in blessing'[79], and Gerard Noel's 'If human kindness meets return', which appeared in the three earlier hymn-books but failed to survive into the twentieth century by securing a place in the *Baptist Church Hymnal*, could both have been sung in other contexts:

> If human kindness meets return
> And owns the grateful tie;
> If tender thoughts within us burn,
> To feel a friend is nigh -
>
> O shall not warmer accents tell
> The gratitude we owe
> To Him who died our fears to quell
> Our more than orphan's woe?[80]

There were hymns, however, that found their focus in the cross as seen and experienced in the sacrament. Some of these appeared in *Psalms and Hymns* but were not re-selected for the 1900 *Baptist Church Hymnal*. Amongst these were Charles Wesley's 'Jesus Master of the feast',[81] 'Communion of my Saviour's blood' by the Moravian hymn-writer, James Montgomery,[82] and the Congregationalist James Conder's hymn:

> Bread of heaven! on Thee I feed,
> For Thy flesh is meat indeed;
> Ever may my soul be fed
> With this true and living bread;
> Day by day, with strength supplied,
> Through the life of Him who died.
>
> Vine of heaven! Thy blood supplies
> This blest cup of sacrifice;
> 'Tis Thy wounds my healing give;
> To Thy cross I look and live:
> Thou, my life! O let me be
> Rooted, grafted, built on Thee.[83]

It is tempting to see in the later omission of hymns such as these the baleful influence of reaction to the Catholic revival and a consequent inhibition to singing about the sacramental elements in the same realist way that earlier Baptists did. On the other hand, similar hymns did survive. For instance, there was Bishop Reginald Heber's hymn:

> Bread of the world, in mercy broken,
> Wine of the soul, in mercy shed,
> By whom the words of life were spoken,
> And in whose death our sins are dead.
>
> Look on the heart by sorrow broken
> Look on the tears by sinners shed,

> And be Thy feast to us the token
> That by Thy grace our souls are fed.[84]

Neither the hymn's sacramental specificity, nor its Anglican parentage, deterred the compilers of the later book from including it. Similarly, the hymn by the Scottish Free Churchman, Horatius Bonar, 'Here, O my Lord, I see Thee face to face', was included and continued to remain popular into the twentieth century:

> Here would I feed upon the bread of God,
> Here drink with Thee the royal wine of heaven;
> Here would I lay aside each earthly load,
> Here taste afresh the calm of sin forgiven.[85]

Perhaps any Baptist fears of such language were reassured by references elsewhere in the hymn to 'the brief, bright hour of fellowship' and

> Too soon we rise; the symbols disappear;
> The feast, though not the love, is past and gone . . .

This hymn was a legacy of the *Baptist Hymnal*, not *Psalms and Hymns*. From the same source the *Baptist Church Hymnal* selected Bishop Robert Baynes' communion hymn, 'Jesus, to Thy table led',[86] with its realist sacramental language:

> Jesus, to Thy table led
> Now let every heart be fed
> With the true and living Bread!
>
> When we taste the mystic wine,
> Of Thine outpoured blood the sign,
> Fill our hearts with love divine.

Amongst hymns that appeared in none of the earlier books were two by the Anglican writer, Elizabeth Charles. One of these tentatively links the Lord's Supper with the resurrection:

> Around a table, not a tomb,
> He willed our gathering-place to be;
> When, going to prepare our home,
> Our Saviour said - 'Remember Me' . . .
>
> Thus round Thy table, not Thy tomb,
> We keep Thy sacred feast with Thee;
> Until within the Father's home
> Our endless gathering-place shall be.[87]

The other ascribes an inferior role to preaching compared with the power of the Lord's Supper to present the Good News with an eloquence not known to human tongue:

> No Gospel like this feast
> Spread for Thy church by Thee;
> Nor prophet nor evangelist
> Preach the glad news so free.[88]

Clearly, Baptists were prepared to go on using sacramental language in their hymns. In the development of their changing repertoire, though they might dispense with some such hymns, they compensated for their removal by the addition of others.

Tracing a theology through the hymns sung by any group of Christians is a hazardous enterprise. Why hymns were selected and continued to be sung, why some faded into oblivion, must be a matter of speculation. As much as the theology of the hymn, it is necessary to consider the flow of its language and, not least in the case of a people for whom singing has been so important, the flow, rhythm and melody, if not the quality, of the tune to which it is set. Certain factors remain consistent, however. The earlier Baptist hymns were robust in the sacramental realism of their language and ardent in their devotion to Christ. It can only be guessed that their later disappearance is more attributable to their dated and unsophisticated language than to any shortcomings in their theology. The later collections continued the theme of devotion to Christ but placed a greater emphasis on memorialism and less on the wider kerygmatic setting of the cross. Hymns with a specific sacramental content continued to be used and, whilst the 1900 *Baptist Church Hymnal* dispensed with some of these, it added others. Most significantly of all, Baptists did not hesitate to draw widely from other denominational sources and, by the end of the century, they were exclusively dependent in their communion hymns upon the compositions of others whose view of the Lord's Supper may not always have been their own.

A study of the nineteenth-century communion hymns sung by Baptists confirms the trends we have detected within their more explicit theological statements. In the earlier part of the century the Calvinist inheritance, evidenced in the realism of their language, continued to influence them and later on remained germane to the beliefs of a minority, of whom Spurgeon was the outstanding example. The majority shared the Zwinglian view of the sacrament, subject as it was to the constant temptation to temper it with a more radical evaluation of the place of sacraments, reminiscent of the earlier Anabaptists. They were saved from the extremes of radical iconoclasm by the influence of main-stream Reformation theology which continued to play a significant part in their attitudes. The hymns they sang, both those from the pens of their fellow Baptists and those drawn from the hymnology of the wider church, confirmed that influence and ensured, at that deep level of consciousness which hymns have the peculiar power to affect, a devout recognition of the place of the Lord's Supper in the life of the church. As some of those hymns reflect, at the table love between Christ and his people found a focal point capable of great intensity. That it did so is astonishing, in view of the often bitter controversies that surrounded the sacrament and the dismissive language that was used of it in the course of them. It is to the first of these controversies that we now turn.

NOTES
[Unless otherwise stated, London is the place of publication]

1. Norwich 1816.
2. Joseph Kinghorn, **op.cit.** p.137.
3. W. Walters, 'Scenes from the Public Life of Jesus of Nazareth', **Baptist Magazine** 44, 1852, p.737.
4. ibid. p.738.
5. T. Pottenger, 'On the Constitution and Working of the Churches', **Baptist Magazine** 49, 1857, p.211.
6. 1882.
7. Charles Williams, op.cit. p.41.
8. ibid. p.44f.
9. ibid. p.49.
10. See pp.182ff.
11. Alexander Maclaren, **Expositions of Holy Scripture: St Paul's Epistles to the Corinthians**, 1909, p.173.
12. ibid. pp.174f.
13. W. T. Whitley, 'The Witness of History to Baptist Principles', **Baptist Magazine** 88, 1896, p.271.
14. ibid. p.272.
15. ibid. p.313.
16. ibid. p.381.
17. Robert Hall, Jnr, **On Terms of Communion**, 1815, in Olinthus Gregory, ed., **The Works of Robert Hall, A.M.**, 1832, Vol.2, pp.63f.
18. John Calvin, **Institutes of the Christian Religion** IV:xvii:1, trans. J. Allen, 1838.
19. William Newman, **A Manual for Church Members**, 1825, p.50.
20. William Button, **An Answer to the Question, Why Are You a Strict Baptist?** 1816, p.93.
21. J. Jarrom, **The Lord's Supper: Its Institution, Uses and the Obligation of Christians to Regard It**, Leicester 1836, p.3.
22. ibid..
23. ibid. p.4.
24. ibid. p.5.
25. Anon, 'Sacramental Meditations', **Baptist Magazine** 39, 1857, p.22.
26. ibid. p.22.
27. ibid. p.23.
28. ibid. p.91.
29. ibid..
30. ibid. p.152.
31. ibid. p.153.
32. ibid. p.215.
33. ibid.
34. ibid.
35. ibid. p.285.
36. ibid. p.286.
37. ibid. p.351.
38. ibid.
39. ibid. p.352.
40. ibid.
41. Edward C. Alden, 'Baptism and the Lord's Supper', **Baptist Magazine** 83, 1891, pp.397-405.
42. ibid. p.399.
43. ibid. p.401.
44. ibid. p.402.
45. J. Hunt Cooke, 'The Lord's Supper', **Baptist Magazine** 91, 1899, pp.516f.
46. ibid. p.519.
47. ibid. p.520.
48. E. A. Payne, **College Street Chapel, Northampton, 1697-1947**, 1947, p.35.
49. See below.
50. Sometimes attributed to Samuel Stennett because it did not appear in the earlier collection of Joseph Stennett hymns, it nevertheless was written by the latter and given to Rippon by his grandson. See 'Joseph Stennett' (W.R.S) in J.Julian, **Dictionary of Hymnology**, 1907, p.1091.
51. Rippon's **Selection of Hymns** (RS) 482; **Psalms and Hymns** (PH) 743; **Our Own Hymn Book** (OOHB) 949. Initials in brackets are used throughout the remainder of the footnotes.
52. RS 489.
53. RS 476.
54. OOHB 937.
55. RS 484.
56. RS 487.
57. RS 488.
58. RS 485.
59. OOHB 938.
60. RS 483.
61. RS 477.
62. OOHB 939.

THE DOCTRINE OF THE LORD'S SUPPER

63 Baptist Hymnal (BH) 654, PH 733, OOHB 944, Baptist Church Hymnal (BCH) 517.
64 BH 647, PH 727, OOHB 936, BCH 519.
65 BH 648, PH 740, BCH 520.
66 BH 649, PH 741, BCH 513.
67 BH 652, PH 738, BCH 516.
68 BH 658, PH 739, BCH 521.
69 BH 655, PH 726, OOHB 945.
70 BH 660, PH 743, OOHB 949.
71 PH 730, OOHB 942, BCH 515.
72 See n.64.
73 See n.66.
74 See n.68.
75 BH 664, BCH 527.
76 See n.63.
77 See n.71.
78 See n.67.
79 PH 735, BCH 524.
80 See n.69.
81 PH 732.
82 PH 737.
83 PH 725.
84 See n.65.
85 BH 653, BCH 525.
86 BH 657, BCH 512.
87 BCH 508.
88 BCH 523.

Chapter Two

THE COMMUNION CONTROVERSY

The issues that have most often attracted the attention of the Christian churches in their discussions of the eucharist proved to be only of peripheral concern to Baptists during the eighteenth and early nineteenth centuries. Questions such as the nature of sacrifice, the real presence and the mode of consecration had no place on their theological agenda. Such questions, as far as they were concerned, belonged to a Catholicism already long rejected. Instead they devoted their energies to an internal controversy that had its roots in the seventeenth century, had continued to trouble them in the eighteenth and was to flare up in renewed intensity in the nineteenth in a way that was to prove divisive, often bitter, always wordy and frequently debilitating. It was a controversy that arose out of the distinctive emphases of Baptist theology and therefore one of which other churches were, for the most part, spectators.

A) BACKGROUND OF THE DEBATE

The communion controversy arose out of a conflict of Baptist views on the relationship of baptism to the church. In common with other separatists of the seventeenth century, they had left the Church of England believing that the church should consist only of those who had made a profession of faith in Christ and had covenanted together with those who had made a similar commitment. They took a further step, which other separatists were unprepared to follow, in allowing their doctrine of the church radically to shape their doctrine of baptism. Whereas Independents and Presbyterians believed that the children of believers were included in the covenant and therefore were to receive baptism in their infancy as a sign of that inclusion, Baptists believed that only those capable of making a profession of faith should belong to the church and therefore only believers should be baptized, baptism being, amongst other things, a rite of initiation into the church. To the baptism of infants they accorded no status whatever. It was a non-baptism, nullified by the absence of conscious faith on the part of the baptizand. Thus far all Baptists walked together in harmony.

The controversy arose out of a different view of the relationship of the Lord's Supper to baptism. On one side, there were those who emphasised the nature of the Supper as a church ordinance and therefore open only to those who had been properly admitted to the church, that is through the sacrament of 'believer's' baptism. These were the 'closed' communionists. On the other side, there were Baptists who believed that profession of faith was always more important than the rite in which it was expressed. These, whilst conceding no validity to infant baptism, were prepared to admit Christians of other persuasions to the table provided they showed evidence of saving faith. These were the 'open' communionists.

The loose structure of the Baptist denomination was conducive to the continuance of the debate over three centuries without any resolution apart from that which resulted from a final sterility. By the end of the nineteenth century, the controversy no longer provided fertile ground for the nurturing of division. Until then it continued to test the emotional energies of the protagonists and to consume volumes of words. There was no central authority to deliver a final judgment on the matter and only the loosest of groupings between those of similar opinion on both sides of the debate. Allegiance to either practice was determined at local level. 'Every church had to make its own decision, and within each church, the opinion of each member had to be considered'.[1] From the beginnings of the seventeenth century, B. R. White has identified three main groups.[2]

The first were the General Baptists who practised both closed membership and closed communion. This meant that both membership and communion within their churches was limited to those who had received believer's baptism. If this restrictive policy seems to be at variance with their title, it has to be remembered that 'General' refers not to their stance on the communion question but to their Arminian view of the atonement. Their position on the communion question is not surprising. Their progress from separatism to a Baptist position under the leadership of John Smyth (d.1612) and Thomas Helwys (d. circa 1616) had been impelled by a development in their understanding of the nature of the church. The church was central to their thinking and from that flowed quite naturally their doctrine of baptism.[3] The purity of the church was secured by the purity of its initiating ordinance. If, as in the case of infant baptism, the ordinance led to the inclusion in the body of Christ of those who had not, indeed could not, exercise saving faith, then the church became a 'mixed' or impure community. If, on the other hand, baptism was limited to those able to profess faith then it was more likely that the church would be in a position to sustain its New Testament purity. The closing of both membership and communion flowed logically from those premises. By the early nineteenth century, however, this position was no longer rigorously held. The 1809 General Assembly of the General Baptists conceded that this was a matter upon which they had no authority to rule and that the decision whether to pursue a policy of 'open' or 'closed' communion rested upon each individual local church:

> ... this Assembly thinks that every individual church must Judge for itself concerning open communion; several churches practice open and several strict communion in our connection - the former admitting persons who are not baptized by immersion as communicants only but not Members of the Church.[4]

The diversity of practice amongst General Baptists is evidenced by an altercation that occurred in the correspondence columns of the *General Baptist Magazine* in 1838, between Jabez Burns of Marylebone and J. Liggins of Hinckley. The former had written that baptism should always precede communion and 'as Paedo-baptism is not baptism' this meant restricting communion to those baptized by immersion. Liggins, taking up the argument in a letter of reply, argued that to close the table in this way amounted to a refusal to recognize other Christians that was nothing short of 'inexcusable churlishness'.[5] Burns replied in the subsequent edition that admitting paedobaptists to communion entailed recognition of 'this foul rival of Christ's Baptism'.[6] The correspondence was brought to a halt by the editor, jolted into action by a letter from a third correspondent who expressed disquiet at the tone of the whole debate and observed that, 'The bigot of every denomination has taken for his text, "first pure, then peaceable"'.[7] It was not to be the last time that the anger excited by the debate was to prompt a magazine editor to close his correspondence columns to it.

The second group identifed by White were the Particular Baptists who owed their origins to the Jacob-Lathrop-Jessey church. This London separatist church had followed a path similar to that of John Smyth, except that they had retained their Calvinist theology (hence the title 'Particular'), and placed more emphasis upon the symbolism of baptism as a rite of death, burial and resurrection in Christ. This group practised both closed membership and closed communion. The Calvinists were to provide some of the most redoubtable defenders of closed communion in the eighteenth century, notable amongst them being Abraham Booth (1734-1806), whose book *Apology for Baptists* (1778) was to be used by Robert Hall, himself a Calvinist, as a taper to ignite the controversy in the early nineteenth century.

The third group also was Calvinist, shared the same views of church and baptism, but argued for open communion. Amongst these were Henry Jessey, John Tombes, Vavasor Powell and, notably, John Bunyan. Bunyan in his *Differences in Judgment about Water Baptism no Bar to Communion* (1673) argued that 'the Church of Christ hath no warrant to keep out of the communion the Christian that is discovered to be a visible saint of the word, the Christian that walketh according to his own light with God'.[8]

At the opening of the nineteenth century the majority of Baptist churches practised closed communion. By the end of the century the tide had turned the other way, though by then a small group, known as Strict Baptists, making closed communion the central tenet of their church practice, had distanced themselves from the main body of Baptist churches and were leading an 'independent, isolated life'.[9] The controversy led to many changes of heart and mind during the course of the century, closed churches becoming open, open churches becoming closed. At times it caused grievous divisions in church memberships. The church at Avenue in Southend-on-Sea is an example. Founded in 1876, the Church Meeting decided in 1878 that

> None but members of Christian Churches be allowed to sit down at The Lord's Table and none but Baptized persons can

join the Church excepting a Doctor's certificate can be given that Immersion would be injurious to health.[10]

As we have seen, open communion and closed membership was a formula that had been followed by some from earliest times. Even these well-charted waters, however, were to be the setting for a storm within six years of the church's foundation. The pastor of the church, John Gavin Wilson, interpreted open communion as an invitation 'to all who love the Lord Jesus', including in this those who had never been baptized at any stage in their lives. It was a position not difficult for Baptists to arrive at, seeing that they recognized no validity in infant baptism and were prepared to receive as communicants those who had never received believer's baptism. An elder deacon, Henry Lester, believed that such an invitation was altogether too open. He wished to limit communion to baptized believers only, even if their baptism was one they had received in infancy. Writing to the *Southend Standard*, a local newspaper which had taken a not unnatural interest in the dispute, he declared his willingness to receive any member of 'any other Christian Church, including of course the Church of England'.[11] Both men, it seems, were guilty of mutually exclusive forms of magnanimity. Wilson would receive anyone who loved Christ, regardless of baptism. Lester would receive anyone who had been baptized regardless of his church allegiance. Unfortunately, their magnanimity did not extend to each other and Wilson departed with six other members to form the Clarence Road Baptist Church.

Where some churches dug themselves into entrenched positions, others were more pragmatic in their approach. The minutes for the Church Meeting held on 2 October 1857 at Queen's Road, Coventry, record that four friends belonging to the Free Church of Scotland 'were granted the privilege of uniting with the church in the ordinance of the Lord's Supper'.[12] The author of the church's history, published in 1925, observes, 'This is a privilege which the church now extends publicly to all who love the Lord Jesus Christ, but our forefathers did not offer it so readily'.[13]

Undoubtedly, local churches were influenced by the stance taken by the Metropolitan Tabernacle, the church of C. H. Spurgeon. Spurgeon's Calvinism was beyond dispute and his influence far-reaching. His own practice was of open communion and closed membership and this was imitated in the churches in and around London in which the men who were trained at his Pastors' College settled.[14] The arrangements at the Metropolitan Tabernacle did not always prevent misunderstandings, however. In 1875, the editor of the *Chicago Standard* attended communion at the Tabernacle having heard that the church did not 'hedge up the path of any soul pressing its way to the sacred feast'. He found, to his dismay, that tickets were issued to communicants and that he was granted one only after he had been questioned closely as to his 'qualification for the Supper'. He concluded that this betrayed a 'closeness which was far more exacting and far less Scriptural than the most restricted communion of regular Baptist churches'. Reporting the incident, the *Freeman*, the weekly Baptist newspaper, sprang to the Tabernacle's defence and, somewhat ingenuously, attributed the incident to 'voluntary zeal to become acquainted with a stranger'.[15]

Of all the disputes in local churches, the *cause célèbre* was that at St Mary's Baptist Church in Norwich. Until his death in 1832, the minister of St Mary's had been Joseph Kinghorn, the leading advocate of closed communion in the controversy provoked by Robert Hall. In his account of the dispute at St Mary's, *Open Communion and the Baptists of Norwich*, George Gould claims that the communion question had been raised from time to time during Kinghorn's ministry but, out of deference for Kinghorn's feelings, the matter had not been pursued.[16] In 1833 the church took the strange step of inviting William Brock, an avowed open communionist, to become its minister, with the proviso that he would not raise the question of open communion in the church. It is clear that, after five years, Brock felt unable to sustain his silence and he raised the matter in the Church Meeting of 23 March 1838. Some felt that he had reneged on a pledge given at the time of his call, a pledge that he denied ever having given. At a further meeting on 30 April he expressed his willingness to resign from the church on the issue, but was dissuaded, the church agreeing that he was at liberty to hold his views as long as he did not introduce the practice of open communion. The matter did not surface again until 1845. Brock received an invitation to become minister of the open communion church at Broadmead, Bristol, which he declined, informing the congregation at St Mary's both of the invitation and of his reply to it. In April of the same year he wrote a letter, sent to every member, in which he laid before them his convictions on the communion question. His ministry had been successful and had clearly drawn people who, whilst identifying themselves with its fellowship and the word proclaimed from its pulpit, were unable to accept the church's ruling on admission to communion. Brock himself referred to one applicant for membership who had been prevented by ill health from being baptized by immersion and was consequently barred from the Lord's table.[17] He interpreted the decision of the 1838 Church Meeting as a warrant to raise the question if conscience so impelled him. He claimed that there was no written constitution that forbade the celebration of open communion at St Mary's and then declared his intention of holding such a service on the third Sunday afternoon of each month. The church's closed communion service on the first Sunday of each month was to continue out of respect for those who believed this to be the right course. When the Church Meeting met on 26 May, Brock was able to inform them that the new service had already been introduced and held twice.[18] The pressures that had been on Brock to introduce the new service are evidenced by a report in the *Primitive Church Magazine* for June of that year, revealing that as many as 160 people had attended the open communion service. At the same meeting a motion that Brock be censured and condemned for his action was put forward but withdrawn, the proposer and seconder 'yielding to the evident feeling of the church'.[19]

Some of those who stood by the church's traditional stance had already sought a judgment in the matter from its trustees. The trustees, in turn, had passed it on to solicitors who judged that the open communion was not a violation of the trust deeds of the chapel. This judgment was reversed when a case was prepared and submitted to them by the closed communionists. Another attempt was made to raise the question in Church Meeting on 30 March 1846 but it was heavily out-voted. During this time eleven members had left the church because of their opposition to the open communion service. The normal procedures were followed for dealing with those who, for any reason, had absented themselves from the Lord's table for an unacceptable period of time. The deputation sent to visit them reported that the dissenters had made it clear that they did not intend to return to the church's communion. The church agreed that their membership had consequently been relinquished 'by their own act'.[20]

The matter was laid to rest again until a Church Meeting on 30 April 1849, following Brock's resignation from the pastorate and removal to London. It had been argued that the open communion service should be discontinued in view of his departure; the church, however, agreed that the communion service on the first Sunday of the month should remain a closed communion service, but that 'brethren [be] left free to meet at other seasons for communion with other Christians, according to their own convictions of duty'.[21] In 1849 the church called to the pastorate George Gould, also an avowed open communionist, who declared that on the communion question 'as upon all other religious questions, I should feel bound to speak as occasion arose'.[22] Peace was preserved until the beginning of 1857. At that time, Elizabeth Bayes applied for membership of the church. Her application was received by the Church Meeting 'cordially', harmony quickly giving way to discord when a letter from her doctor was read to the meeting, certifying that she was not in a state of health 'to justify her being exposed to the consequences which might possibly result from immersion in cold water'.[23] The meeting was adjourned and reconvened on 26 January. It was then proposed that 'Christians are bound to receive one another as believers in the Lord Jesus, and to partake of the Lord's Supper together'.[24] It was argued in reply that a difference had to be observed between admitting the unbaptized believer to the Lord's table and to membership of the church. A compromise formula was moved, recommending that Elizabeth Bayes be received, as a member, at the monthly communion service of the church 'on the ground of her willingness to be baptized as soon as the providence of God allows'.[25] An amendment was put that she be not admitted to the Lord's Supper until such time as she was baptized. The amendment was lost by twenty-three votes to six; the compromise formula, based on 'intentional baptism', was carried. Elizabeth Bayes received communion on the first Sunday in February and was baptized on 1 July when the warmer water, no doubt, posed less threat to her health. Her case had, by then, re-opened the whole question and at the March Church Meeting an adjournment was needed after a 'long and desultory conversation' in which the church had been faced with a proposition that it continue to be closed in its membership but that the communion should be open to all 'believers in the Lord Jesus', and an amendment that only baptized believers be admitted to the communion on the first Sunday of the month, 'according to the practice of this Church for the last 170 years'.[26] Gould, who had remained commendably restrained during the whole dispute, was given the unhappy task of delivering 'his judgment upon the question' when the Church Meeting was reconvened on 11 March. The scent of battle drew one hundred and thirty-two members, seventy-eight of whom, after hearing Gould's paper, voted against the amendment tabled at the previous meeting and fifty-four in favour. The original resolution was then carried *nem con*. Thus, St Mary's Norwich, nudged by a doctor's certificate, accepted the practice of open communion. A further Church Meeting on 30 March agreed that those believers who had hitherto gathered at the open communion on the third Sunday afternoon of each month should not be invited to the regular communion held on the first Sunday. The space vacated by them was offered to those strict communionists who would 'conscientiously object to commune with unbaptized believers at the table of the Lord'.[27] The church declined to exert its authority by specifying that these brethren should meet on the third Sunday, preferring to leave them to determine their own choice of day. In his account of the dispute, Gould expressed the sanguine, but unrealistic, hope that 'this series of resolutions would effectually provide for all parties'.[28] He was to be disappointed. The closed communionsts seceded, hired an unused chapel and there celebrated the Lord's Supper according to their convictions. Convinced that they had been dispossessed, they called on William Norton, a trustee and leading figure in the dispute, who was then living in Egham in Surrey, to act as their spokesman. Norton and two others called on Gould, requested him to vacate the pulpit of St Mary's at once and for all those who shared his views to vacate the chapel as soon as possible. Gould declined their invitation. The seceders continued to celebrate the Lord's Supper in their hired chapel but claimed that they were the true membership of St Mary's. They also made it clear that they intended to continue attending Church Meetings at St Mary's which they did in large numbers. Their right to take part in the meetings was challenged in view of their secession. It was finally agreed that the matter be submitted to the arbitration of persons acceptable both to Gould and Norton. A long correspondence between the two men followed, Norton moving to the opinion that the dispute should be submitted to the Charity Commissioners for their judgment. Gould was advised that the Commissioners had no jurisdiction in such doctrinal matters.

THE COMMUNION CONTROVERSY

At the Church Meeting on 1 March 1858, Gould intimated his intention of bringing before the church the names of absentees from the monthly communion service. It was felt that one last effort should be made to restore the seceders to fellowship. A closed communion service was arranged for the afternoon of 11 April and the seceders invited to attend. None of them accepted. At the Church Meeting of 26 April a deputation was appointed to call on the seceders in accordance with the church's usual procedure for lapsed communicants. They reported back to the church on 30 July that forty-one of those whom they had seen expressed their intention not to return to the fellowship of the church. They were deemed to have severed their membership by their own act and it was agreed that their membership be terminated. On 13 May the controversy was shared with the public at large, when Norton filed a petition in Chancery claiming that St Mary's, being a Particular Baptist church, should admit to the table only those who were baptized believers and held a doctrine of limited atonement.[29] Norton argued that a Particular Baptist church consisted of those who had been baptized by immersion, on profession of faith and who held that 'Christ, as the surety of God's elect, bore their sins, and died exclusively for their redemption'.[30] He endeavoured to state, through his counsel, an argument from historical precedent that failed to take into account the diversity of practice amongst Particular Baptists. Particular Baptists, he claimed, held that atonement and redemption were co-extensive. It was not true to say that the atonement was for all but effective only in the case of the elect. The atonement was limited to the elect. Only those who held this view and what he took to be its corollary, that believers should be baptized by immersion upon profession of faith, could claim to be Particular Baptists. Arguing on the basis of that definition he claimed that Robert Hall, the Particular Baptist champion of open communion, was not in fact a Particular Baptist as he held a general view of the atonement though limited in its effect to the elect. The seceders clearly saw the decline from closed into open communion as part of a wider liberalizing of what they believed to be the Calvinist tenet of limited atonement.

The case was heard over three days, judgment being given by the Master of the Rolls on 28 May 1860. He ruled that:

> a) The Trust Deeds of the church stated that the premises of St Mary's were to be used for the 'Congregation of Particular Baptists' and made no mention of what was to be the church's practice in the matter of communion.[31]

> b) The present practice of the church did not compel any who held strict communionist views to participate in open communion. Nor, in view of the provision of a closed communion service for those who desired it, were the strict communionists deprived of the sacrament.[32]

c) The argument that to be a Particular Baptist church carried the invariable corollary of closed communion was historically inaccurate. Henry Jessey, John Tombes and John Bunyan in the seventeenth century were quoted as examples of Particular Baptists who practised open communion.[33]

d) It was part of Particular Baptist practice and belief that no congregation or group of congregations had jurisdiction over another, each congregation ordering its affairs as it thought fit.[34]

e) It had been argued that the practice of the church had been established by long usage and that this weighed against the introduction of open communion. The Master of the Rolls ruled that there was involved no change of practice involving an 'essential or fundamental doctrine of the faith of Particular Baptists', further there was no contravention of the Trust Deed. Therefore, it could not be argued that a practice involving neither fundamental doctrine nor legality could 'become so fixed by custom as to be incapable of alteration'.[35]

The judgment concluded that 'the full Members of the Church or Congregation of Particular Baptists, within the city of Norwich, are entitled to adopt the practice of Free Communion, or of Strict Communion, as they shall, from time to time, think fit to Determine'.[36] So ended a dispute that had laid such uncompromising claims upon the energies of the church for a period of twenty-seven years.

The case in Chancery served dramatically to highlight turmoils through which many churches must have passed during this period. Various deductions may be drawn from it. Firstly, it demonstrates the autonomy of local Baptist churches in making decisions affecting the ordering of their corporate life. St Mary's may have been a microcosm of a wider conflict but it had finally to resolve the dispute in its own way, even if that involved the drastic recourse to the due processes of law. Gould had sought the opinions of men as distinguished as Joseph Angus, William Landels, the Secretary of the Baptist Union, J. H. Hinton, Baptist W. Noel and Edward Steane, but their word carried no more weight or authority than that of individual opinion and had finally to be adjudged by the corporate decision of the church. Secondly, the St Mary's affair reveals the impact that ministers had upon the beliefs embraced by the members of the church. Joseph Kinghorn's commitment to and public advocacy of closed communion placed a restraint upon discussion within the church, if it be the case that such discussion was ever desired. The ministries of Brock and Gould carried the church to an open communion position and it was naïve in the extreme if the strict communionists believed that the church's practice could go unquestioned whilst calling such men to the pastorate. Undoubtedly, the influence of the minister was counterbalanced by the presence of men of contrary opinion within the congregation, capable of powerfully expressing their beliefs. It required a strong spiritual constitution for a man like Gould to face up to a figure as powerful and articulate as William Norton but, given that he possessed the strength, a minister could deeply influence his church. Thirdly, the practice of a Baptist church was affected by changes within its membership. The impressive number of people who attended Brock's early open communion services is evidence of a congregation that had drawn people from a wide constituency. The one hundred and sixty communicants on that occasion are to be compared with the one hundred and thirty-two members who attended the Church Meeting of 11 March 1857 when the controversy was at its height. Fourthly, the case presented by the seceders at the Chancery Court reveals the difficulties faced by Baptists in drawing upon the precedents of their own history. The link that Norton tried to establish between the soteriological beliefs of a Particular Baptist church and its practice in the matter of admittance to communion was untenable from the outset. Baptist history, not unlike the Bible, can be employed to prove anything, provided that the text is not examined too closely. The full public glare of a court of law was not the place to embark on such a hazardous enterprise.

A theological controversy, fought within a frame of reference so domestically Baptist, as emotionally costly as was the communion debate, miraculously left energies for other enterprises, as is evidenced by the vigorous tempo of Baptist church life in the latter half of the nineteenth century. Perhaps many washed their hands of it, as did the editor of the *Baptist Reporter* who declined to allow the matter to be discussed in his columns.[37] The difficulties facing Baptists were succinctly expressed by J. H. Hinton in his presidential address to the Baptist Union in 1863. The Baptist denomination, he said, might well name itself 'Legion':

> In the first place, it is divided into two by a difference of doctrinal sentiment, some churches holding the Calvinistic system, some the Arminian. These constitute respectively the General Baptists and the Particular Baptists . . . Of these two bodies the larger, or the Particular Baptists, is itself divided by a doctrinal diversity, according as the Calvinistic system has been found capable of being modified into two forms, which have been called High and Moderate Calvinism. The Particular Baptist body is further divided by a practical diversity on the subject of Communion. It contains churches which restrict fellowship at the Lord's Table to persons who have made profession of their faith by Baptism, and churches who admit to Communion professed believers in Jesus, although unbaptized. These are called respectively Open-Communionists and Strict Communionists . . . We have then six parties.[38]

B) THE HALL-KINGHORN DEBATE

The communion debate had occupied the mind of the Baptist churches, to a greater or lesser extent, since the seventeenth century. The fact that it flared up so vigorously in the opening years of the nineteenth is not to be attributed to spontaneous ignition. The closing decades of the eighteenth century had witnessed a cracking, if not a breaking, in the mould of Baptist church life. Almost a century of petrification had followed the exhausting clash of the Civil War. The Restoration, no matter how disadvantageous to the Nonconformists, had provided a stability which all valued, whatever its effect upon their religious profession and practice. Within the constraints imposed by King and Parliament, churches settled into patterns of corporate life that ministered to their own needs and increasingly reinforced their complacency. In the latter half of the century that settled order began to be disturbed by events both outside and inside the church. John Wesley was the herald of a new Evangelicalism that exuberantly called all and sundry to share in a gospel that had again become Good News. The French Revolution sent its tremors throughout Western Europe, signalling the crumbling of the old social order, a process that in Britain was happily gradual and bloodless. The Industrial Revolution was changing the face of Britain's cities and the pattern of its corporate life. The gradual urbanisation of the working masses heralded a new age of mobility and its often attendent rootlessness. Congregations ebbed and flowed with the tide of human movement, the relative importance of various doctrines shifting as well.

Within the Baptist churches, various pressures led to the re-opening of the communion question with all its attendent agitation. The General Baptist churches had been jolted into life by Dan Taylor and his New Connexion, Taylor himself having come under the influence of John Wesley and the Methodist movement. The Particular Baptist churches, clutching their own throat in the ever-tightening grip of a high Calvinism, had persuaded themselves that preaching the gospel was God's work and not theirs, as he alone could discern the elect and give them saving faith. This recipe for certain death had been replaced by another that gave some hope of life. Andrew Fuller, dismayed by the consequences of the hyper-Calvinism of his fellow Baptists, wrote *The Gospel Worthy of all Acceptation* (1785), an eloquent plea for recognition that the gospel had to be preached and, being preached, required a response. What he argued theologically fired the imagination of William Carey with the possibility of preaching the gospel to the whole of mankind. The Missionary Society was to carry the logic of Fuller's theology to India and to shape the perspective of Christians through to the twentieth century.

The Missionary Society was to prove one among many societies that were to spring up in the nineteenth century. It was the age of initiative, a time of causes, an epoch of battles fought with enormous energy on many fronts. Inevitably, Christians were not so much drawn together as thrown together. Combined action promised greater results than unilateral enthusiasm. If Christians wanted to achieve the many estimable goals they set themselves, then there had to be greater co-operation. Where practice led, piety followed. Christians who worked together increasingly felt the constraint to pray together. A glance at Robert Hall's involvement in movements of this kind will go some way to explain the passion with which he re-opened the communion controversy. Amongst them were the Bible Society, the London Missionary Society, the British and Foreign School Society, the Anti-Slavery Society, the Cambridge Benevolent Society, the Frame-Knitters' Society and the Committee for the Relief of Distress in Germany, as well as other similar causes.[39]

For Baptists, these changes called for a reappraisal of their doctrinal position. Their doctrine of the church drew a clear line of demarcation between the church and a world in whose life and welfare they were increasingly engaged. Their doctrine of baptism, especially when accompanied by the corollary of closed communion, separated them from Christians with whom they increasingly worked in common cause. The communion controversy can be viewed as a dispute about the way in which the church should respond to a situation that was vastly different from the setting of the seventeenth century and was breaking the mould of the eighteenth. It has been seen as a dispute in which Baptists were divided on how far they could replace symbolism with empiricism.[40] Hall spoke for those who believed that doctrine and the symbols in which it was expressed had in some way to respond to what was happening in the church and world of their time. Kinghorn spoke for those who believed that the significance of the symbols remained unaffected by the shifts and changes of the environment in which they were observed.

It was these different approaches that accounted for the ways in which Hall and Kinghorn approached the communion question when the controversy was re-opened at the beginning of the nineteenth century. Hall faced the empirical question of how the Baptist churches were to respond to the new relationships between Christians drawn together in common action in an ever-increasing number of projects. For him, the inter-relationships of Christians in the loose structures of the many societies that were being formed raised the question of their unity within the structures of the church itself. Could Christian men and women, bound together by common action, stand apart in matters of prayer and worship and, if they had learned to pray and worship together, could they continue to hold each other at arm's length in the eucharist? For him, then, the communion issue was about the unity of the church, a unity that was created by the multilateral response of the churches to the challenges posed by society. Kinghorn, on the other hand, argued for the validity of those symbols that he believed existed to preserve the integrity of the church. To Baptists, the sacrament of baptism was not an isolated ordinance characterised by the age of the candidate and the quantity of water employed in its administration. Those aspects of it were derivative from its deeper theological meaning. A proper understanding of baptism involved a proper understanding of the nature of faith and of the Christian life; it defined the church and safeguarded its true character as a gathered community, a covenant people bound together in the free and conscious assent of faith. For Kinghorn, the communion issue was about right order, an order that was in no way affected by the temporal tides through which the church had to chart its course.

The difference between the two men is apparent in the way that each begins his first book on the issue. Hall, in his introductory remarks, says:

> Whoever forms his ideas of the Church of Christ from an attentive perusal of the New Testament, will perceive that *unity* is one of its essential characteristics.[41]

Kinghorn perceives the question as being one of

> . . . whether persons who are acknowledged to be unbaptized ought to come to the Lord's table.[42]

Because they both started from different points it can be questioned whether there was a real meeting of minds beneath the argument and counter-argument of their dispute, or whether either faced up to some of the consequences of their own convictions. Where they both succeeded was in setting down the markers that were to plot the course of the debate in the coming years. The implications of some of their arguments were not really faced until the twentieth century; some remain to be faced to this day.

The two men were very different in their gifts, in their style and in their interpretation of the Christian ministry. Robert Hall, Jnr (1764-1831), was the son of one of the eighteenth century's leading challengers to the hyper-Calvinism of the time. He displayed an early intellectual brilliance, eventually graduating from King's College, Aberdeen, following a period at the dissenting Bristol Academy. He had pastorates in Cambridge, which he loathed, in Harvey Lane, Leicester, where he ministered for eighteen years and which became an open communion church within a year of his leaving, and the Broadmead church in Bristol where his preaching abilities drew large congregations. He was an outstanding orator, being described by a later historian as 'the Chrysostom of the English pulpit'![43] He was an ebullient and witty conversationalist, at times expressing his forceful opinions with a trenchant and, to an adversary, crushing humour. In contrast, Joseph Kinghorn (1766-1832) was a man whose pastoral gifts far exceeded his preaching abilities. He had only one pastorate, that at St Mary's, Norwich, where he was deeply loved by his people, a fact that probably goes further than any other in explaining their apparent silence on the communion issue whilst he was amongst them. The two men respected each other, though Kinghorn was later offended by Hall's somewhat bruising literary style.

Hall opened the controversy in 1815 with his book *On Terms of Communion*, which took as its opening point of dispute Abraham Booth's *Apology for Baptists*, written nearly forty years earlier in 1778. Kinghorn took up the challenge that had been presented to the closed communionists, publishing his reply, *Baptism a Term of Communion at the Lord's Supper*, in 1816. This was replied to by Hall's *A Reply to the Rev. Joseph Kinghorn, being a Further Vindication of Free Communion* in 1818. In 1820, Kinghorn published *A Defence of Baptism a Term of Communion in Answer to the Rev. Robert Hall's reply*. Once the chief arguments had been made on both sides, the controversy became tedious, academic and repetitive. Others joined in the debate on both sides, but added little to the points argued by the two chief protagonists. To these arguments we now turn.

C) THE UNITY OF THE CHURCH: ROBERT HALL

In a literary debate as wordy as that between Hall and Kinghorn, simply to review and re-state their arguments would be an unnecessary and fruitless enterprise. Inevitably, as much space is given to the nature of baptism as to the nature of the Lord's Supper and, whilst the two are inseparable, our chief concern must be with the latter. Our ends will be better served by extrapolating from the writings of both men those theological ideas that were at the heart of the issue or were to prove most influential in the coming years. Reference will also be made to the way in which these points were handled by other participants in the debate.

In Hall's work there are three areas of major interest in his approach to the subject of the Lord's Supper. The first is his basic conviction that it is a sign of the church's unity. The second is his argument that faith takes precedence over 'ceremonial'. Thirdly, Hall deals with the way in which the church is historically conditioned, thus making it impossible in any dispute to return to an original and pristine state in which the world of the New Testament is reproduced in later centuries.

i) The Lord's Supper as a Sign of the Church's Unity

The Lord's Supper, however it be interpreted theologically, centres on the passion and death of our Lord Jesus Christ, an event which all Christians confess as the means of their salvation and in which they believe they have a share. In that death they know themselves to be face to face with a mystery which they have tried to explain in different ways, their differences running along theological rather than confessional lines. That Christ 'suffered under Pontius Pilate, was crucified, dead and buried' and that his death was 'for us men and our salvation' has not been a matter of dispute amongst Christians. Yet the sacrament that is the sign of that atoning death has become the place where Christians experience most grievously their divisions. Hall felt the burden of division as much as any twentieth-century ecumenist committed to the cause of unity amongst all Christians. He was angered and baffled that the place where Christians celebrated the salvation that made them one was the place where they most zealously paraded their divisions. Eloquently, he expresses the dilemma:

> It must appear surprising that the rite, which, of all others, is most adapted to cement mutual attachment, and which is in a great measure appointed for that purpose, should be fixed upon as the line of demarcation, the impassable barrier, to separate and disjoin the followers of Christ.[44]

To Hall, schism was abhorrent. The Holy Scriptures knew nothing of a 'plurality of true churches, neither in actual communion with each other, nor in a capacity for such communion'.[45] His abhorrence has to be viewed in the context of the communion debate in which he was engaged. He saw the closed communionist practice of excluding Christians from whom Baptists were divided, 'on matters confessedly not essential to salvation',[46] as nothing less than schismatic. Hall believed that Baptists were divided from their fellow Christians on the issue of baptism and nothing more. In his eyes, differences of baptismal belief and practice were not sufficiently fundamental either to justify separation at the Lord's table or even, as he was to reveal later, the existence of a separate denomination.

In allowing baptism to cause division at the Lord's table, the closed communionists were also denying the corporate nature of the Lord's Supper. It was a federal rite, the very essence of which lay in the corporate participation of all Christians. It was given as a 'token of our reconciliation', a place of spiritual participation in the blood and body of the crucified Saviour,[47] in which Christians share together. At the Lord's table

> ... we are actual partakers by faith of the body and blood of the Redeemer offered upon the cross ... [we share in] a *federal rite*, in which we receive the pledge of reconciliation, while we avouch the Lord to be our God, and surround his table as a part of his family.[48]

This was no place to draw lines of demarcation or to erect barriers, especially in matters considered to be not essential to salvation.

Clearly, that was not the light in which closed communionists saw the Lord's Supper. The great Welsh preacher, Christmas Evans, confessed himself attracted by Hall's advocacy of Christian unity. The barriers that divided Christian men at communion were not, however, put there by Baptists but by the paedobaptists, on the one hand, and heaven itself, on the other. The barrier of the 'immersion of all believers on profession of their faith, as an initiating ordinance to communion into the kingdom of Christ' had been erected by heaven, and the Messiah 'expects to find this barrier in good repair at his second coming'.[49] The paedobaptist barrier could easily be removed since it had no sanction in scripture. It was now easy to see where the blame lay, for keeping up the bar to communion. The barrier on this side, is instituted by heaven, and cannot be removed; and the barrier on the other has no written patent in the word of life and ought not to be preserved.[50]

Evans' belief that baptism should be by immersion upon profession of faith was one that was shared by all his fellow Baptists. Indeed, it was the *raison d'être* of their denomination. It was certainly arguable that it was not essential to salvation, but it was essential to a great many other aspects of Christian truth. Take away believer's baptism and the Baptist churches were robbed of their chief characteristic and sole motive for existing as a separate body. A later protagonist in the debate, Joseph Ivimey, minister of the Eagle Street Baptist Church in London, believed Hall was a threat to the very existence of the Baptist denomination:

> The manner in which Mr. H contemplates the destruction of the denomination to which he belongs, and from which he has derived all his comforts, reminds one of that event in history, when the Emperor who had caused Rome to be fired, was the only person who enjoyed the general conflagration.[51]

Hall, no less than his fellow Baptists, believed that baptism by immersion upon profession of faith was the only valid interpretation of New Testament baptism and, like them, he believed that infant baptism could 'never be mistaken for baptism',[52] but he had to balance that commitment, on the one hand, with his total aversion to schism on the other. He refused to be committed to any doctrine of church order that entailed separation from Christians of whose sincerity he was in no doubt whatever. He would not allow even the most hallowed of Christian traditions to stand in the way of the swift step which he invariably took towards any Christian in whom he recognized a devotion to Christ. His opponents pointed out, as they were entitled to, that Hall was departing from the universal practice of the church that had, from earliest times, unanimously concurred in requiring baptism as a necessary preliminary to communion. As universally recognized as was the practice, it was of more concern to Hall that it stood in the way of Christian unity and, further, perpetuated error in the church. Roman Catholics, Lutherans, and members of the Church of England alike stood by the necessity of the sacrament of baptism before communion because they believed that it was by baptism that 'we become the children of God, and heirs of his kingdom'.[53] If, in his desire to open the Lord's table to all Christians, Hall could be accused of going against universal practice, then a similar charge could be laid at the door of the closed communionists who, in their zeal, sought to exclude other Christians from communion. This was, he claimed, a practice without precedent in the church:

> The right of rejecting those whom Christ has received; of refusing the communion of eminently holy men, on account of unessential differences of opinion, is not the avowed tenet

of any sect or community in Christendom, with the exception of the majority of the baptists . . .[54]

Hall believed that it was preferable to set on one side a tradition, conducive as it was to division and tainted with the error of baptismal regeneration, than to further schism, which he considered to be nothing less than

> . . . a causeless and unnecessary separation from the church of Christ . . . a breach of communion . . . fraught with scandal . . . utterly repugnant to the genius of the gospel.[55]

The exclusion of paedobaptists from the Lord's table was tantamount to excommunication or, in other words, a form of punishment. Hall argued that excommunication had been reserved in the church only for the most 'openly vicious and profane';[56] it was appropriate only to behaviour that could be adjudged to be criminal. It was hardly fitting that such an instrument of punishment should be applied to fellow Christians who would normally, as much by strict communionists as by others, be held in the highest esteem. Excommunication was a wound to the soul that

> . . . no balm can cure, no ointment can mollify, but which must continue to ulcerate and burn, till healed by the blood of atonement, applied by penitence and prayer.[57]

Punishment, he said, was always meant to reform the offender. Such punishment, however, could not have that effect on a paedobaptist because he believed in the rectitude of his own conduct and could be reassured that the approach of by far the greater part of Christendom to these matters was the same as his. There could be no justification for singling out this one error in doctrine as the grounds for excommunication, the punishment being totally unfitted to the crime. It was the contention of open communionists, he says,

> . . . that it is impossible, without a total disregard of truth and decency, to assert, that [infant baptism] is *intrinsically* and *essentially* more pernicious in its effects than the numerous errors and imperfections which the advocates of strict communion feel no scruple in tolerating in the best organized churches.[58]

Further, if it could be argued that baptism was an invariable part of the Christian profession, then its neglect or malpractice could only lead logically to exclusion from salvation.[59] That was a conclusion that Hall accused the closed communionists of refusing to face.

Baptists on both sides of the divide, however, faced unenviable dilemmas. They had rejected infant baptism as null and void and invested their own practice with a symbolism that had implications for their understanding of the nature of the Christian life and their definition of the church. Hall was prepared to open the Lord's table to other Christians and to pay the price of magnanimity. His action at once brought him closer to other Christians but also distanced him from them, since he was compelled to reject beliefs still held by the majority of Christians. These were that infant baptism was a valid sacrament and that baptism should precede admission to the Lord's Supper. Hall was compelled to reject the former and deny the latter. He was consequently in the unhappy position of making baptism of less importance for Baptists that it was for paedobaptists. Paedobaptists could argue, and did, that if they were to be admitted to Baptist communion tables then it should be on the basis, not of magnanimity, but of a due recognition of their baptism and thus of their churchmanship.

The strict communionists faced a different dilemma. They held to the traditional belief, shared by all other Christians, that baptism should precede communion. They too, however, belonged to a denomination that rejected infant baptism and re-defined baptism. Their dilemma was that few Christians had been persuaded by their example or convinced by their reasoning, leaving them a small and comparatively insignificant minority when placed in the setting of all the Christian churches. As a minority they were under the unfortunate necessity of excluding the greater part of Christendom from communion on the grounds that it was unbaptized.

If the admittance of the unbaptized to communion was a denial of the universal practice of the church, the exclusion of professing Christians of other persuasions was a denial of that forbearing brotherly love that was the hallmark of the New Testament church. From the earliest days of the denomination, when Thomas Helwys, in his book, *The Mistery of Iniquity* (1612), had pressed the merits of religious tolerance on James I, many Baptists had identified themselves with the cause of religious liberty. They had coveted freedom not only for themselves but for others also. But they also found that religious tolerance had to be balanced with devotion to the gospel. Was it possible to tolerate error? Though they might argue for tolerance towards Jews, Turks or heretics,[60] could they countenance deviance within their own ranks? Hall believed that they could. Had not Christ, in his high-priestly prayer, prayed that all Christians might be one?[61] To exclude other Christians from the Lord's table was 'to inflict a wound on the very heart of charity'.[62]

The New Testament way of handling conflict and differences within the church was not exclusion from the table. Hall used as examples two illustrations from the New Testament, the Jerusalem Council and the case of the 'weaker' brother in Romans 14. The Jerusalem Council met to arbitrate between those Jewish Christians who believed that it was wrong to eat certain kinds of meat forbidden by Mosaic law and those Gentile Christians who believed that obedience to this particular part of the Mosaic law was not incumbent upon Christians. The dispute was part of the wider conflict between Paul and the Judaizers, Paul holding that the imposition of Mosaic law on Gentile converts to the Christian faith was a denial of the sufficiency of Christ and his redeeming work. The Judaizers, on the other hand, believed that the Christian gospel demanded moral obligations which were embodied in Mosaic law and had not been abrogated by Christ. The divide between the two was deep and bitter[63] yet, Hall claimed, it did not lead to the excommunication of one party by the other:

> ... a contrariety of opinion and of practice prevailed in the church respecting Jewish ceremonies and observances, which considerably impaired its harmony. But instead of attempting to silence the remaining differences, by interposing his authority, St. Paul enjoins mutual toleration.[64]

The second example used by Hall was that of the 'weaker brother' in Romans 14. The argument in the early church was again about food, this time whether or not Christians were to eat meat that had been offered to idols. Paul's inclination was to stand with those who claimed that idols had no reality, that all food was the gift of God, and that the man of faith may eat. He recognized, however, the dilemma of the 'weaker brother' who, in his new life in Christ, found such meat, and all its associations with a way of life now renounced and left in the past, disturbing to his faith. The counsel of Paul was that the strong should show forbearance to the weak. The 'weakness' here described, claimed Hall, was synonymous with error. Tolerance is advocated on the principle that

> ... the errors and mistakes to be tolerated are not *fundamental*, not of such a nature, in other words, as to prevent those who maintain them from being accepted with God.[65]

The Apostle recognized the integrity with which the opposing parties held their opinions:

> Both were equally conscientious, and therefore neither deserved to be treated with severity.[66]

The analogy of the 'stronger' and the 'weaker' brother was to be used some years later by William Innes in his book, *Open Communion and Christian Forbearance*.[67] He, like Hall, believed that the baptismal issue was not fundamental: it was in the same category as the dispute relating to meat offered to idols. He saw mutual forbearance as beneficial to the individual, to the church universal and to the world. It was beneficial to the individual because, without forbearance, he would suppress his own questions and violate his conscience. A man in this situation had the alternative of submitting to a degree of external conformity, even though not persuaded in his own mind, or separating from a church which he might otherwise love.[68] In the church universal, mutual forbearance compelled Christians to concentrate on the most important matters and not on 'matters of mere outward arrangement':[69]

> It is melancholy to see persons contending with the utmost eagerness, for some mere matter of form, where the leading features of the Christian character, spirituality of mind, and personal godliness, are very partially, if at all to be seen.[70]

Under his third point, Innes argued that mutual forbearance was beneficial to the world. He advanced a view shared by all who have cherished the cause of Christian unity, namely, that the unity of Christians would speak powerfully to a world torn by dissensions. If such a world could see a community that was irradiated by a spirit of union and of mutual love and forbearance, by a readiness to make sacrifices and to promote each others' happiness, it would be

> ... so extraordinary, so completely different from every other association of human beings, that it might be justly considered a sort of *moral miracle*, as such a deviation from the general laws of our moral nature, as opening the blind eyes would be from those of our physical nature.[71]

The exclusion of fellow Christians from communion was an impediment to the progress of the spiritual kingdom of Christ and delayed the day when the world would believe that 'Jesus came from God'.[72] Like Hall, Innes found it impossible to deny the validity of other peoples' religious experience and, like him also, he saw the implications of Christian practice for the ongoing mission of the church in the world. A church that could not deal with its own wounds was in no position to bind up the wounds of a broken world. He paid the same price for charity as had Hall, however. Baptism was not to be regarded as essential and matters of church order were no more than 'matters of mere outward arrangement'. He was no more successful than Hall in devising some means of balancing charity with loyalty to the beliefs he shared with his fellow Baptists. Open communionists found that they could not rigorously adhere to their Baptist convictions whilst arguing for the admission of other Christians to the Lord's table on the basis of their membership in the true church. To refuse communion was to refuse recognition.

For Hall, membership of the true church rested upon faith. All orthodox Christians, he argued, uniformly maintained that 'union to Christ is formed by faith'.[73] As Baptists required faith prior to baptism they were testifying that it was not the sacrament that effected the union. Paedobaptists, therefore, equally with Baptists, had the means of union available to them; they too, were joined with Christ by faith, therefore:

> ... it seems impossible to deny that they are fully entitled to be considered, in the catholic sense of the term, as members of the christian church.[74]

Given Hall's premises, that was a conclusion with which the closed communionists could not disagree. They, no more than he, would not claim that it was anything more than faith that gave access, through grace, to Christ and his church. Baptism was not an effective sacrament in the sense that it made Christians. Faith, on the human side, was the agent of salvation, and baptism was the sign of that faith.

If faith was more important than baptism, the thing signified more important than the sign, love took precedence over both as over all else. It was belief in the pre-eminence of love that motivated Hall to contend for a communion table open to all Christians. Nothing more powerfully expressed the relationship into which Christians had been brought in Christ than did the love which existed between them. It was with an eloquent plea for love that Hall finished his own contribution to the controversy:

> ... when the Spirit is poured down from on high, he will effectually teach us that God is *Love*, and that we never please him more than when we embrace with open arms, without distinction of sect or party, all who bear his image.[75]

Having staked out his claim that the way of the open communionists was the way of love, Hall left his opponents the unenviable task of defending themselves against the imputation that their way was the very opposite of loving. Joseph Ivimey rebuked Hall for bringing public opprobrium on his 'strict' brethren and causing them to be labelled as bigots.[76] This charge, he believed, could as well be laid at Hall's door for, whilst admitting paedobaptists to the Lord's table, he did not alter his opinion that they were 'imperfect Christians' and 'erring brethren'. Kinghorn and those who stood with him had to argue a rationale for schism that would demonstrate that they were not motivated by a lack of love, nor nurtured on the baleful fare of bigotry, but were acting purely out of concern for the truth. They could rightly claim that schism had always proved a necessary means of defence of truth in the history of the church and that the very existence of the Baptist churches themselves was evidence that, in the interests of theological convictions, there was at times no alternative but to break away from other Christians and begin again. As important as was unity amongst Christians, truth took precedence over all else. If Hall's plea was to be heeded, argued Kinghorn, then there would be 'an end of all reformation in the church for the purposes of fulfilling the will of Christ'.[77] In Kinghorn's eyes, the process of reformation and renewal always entailed schism: it was an inevitable process that had its origin in the fragmentation brought about by the Reformation:

> Every cause which leads any class of Christians to establish a separate communion, may be denounced ... and we must never, on this plan, follow the commands of Jesus Christ, by

departing from a corrupt society, lest we should 'destroy the unity of the church'! We can neither be Baptists, nor Dissenters, nor even Protestants, without incurring this charge. The great question is, are we doing the will of Christ? If we are we may leave the rest to him ... In every reformation, some breach of unity is unavoidable.[78]

Both men would have argued that they were concerned for the truth. In Kinghorn's case, it was the truth of the symbol and all that it represented, in Hall's case it was the empirical truth of the situation in which Christians found themselves at the dawn of the nineteenth century that compelled them to recognize the validity of one anothers' confession of Jesus Christ. As convincingly as Kinghorn might argue for the necessity of schism, the situation then facing Christians in England could not be paralleled with that facing Luther's followers in Germany in the sixteenth century. A constant process of splintering was leading to ever smaller groups incapable of exercising any appreciable influence either upon the churches from which they had broken away or upon the society by which they were surrounded.

Some closed communionists were not insensitive to the charge of schism and countered by arguing that it should properly be laid at the door of the open communionists. Baptists had broken away from other churches on the grounds of their convictions in the matter of baptism. If baptism was to be set on one side then there no longer existed any justification for a separate existence. Indeed, argued Ivimey, to set up an open Baptist church in an area where there was already an evangelical paedobaptist church was a blow to the work of the ministry in that place.[79] Paedobaptists might be encouraged to leave their own churches on grounds other than those of principle. If between a paedobaptist Independent congregation and a Baptist open congregation there was no clear difference of principle, then it was a clear act of unnecessary schism for them to go on existing separately. Casual schism of this sort, it could be argued, was more damaging to the church than the schism caused by those who believed that there had been a clear violation of New Testament principles.

That infant baptism involved such a violation, in the eyes of the closed communionists, is apparent in their rejoinder to Hall's use of the analogy of the 'weaker brother' in Romans 14. The 'weaker brother', said Kinghorn, could not be be identified with the paedobaptists. 'Weak' was not synonymous with 'erroneous'.[80] Jews and Greeks held very different views concerning meats and drinks, but the gospel did not enjoin a common pattern of behaviour in such matters. It was another matter altogether, however, where the practice in dispute was 'a part of the revealed will of Christ, which was binding both on Jews and Gentiles'.[81] Ivimey, too, challenged Hall's use of the Romans passage:

> ... H[all] cannot discover the difference between abrogated ceremonial rites and unabrogated positive institutes; between

a superstitious attachment to things not religious, and the non-observance of a divine precept...[82]

The degree of tolerance that existed between Christians had to be measured by the gravity of the issue that divided them. The controversy relating to meat and drink in the early church proved to be transient because the changing circumstances of the church eventually made it redundant. By the close of the first century it was no longer an issue. Baptism, however, like the Lord's Supper, was a dominical insitution and its status as one of the signs of the church had remained unaltered either by the Protestant Reformation or the majority of dissenting movements that grew out of it. Hall was able to use the analogy of the 'weaker brother' because he equated baptism with the meat and drink controversy. Neither, he claimed, was of primary importance or essential for salvation. Hall in effect cut the dominical ground from beneath the sacrament.

The closed communionists were not prepared to devalue the symbol, and so for them tolerance could be reached only by a far more circuitous route. Kinghorn stoutly denied that the closed communionist position amounted to excommunication of paedobaptists. To establish a separate communion was not to deny the existence of other communions based upon different interpretations of the symbol. The closed communionists simply claimed that the two interpretations were incompatible, where Hall had argued that they were unimportant. Kinghorn urged that it was perfectly proper for paedobaptists to celebrate communion, for in doing so 'they do not unite together with those whom they deem unbaptized'.[83] Strict Baptists and paedobaptists alike followed a principle recognized by both, i.e. 'that the subjects of Christian communion should be baptized'.[84] Others, setting less store by tolerance, argued that it placed a muzzle on truth. G. Pritchard, writing in reply to Hall's *Terms of Communion,* referred to the open communionist claim that the occasional exchanges between Baptist and paedobaptist pulpits provided a precedent for shared communion. The success of these exchanges, argued Pritchard, depended upon the avoidance of divisive subjects, a constraint conducive to short-term affability but unlikely to promote long-term spiritual health.[85] William Button believed that tolerance purchased at the expense of truth extorted too high a price:

> Love, charity, peace, candour, forbearance, are pleasing, plausible words; but when applied to the subject before us, they are delusive ones. Do you not know, that there is such a thing as false charity? Is that wholesome, evangelical peace, which is made with men at the expense of truth?[86]

Hall had argued for the recognition of paedobaptists at the Lord's table on the grounds that they were members of the true church, though in error. Kinghorn disputed neither claim: they were indeed members of the true church and, equally, they were in error.[87] It was error of such magnitude, however, as to have justified the establishment of Baptist churches in separate communion. Ivimey contended that it was paedobaptists who had departed from the original faith and practice of the apostolic church and therefore it was they who were the real separatists and guilty of the worst schism.[88] Others, agreeing that it was the paedobaptists who had departed from the apostolic faith, were not prepared to concede even the scant and grudging recognition that Kinghorn had afforded them. John Stevens held that to admit them to the communion would be 'to allow of known disobedience and error in the church'.[89] They could claim no more than the pretence of having been baptized:

> Therefore, they are not fit persons to admit into the church of Christ, not having put on Christ, or confessed his name, in that way of obedience which is prescribed in the scriptures, and was adhered to by the churches formed under the ministry of the Apostles of our Lord.[90]

In 'Free Communion Examined', W. Palmer claimed that mixed communion was nothing less than 'promiscuous intercourse' and indefensible, in that recognition of individual members of other churches implied recognition of the churches to which they belonged.[91] Conversely, they could not reject institutions without rejecting those who belonged to them. Clearly, the degree of recognition that closed communionists were prepared to grant to other churches varied.

ii) The precedence of faith over symbol

Dismayed by the division caused by differing interpretations of the ordinances, Hall cut his way through the hedges that surrounded the Lord's table by the simple expedient of opening it to all 'sincere' Christians. The notional simplicity of this solution was less apparent in practice, however. The closed communionists could argue that their definition of those who should be admitted to the Lord's table was unambiguous and consistent with their Baptist beliefs. Only those baptized by immersion, on profession of faith, should be allowed to receive communion. Though this might exclude the greater part of Christendom it had the benefit of consistency and clarity. Hall's invitation to 'sincere' Christians, whilst consistent with his own vision of the church, was to prove less so with certain cardinal points of Christian practice. It was also far from clear who were to be regarded as 'sincere' Christians. What is a 'sincere' Christian? How is 'sincerity' gauged?

As we have seen,[92] Hall argued that Baptists were agreed, in common with many Christians of other persuasions, that baptism did not make a person a Christian. Baptism was a sign of the baptizand's surrender to Christ. It was administered where evidence of faith was discernible in the life and profession of the one who sought baptism. Presumably, if it was possible to trace the presence of believing faith in the life of a candidate for baptism, it was no less possible to recognize its presence in the life of a devout paedobaptist seeking communion at the Lord's table. The church was in no different position in deciding whether to grant communion to those who sought it than in deciding the suitability of a candidate for baptism. In both cases it looked for faith, the marks of discipleship, consistency of life with profession or, in other words, for 'sincerity'. The question for Hall was whether the sign was more important than that which it signified. Clearly, for him there could be only one answer: living faith took precedence over a scrupulous observance of the sacrament of baptism. The closed communionist challenge to this position was that failure to heed the dominical command to be baptized on profession of faith entailed a disobedience which could not be set aside, even in the interests of charity. Non-Baptists were to be granted only the qualified recognition of disobedient Christians. Abraham Booth, the posthumous adversary against whom Hall argued his case for open communion, had claimed that only those should be admitted to communion who 'revere [Christ's] authority, submit to his ordinances, and obey the laws of his house',[93] taking it as read that this precluded paedobaptists. Hall argued that Booth's strictures were not applicable to paedobaptists and therefore provided no grounds for their exclusion from the Lord's table:

> Every conscientious adherent to infant baptism reveres the authority of Christ not less than a baptist, and is distinguished by a spirit of submission and obedience to every known part of his will; and as this is all to which a baptist can pretend, and far more than many who, without scruple, are tolerated in our churches, can boast, we are as far as ever from ascertaining the *specific difference* betwixt the case of the paedobaptist, and other instances of error supposed to be entitled to indulgence.[94]

This in no way implied a recognition of infant baptism on the part of Hall. On that matter he could not have been clearer:

> While we universally maintain the nullity of infant baptism, the persuasion which our paedobaptist brethren maintain of their being baptized, can never be mistaken for baptism.[95]

Absence of baptism did not, however, diminish sincerity on their part and nothing more was required of them before admittance to the Lord's table.

By pressing the necessity of baptism before admission to communion, the strict communionists unwillingly found themselves associated with those Christians who made baptism a necessary prerequisite of salvation. The universal practice of infant baptism had grown out of the error that to be unbaptized was to be unredeemed, whilst to be baptized was to be numbered among the children of God. By arguing that baptism was an invariable part of the Christian profession, the closed communionists were faced with a conclusion they vehemently denied. Admittance to

God's kingdom, argued Hall, was upon profession of faith; if baptism was required as an essential part of that profession then it followed that, where it was neglected or wrongly practised, those guilty of such neglect or malpractice were effectively precluded from salvation. Hall knew that such a deduction was totally unacceptable to people like Kinghorn, whom he taunted with the dilemma:

> He travails in birth, but dares not bring forth; he shrinks from the sight of his own progeny.[96]

The strict communionists were faced with the alternative of either limiting salvation to those who shared their beliefs or admitting that what they required for admission to the Lord's table was not of the essence of the Christian faith.[97] To insist upon baptism as an indispensable part of Christian profession laid them open to the charge of placing the sacrament on the same footing as Catholics who regarded the sacrament as an *opus operatum*. Such a belief was unacceptable to 'consistent protestants' who,

> ... while they conscientiously attend to every positive institute, according to the measure of their light, look upon the few and simple ceremonies of the gospel as incapable of affording the smallest benefit apart from the disposition and intentions with which they are performed.[98]

The closed communionists, averred Hall, were kin to Roman Catholics who believed themselves to be the only true church. Whilst Romanism confined salvation to those who came within its borders, the strict communionists rescued themselves from such an un-Protestant conclusion by a familiar theological sleight-of-hand, distinguishing between the mystical body of Christ and his visible church.[99] Hall knew well enough that the closed communionists made no connection between salvation and a proper ordering of the church. He had forced the connection himself by the manner in which he had framed the dispute. Are paedobaptists 'sincere' Christians? he had asked. If they were they should be admitted to communion. The strict communionists replied that the matter at issue was not whether paedobaptists were 'sincere' Christians, and certainly not whether they were saved. The question was, How is the church to be rightly ordered? A right ordering of the church required baptism on profession of faith as a necessary qualification for admittance to the Lord's table. They argued that there was nothing novel or innovative in this requirement. Baptists were not distinguished by requiring baptism before communion but by the mode in which the sacrament was administered and those who were considered to be the proper recipients of it. Others, like Hall, could draw the inaccurate and unhappy inference that by barring the way to the Lord's table they were barring the way to eternal life. It was, however, an inference from which they were quick to dissociate themselves and one that was not invariably supported by the practices and beliefs of the historic church. The bar to the table was erected against those deemed to be disobedient Christians, not against unsaved sinners. All the leading Reformers had defined what they believed to be the marks of the church without confusing them with the limits of salvation. Division between Protestants had been caused and perpetuated by differing interpretations of the marks and not by doubts about other people's saving experience.

In the course of his argument, Hall had to concede a good deal on the question of church order. If faith in Christ was primary, did it follow that matters of church order were emptied of all importance? If the closed communionists were in the unenviable position of seeming to unchurch the greater part of Christendom, Hall was in a hardly less unhappy position of seeming to treat a dominical sacrament as of little importance and to act in a way that was contrary to long established Christian tradition. Had he argued that infant baptism had some validity, however erroneously it was practised and theologically interpreted, then he could have claimed that what was at stake was a difference of opinion on the meaning of a sacrament. Infant baptism, however, he considered null and void, a no-baptism. He was consequently defending the right of 'sincere' but unbaptized Christians to be admitted to the table. This inevitably raised the question: How important is baptism? To this, Hall had no other answer than that it was a doctrine over which differences were 'unessential'.[100] Whatever the emphases of apostolic times, baptism was no longer necessary as a basic evidence of faith.[101] Thus Hall had moved from the perfectly proper observation that baptism was not a condition of salvation to the far more dubious argument that baptism was not essential to church order.

This he sought to justify by claiming that there was no necessary connection between the two sacraments of baptism and the Lord's Supper. The traditional ordering of the church that had required the administration of the former before participation in the latter had, Hall claimed, no basis in the New Testament.[102] John's baptism being a baptism of repentance and not Christian baptism, it followed that the institution of the Lord's Supper preceded baptism, which had its origins in our Lord's Great Commission (Matthew 28.31). Christian baptism came into being at Pentecost when it was accompanied by the spiritual benefits of the Holy Spirit.[103] The Lord's Supper, he argued, had not required the prior administration of baptism; therefore paedobaptists, though effectively unbaptized, could be admitted to the Lord's table.

In the matter of baptism, Hall aligned himself with those who, believing that they acted within a prophetic tradition going back to the Old Testament and confirmed in the New, have placed more emphasis upon inner dispositions than outward acts. Here Hall voiced an approach to sacraments that was to be more loudly echoed as the century progressed and, for some, was to become a mark of Baptist orthodoxy. He applied a description of sacramental practice to baptism that others, after him, were to apply with equal zeal to the Lord's Supper. He assigned it to the 'ceremonial' aspect of religion which was to be held as inferior to the 'inner' or 'moral' aspects of religion.[104] Faced with a paedobaptist who was clearly 'a humble follower of Jesus Christ', the question arose:

> If, to tolerate such, must subject us to the reproach of repealing the law of Christ, let us remember we are not the first who have been condemned for undervaluing the ritual part of religion, and for preferring mercy to sacrifice.[105]

A scriptural allusion so beguiling, Hall well knew, could not easily be queried by his fellow Baptists. It still left an unresolved question, however. If infant baptism had no validity and thus the unbaptized could be admitted to communion, given evidence of their 'sincerity', how important was baptism? Was it a mere ceremony that belonged to 'the ritual part of religion'? Hall, it seemed, was willing to take a final and fateful step. Not only would he admit paedobaptists whom he considered to be unbaptized, he was prepared also to admit to communion those who denied the necessity of baptism in any form:

> ... for my own part, I should feel as little hesitation in admitting such as deny the perpetuity of baptism, whenever the evidence of their piety is equally clear and decisive.[106]

Hall was, of course, loyal to the Baptist emphasis on baptism, but, driven by a passionate resolve to recognize other Christians as part of the church and therefore fellow communicants in Christ, and caught in verbal conflict with his closed communionist brethren, he contributed to a theological bequest that was to play a maverick role amongst the Baptists who followed him. If baptism was a ceremonial expression of faith, if it was a 'ritual part of religion', then why should not the same judgment be made of the Lord's Supper? Was that, too, a ritual paling into insignificance before the weightier matters of inward faith and pious living?

The relegation of the sacraments to a minor and, sometimes, inessential role in the Christian life was to gather momentum later in the nineteenth century in reaction to Tractarianism and the Catholic revival. Hall was enthusiastically embracing this approach in his approach to baptism, however, some two decades before the appearance of the Tractarians. His enthusiasm poses a conundrum. His theology of the Lord's Supper was, as we have seen, deeply influenced by the Calvinism that played a large role in the rest of his beliefs. He rejected Zwinglian memorialism and argued that the sacrament was a real participation in the body and blood of the Lord. In his doctrine of baptism, however, he was to be found in that theological hinterland where Zwinglianism shaded off into Anabaptist radicalism. Various explanations are possible. In the first place, though it was possible to take a Calvinist understanding of the Lord's Supper into a Baptist theology of the church, the Reformer's doctrine of baptism comprised a weighty defence of infant baptism, driving Baptists into other theological pastures. Secondly, however carefully Zwingli may have safeguarded himself from reducing sacraments to *signa nuda*, he could not prevent others who started from his presuppositions pressing down other roads. He was at variance with Anabaptists in the matter of baptism, but he was seen by them as a kindred spirit in his understanding of the relationship between sign and thing signified. Once the wedge had been driven between the two, as between material and spiritual, there was nothing to prevent radicals from reducing sacraments to the status of parables depicting spiritual realities whose location was the believing heart. An unbroken line could be traced from Zwingli to the radicals along which subsequent Protestant Dissenters could place their own marker, either, at one end, close to Zwingli or, at the other, to the Anabaptists. Hall, a Calvinist at the table, proved a radical at the font.

A possible explanation of this was provided by the Baptist historian, Thomas Armitage, who, writing in 1886, attributed Hall's advocacy of open communion to Socinianism. Socinus was an Italian who had found refuge amongst Polish Anabaptists in the early seventeenth century. His teachings, with their defective Christology and deference to reason above all things, representing 'religion in a form so rationalistic that it seemed hardly to deserve the name of "faith"',[107] had found a congenial air in which to flourish in the deistic climate of the eighteenth century. Its baleful influence had spread to the General Baptist churches in particular, many of which had drifted into Unitarianism. A young minister, Andrew Leslie, perhaps spoke for others when he had the honesty to admit during his ordination affirmation of faith in 1823 that he had been somewhat fearful of Socinian teaching since 'if at any time I happened to take up any of the Socinian writings . . . my peace of mind instantly departed and I began to doubt'.[108] Armitage drew parallels between Socinianism and Hall's teaching on open communion. They both numbered baptism as amongst the 'unessential' truths of the Christian faith; both argued for love and liberality at the Lord's table and both held 'sincerity' to be the chief qualification for admittance to the Lord's Supper; both denied the necessity of external acts and stressed the 'internal and spiritual' character of the church.[109] Knowing the dire influence of Socinianism on some of the Baptist churches, Armitage perhaps hoped to establish that Hall's advocacy of open communion was guilty by association.

Hall's Christology was irreproachable and, as we have already traced, the religious climate of the early nineteenth century provided reason enough for him to re-open the communion issue. Socinianism may, however, have revived the attraction of ideas that had circulated amongst radical Protestants since the dawn of the Reformation. Luther's turbulent contemporary, Carlstadt, and, together with him, many of the continental Anabaptist groups, had democratised the sacraments and made them marginal to what they considered to be the more important matters of faith and inward attitudes.[110] The Quakers of the seventeenth century had travelled even further down the radical road, dispensing with sacraments and ceremonial religion altogether, turning instead to the inward light of the Holy Spirit as he stirred in the hearts of God's people. The General Baptists had avoided non-sacramental radicalism, their concept of baptism being tightly tied in with their view of the church and the nature of Christian commitment, whilst the Particular Baptists had grown under the constraints of Calvinism, with its emphasis upon word and sacrament in the ordering of the life of the church, quite apart from their distinctive emphasis on the death, burial and resurrection motif in Christian baptism.

In the changing situation of the late eighteenth and the nineteenth centuries, however, the radical Protestant legacy developed a new importance. Hall appealed to it because he found the baptismal barrier to full communion between Christians both tiresome and unnecessary. Later Baptists were to appeal to it because it placed them even further at the opposite pole from a Catholicism from which they wished to be completely dissociated. Hall, however, had identified only baptism with the 'ceremonial' side of religious practice, whilst holding a 'high' view of the Lord's Supper. He was in no position to prevent his successors doing with the latter what he had done with the former. Kinghorn was perceptive enough to detect the dangerous position into which Hall was leading them:

> ... is baptism to be thrown into the shade as a mere ceremonial, to make way for another institution which is equally ceremonial? The direct effect of mixed communion, as far as I can discover, justifies this expostulation. The Lord thought fit to appoint a ritual observance, as the declaration of our trust in him, and subjection to him; and thus obedience to one rite, opens the way for attention to another. Nor can any object, that men are debarred from communion on account of a rite, when communion itself is supported by ritual observances.[111]

With the coming of the Catholic revival later in the century, words such as 'ceremony' and 'rite' were to be used in an even more pejorative way. The Catholic approach to the sacraments was also to attract such epithets as 'carnal' and 'materialistic'. In the heat of theological battle some Baptists were to become ensnared in their own vocabulary, allowing their repugnance for Catholic sacramentalism to colour their attitude to the sacraments within their own church life. Writing of the open communionist attitude to the sacraments, Kinghorn penned words that were unwittingly prophetic, describing as they did an outlook that was to become fairly commonplace by the end of the century. Such congregations, he said,

> ... think themselves in an advanced state, when they consider the ritual parts of religion as of comparatively little

importance, like the ceremonial observances of the Jewish law, which once, in the infancy of religious society, had their use, but now, when it has become advanced, may be laid aside, or, left to the determination of every individual, as an unimportant private speculation.[112]

In his debate with Hall, Kinghorn had here discovered an unguarded flank. It is certain that Hall never intended that his sometimes dismissive attitude to baptism should be extended to the Lord's Supper. But once one sacrament had been relegated to the status of 'mere ceremonial', it could not be long before the other followed in its wake.

iii) The historical factor in the communion debate

One of the main features of radical Protestantism, of which the Baptist churches form a part, has been an overriding commitment to the Holy Scriptures and what they were held to teach in matters of doctrine and practice, coupled with a comparative lack of interest in the history of the church and the way belief and practice have been affected by the context in which they have been received. Bible in hand, each new schism has been moved by the conviction that what it saw described in the story of the New Testament church could be reproduced in the present. Schism is, in part, the story of repeated attempts to make a new beginning, to establish a church conforming to that found in the biblical ideal, to rid it of the deformities of time and to restore it to its original purity. This exalted enterprise has often stumbled on certain stubborn facts. The first is that the church of the New Testament was not an ideal community and had itself to wrestle with imperfection and incompleteness. The second is that it was in a process of growth and development in beliefs about its own nature; its ministry and the meaning of its sacraments did not arrive ready formed on the day of Pentecost. The third is that the church cannot disengage itself from history nor can individual Christians discern scripture through spectacles uncoloured by their own theological environment, or the circumstances of their own time, or their own hopes and expectations.

The closed communionists represented the radical tradition in their approach to churchmanship. They believed that a clear model was to be found within the New Testament and the life of the church was to be based upon that model. The gospel was to be preached, those who responded in faith and repentance to be baptized by immersion and then, and only then, admitted to the full privileges of church membership, amongst them the right to share in the communion of the Lord's Supper. Robert Hall, on the other hand, argued that the passage of history had altered the perspective in which the teaching of the New Testament was to be seen. Christians could not avoid the conditioning of history. It was impossible to leap across the centuries and inhabit again the world of the early church.

He recognized, first of all, that with the passage of time religious groups had a vested interest in maintaining the *status quo*, making objective theological thinking increasingly difficult. He drew an interesting parallel between the way in which science arrived at its conclusions and the way that Christian groups arrived at theirs. In scientific research, he argued, there were no groups with a vested interest in the perpetuation of particular truths, and so the method of research was marked by a greater disinterestedness.[113] Since the church, however, had divided into parties and sects, theology had sacrificed some of its freedom in the interests of party advantage:

> Religious parties imply a tacit compact not merely to sustain the fundamental truths of revelation, (which was the original design of the constitution of a church,) but also to uphold the incidental peculiarities by which they are distinguished.[114]

The forming of schismatic groups made truth more difficult to arrive at. Those who wished to restore an 'obsolete practice' to the place it held in the early church, as had the Baptists who wished to restore baptism, should never allow themselves to be manoeuvred into separatism.[115] The Baptists had suffered the consequences of their history. They were associated in the popular mind with the Anabaptists of Munster, their withdrawal into sectarianism doing nothing to dispel the infamy of that association. The formation of a separate sect had meant that the powerful case for a New Testament theology of baptism had gone by default, since, as far as other Christians were concerned:

> It was seldom examined by an impartial appeal to the sacred oracles, or regarded in any other light than as the whimsical appendage of a sect, who disgraced themselves at the outset by the most criminal excesses, and were at no subsequent period sufficiently distinguished by talents or numbers to command general attention.[116]

The isolation of Baptists had become a means of self-perpetuation in which denominational survival had ranked as of greater importance than seeing the relationship of the part to the whole or of persuading other Christians of the validity of their baptismal beliefs.

He argued, in the second place, that what had happened to Christian beliefs in the passage of history could not be ignored. He conceded that, in apostolic times, it was a law that those who believed were baptized. To have denied baptism in those days would have been to flout apostolic counsel and to act contrary to the word of Christ. Those who so acted would have been regarded, and rightly so, as proud and contumacious heretics. Now, however,

> ...a new state of things has arisen, in which, from a variety of causes, the doctrine of baptism has been involved in obscurity.[117]

There was, he argued, a marked distinction between wilful rejection of believer's baptism in the early church and the practice of infant baptism in the contemporary church. To misinterpret was not the same as wilfully to contradict.[118] Hall here stood at the threshold of an argument that he hesitated or was unwilling to cross. The practice of baptism had not fallen into obscurity; it was still the universal practice of all Christians. Baptists were a minority in believing that the baptism of infants was a departure from apostolic practice and, a belief with even greater consequences for their relationships with other Christians, that it was a non-baptism. The great majority of Christians believed that infant baptism was both consistent with Holy Scripture and had been the universal practice of the church from comparatively early times. Hall, while not conceding any validity to infant baptism, recognized the difficulties faced by a minority endeavouring to set on one side the practice of centuries and, in the process, unchurching and barring from communion the great majority of practising Christians. However much Baptists might wish to return to what they believed to be the purity of New Testament practice, they could not ignore the fact that the church had not come into existence the day before yesterday and that long centuries of Christian practice had found in another mode of baptism a means of grace and a vehicle of truth. Hall faced that scenario, but even he refused to come to terms with it. In the eyes of some paedobaptists the magnanimity of the open communionists in accepting them at their communion tables was diminished by their complete unwillingness to recognize any validity in their baptism. This view was expressed by the Congregationalist editor of the *Christian Witness*, Dr John Campbell, in 1845. The point in dispute, he claimed, was not

> ... whether baptism be necessary to fellowship, but whether affusion or sprinkling be scripture baptism. We do not contend for the right of the paedobaptist to sit down at the Lord's table in a Baptist church, simply on the ground that he is a child of God, but on the ground that he is a believer baptized, in his own view and conscience - baptized in a manner agreeably to the Scripture.[119]

Even the most ardent advocate of open communion would not have been prepared to concede that much.

In the third place, Hall made the daring claim that what prevailed in New Testament times was not necessarily binding upon subsequent generations. He argued that time modified what the New Testament saw as essential for salvation. He took as an example the ruling of the Jerusalem Council that Gentile Christians should refrain from eating things strangled and containing blood, a command nowhere repealed within the pages of the New Testament but no longer held to be binding upon Christians.[120] The 'piety of the paedobaptists', which Kinghorn himself had been compelled to recognize, was evidence that baptism was no longer to be numbered amongst the basic evidences of faith.[121] Hall was making the perfectly defensible point that the world of the New Testament could not be placed whole and unmodified in subsequent times and in other places. Few, however, would have agreed with him on the matter of baptism. Paedobaptists and Baptists alike accepted that baptism was a dominical institution binding on all Christians to the end of time. We have seen that Hall was prepared, in the interests of unity and magnanimity, to set it aside altogether. It is doubtful whether any reading of the New Testament would lend support to such an action, no matter how loftily motivated.

D) THE INTEGRITY OF THE CHURCH: JOSEPH KINGHORN

A number of the points contended by Kinghorn have already been noted in the arguments he advanced against his adversary, Robert Hall. Compared to Hall, Kinghorn occupied the middle ground of the Baptist tradition, defending beliefs that had been germane to the thought and very existence of the Baptists as a separate denomination. Whereas Hall took a pragmatic view of the situation at the beginning of the nineteenth century and the way Baptists should respond to it, Kinghorn defended a view of the church that he believed should remain unaltered by time or circumstance. Baptism was the *raison d'être* of the Baptists' separate existence and could not be pruned away as a theological extravagance because the changing face of the times required it. It embodied what Baptists believed about the Christian life and the nature of the church, truths that might easily be set aside once the sacrament itself had been relegated to an inferior and non-essential role in the ordering of the church's life. For Kinghorn and the closed communionists the difficult consequence of being consistent in their loyalty to that position was that they were compelled to close the Lord's table to those they deemed to be unbaptized. To their mind that was preferable to admitting error and disobedience to the heart of the church's life, making Baptist churches no different from the churches from which they had first departed.

i) Only those properly baptized may be admitted to the Lord's Supper

Kinghorn contended that the Lord's Supper was an ordinance of the church; therefore only those who belonged to the church could be admitted to it. In arguing this position he could appeal both to Baptist tradition and the wider tradition of the Christian church. The Baptist belief about the importance of baptism did not stem from any conviction of sacramental efficacy, although the early General Baptists would appear to have held that baptism marked the point of entry into the church.[122] Their central concern was to ensure that the church was composed of those who had made a free and conscious response of faith to the preaching of the gospel and, following repentance, were resolved to lead a new life characterised by piety and sanctity. Baptism was the sign of that response and resolve. Understood in those terms, it clearly did not apply to infants who were unable to respond to the gospel or to resolve to order their lives according to its precepts. Baptists believed that their baptismal practice safeguarded the integrity of the church within the parameters by which they had defined it. To admit infants to the church was, in their view, to sacrifice the priority of faith and to dilute that corporate commitment that they believed to be the hallmark of a true church.

Kinghorn also claimed that he was being consistent with the traditional stand of the Christian church as a whole. To the question whether baptism or its absence had any bearing on admission to the Lord's table, the paedobaptists, Kinghorn claimed, would almost universally maintain that only the baptized might properly be admitted.[123] If they themselves were to be convinced that their own baptism, received in infancy, was invalid, then

> ... they would shrink at the thought of coming to the Lord's table unbaptized; and would appear there no more, till they could come with minds satisfied on the subject.[124]

Since Baptists regarded paedobaptists as unbaptized, their refusal to admit them to the Lord's table was simply acting upon a principle shared by both. Any paedobaptist seeking admission to communion in a Baptist church should be deterred by his own beliefs. In Kinghorn's view it would be equivalent to paedobaptists arguing:

> WE would not admit a person whom WE thought unbaptized, but we wish you to admit US, though on your own principles you must deem us so.[125]

It was this principle, shared by Baptists and paedobaptists alike, that Hall had set on one side. As we have seen, Hall did not accept the validity of infant baptism. Knowing that, paedobaptists receiving communion in an open communion Baptist church would be acting against their own beliefs:

> According to Mr. Hall's statement, you are not baptized; if he be correct, are you doing right in receiving the Lord's supper?[126]

As Ivimey had charged Hall, the hospitality of open communion tables was extended not on the ground of recognition but that baptism was not essential to communion.[127]

Kinghorn, then, found himself in agreement with Hall on this one point, that infant baptism was a non-baptism. What the former claimed was that he was being consistent with that principle by refusing admission to those he deemed to be unbaptized. Hall, by admitting them to the table, was acting in a way that was contrary to Baptist and the broader Christian traditions. As John Aldis, the minister of the Maze Pond church in Southwark, argued, the closed communionists were acting in a way consistent with a universally shared Christian conviction:

THE COMMUNION CONTROVERSY

> Even the straitest of the strict communionists does but act upon a doctrine firmly held, and uniformly enforced, by the greater proportion of all paedobaptists ... that baptism is a pre-requisite to the celebration of the Lord's Supper, and nearly all Christendom affirms that they are right; but if so, they must violate their consciences, or practice strict communion, for they do not believe that the sprinkling of infants is Christian baptism.[128]

To this unyielding position there were three possible objections: the first, that among paedobaptists there were many of godly character; the second, that whatever opinion Baptists might hold of infant baptism, those who had received it considered themselves properly baptized; and the third, that the New Testament did not specify baptism as a necessary prerequisite of communion.

To the first of these, Kinghorn replied with an appeal to the apostolic tradition. Though he would not deny the excellence of character of many paedobaptists, Kinghorn stressed that it was not their excellence that was in doubt, nor could their excellence be made the grounds upon which their claim to full communion was established:

> ... until it be shewn, that the apostles pleaded for the admission of men into the church, on the ground of their being good men, while they refused obedience to a command of Christ, the principle on which mixed communion is placed, as founded on toleration and forbearance, is NOT established.[129]

Kinghorn and others were not blind to the Christian virtue of paedobaptists but, unlike Hall, they saw obedience and not a Christ-like character as the crucial issue. As William Newman claimed:

> We readily grant, that true believers of all denominations. whether they be protestants, catholics, or members of the greek church; whether they be baptists, paedoBaptists or kataBaptists, shall all be happy together in heaven. But shall we hence conclude that they may all unite at the Lord's Table?[130]

On the second objection, that paedobaptists believed themselves properly baptized, Kinghorn responded that it was not enough that a person deemed himself baptized. If Baptists accepted a baptism that they believed to be inconsistent with the teaching of the New Testament, then they were doing nothing less than allowing men to write their own conditions of entry to the church of Christ, a principle that would be as unacceptable in secular life as it was in the religious. Baptists were not free to dispense with that which they believed was authorized by the example of Jesus in his baptism in the Jordan, by his last commission to his disciples and by the clear witness of the New Testament as a whole.

To set believer's baptism on one side was to lay claim to an authority not within the province of human beings. Baptism, said Kinghorn,

> ... is the Lord's ordinance, not ours; his church which we enter on our baptism, not a society of our own forming.[131]

The third objection to the exclusion of the unbaptized from the Lord's Supper was that the New Testament did not command it. Hall had argued that, since the baptism of John was a 'naked ceremony', the first eucharist, supposing the Last Supper can be viewed in those terms, preceded the institution of Christian baptism and was shared by those who were yet to receive it.[132] Hall located the institution of baptism in the Great Commission of Matthew 28.31, fulfilled in the baptism of water and the Spirit which was initiated on the day of Pentecost. He further claimed that the New Testament presented no contingent link between the two sacraments. Nowhere, he argued, was it stated that communion was dependent upon first having received baptism.[133] In his reply, Kinghorn linked the terms of admission to communion with those required at a first profession of faith. The New Testament, he argued, consistently taught that baptism was an integral part of profession in Christ and initiation into the Christian church:

> ... in every instance, where the history of the first planting of a church is detailed, we see it composed of those who believed in Christ, and were baptized in his name.[134]

This being the universal practice of the early church, the question of the unbaptized simply did not arise:

> The New Testament does not prohibit the unbaptized from receiving the Lord's supper because no circumstance arose which rendered such prohibition necessary.[135]

Kinghorn's argument was the reverse of Hall's when he had claimed that it was impossible to ignore the passage of history and to transplant the world of the first century into that of the nineteenth. Kinghorn was arguing that questions of the nineteenth century could not be addressed to the New Testament in the hope that answers consistent with a nineteenth-century milieu would be found. If the church had reached a point in its development for which the New Testament provided no guidance, it had to be questioned whether the church had remained true to its original calling. There were no maps to guide the open communionists because they had wandered into alien and uncharted land. The New Testament did not offer guide-lines for those who walked in disobedience to Christ and his laws. As far as Kinghorn was concerned the admission of the unbaptized to the Lord's table involved a triple disobedience. It implied that the church had a right to dispense with a clear command of Jesus Christ,[136] it was a deviation from what was acknowledged to be the universal practice of the apostolic church,[137] and it introduced a practice that altered the constitution of the church from that which had been laid down in apostolic times:

> If we collect some who are, and others who are not baptized, we cannot maintain, that such an assembly resembles the apostolic church in its unity; for they had ONE Lord, ONE faith, ONE baptism.[138]

ii) The church is weakened by 'mixed' communion

The closed communionists saw two consequences of a policy of open communion that would tend to weaken the church. The first was that ministers and members of 'mixed' churches would temper their witness to the New Testament in order not to give offence to one another. The second was that the introduction of 'mixed' congregations undermined the existence of Baptist churches as a separate entity.

The first was to become a matter of urgent debate as churches that had been traditionally closed opened their tables to other Christians, thus creating situations in which actual practice gave added urgency to theological questions. Ivimey claimed that, in 1824, there were nearly 700 Baptist churches in England and Wales with an average membership of about 100 and congregations of twice that number. Of those churches he estimated that no more than fifty admitted unbaptized persons to the Lord's table.[139] By the end of the century the open communion churches outnumbered the closed. The change from one to the other inevitably caused divisions and hostilities. Kinghorn saw the effect that such a change would have upon some congregations. Faced with a 'mixed' congregation ministers would tend to trim their preaching in order not to give offence to either side of the baptismal divide:

> Where the mixture of Paedobaptists is considerable, and the minister is a Baptist, he not only runs the risk of giving umbrage, if he does speak his sentiments on the subject of baptism, but he is tempted to do so in the style of a person who begs pardon for presuming to think differently from so many better and greater than himself.[140]

Ivimey also saw the danger and urged younger ministers to seek no change in the constitution of their churches, warning them that:

> ... there is a great danger lest it should prove very injurious to your own peace, and the tranquillity of the churches over which you may be settled as pastors.[141]

In situations such as St Mary's, Norwich, his words were to prove grimly prophetic.

The second consequence of open communion, claimed Kinghorn, was that it undermined the grounds on which Baptists had dissented from other Christians. Baptists had first separated from the established church in the belief that it practised an erroneous baptism which, by being administered to infants indiscriminately, created a national church. If it was universally agreed that baptism was the only mode of entry to the church and all its privileges during apostolic times, then to put it on one side was to abandon the principle of scriptural authority. If the recipients of an erroneous baptism were to be admitted to the Lord's table, then there remained no grounds for dissent. Kinghorn challenged his open communion adversaries:

> ... how can you plead for your separation from the Establishment of your country, on the ground of attachment to the primitive church, when you set up a church, which practically dissents from what you yourselves believe was the practice of the purest ages?[142]

Ivimey painted an even bleaker picture of the consequences of open communion. Because of the communion controversy many Baptists had left their denomination and joined the Independents. Conversely, paedobaptists joining Baptist churches had been admitted to communion but not to membership, thus being deprived of a vote and any say in the appointment of succeeding ministers. Mixed communion, he claimed, tended to destroy the Dissenting as much as the Baptist churches.[143] Surveying that troubled landscape, Ivimey was roused to make an impassioned condemnation of Hall:

> I certainly consider him the greatest and most powerful enemy that the baptized churches have ever had; as an enemy in the camp is more to be dreaded than one in the lines of the hostile army.[144]

Ivimey's attack was not untypical of the anger and hostility that were to be roused on both sides of the debate. The war of words increased but nothing was written that was able to carry it beyond the impasse reached by Hall and Kinghorn. Both men had been able advocates of their respective positions, they had clearly stated the issues, they had provided the ammunition that was to be put to use by many others, the majority less able than the original protagonists. As with much else in the development of the Baptists, as well as other churches, theology was overtaken by events. The issue of unity would not go away and became more urgent as the century progressed. The increasing mobility of the population was to raise problems for the provision of the different needs of closed and open communionists. For all that the closed communionists accused the open of furthering schism they were themselves to become its agents. To these two developments we must now turn.

E) BAPTISTS AND UNITY

The attitude of Baptists to questions of Christian unity was subject to a new appraisal at the founding of the Evangelical Alliance in 1846 and in the following years. The 1840s saw the grouping of Christians across denominational boundaries, the 'horizontal' divisions of the church raising more pressing questions, for the time being, than its 'vertical' divisions. In 1843 Pusey preached his sermon on the eucharist in Christ Church, Oxford, and the increasingly insistent and popular demand for a return to its catholic roots was heard within the Church of England. It was greeted with dismay both by Dissenters and Evangelical Episcopalians whose first loyalty was to the Protestant heritage of the established church. The growth of Evangelical and charitable societies, drawing together Christians from different traditions, so influential in the thinking of Robert Hall, was continuing to have its effect on the thinking of Christians of all persuasions.

The Evangelical Alliance was formed to give visible and corporate expression to this convergence of Christian action. The initial aim of bringing Evangelical churches together into a form of visible unity had to give way to the lesser, and far more realistic, ambition of drawing together like-minded individuals. It included Evangelical Episcopalians as well as representatives from the churches of historical Dissent, including, from amongst the Baptists, Edward Steane, one of the co-secretaries of the Baptist Union, and Baptist Wriothesley Noel, one of their leading ministers. The Alliance was formed on the basis of a doctrinal statement of nine points, sufficiently broad to embrace different denominations, but sufficiently specific to exclude, by implication, Unitarians and Roman Catholics. Beginning with the divine inspiration of the Holy Scriptures, the agreed basis was a statement of beliefs held in common by Evangelicals.

In London, two meetings convened by Dr John Leifchild, a leading Congregationalist minister, led to a united communion service, held at the Surrey Chapel on 1 January 1844. Members of Evangelical churches were invited to join with members of the chapel in order to 'unite in the hallowed exercise'. Admission was to be by ticket and, in the event, the occasion was oversubscribed. At the same time, Leifchild published his pamphlet on *Christian Union*.[145] In this he argued for a greater unity by more frequent meetings between Christians, especially for the purpose of corporate worship. A unity which would remove at least one of the stumbling blocks to faith encountered by an unbelieving world might be achieved by prayer, by talking about it, by a conviction of its necessity on the part of ministers, by reading that crossed the traditional boundaries, by interchange of ministerial services and by more frequent united communion services. The New Year's communion service and Leifchild's commitment to united communion services clearly envisaged the Lord's Supper as a means towards unity rather than its goal. Leifchild described its power to draw Christians together:

> If ever a tender feeling of sympathy pervades all the portions of the mystical body of Christ, it is when assembled on such an occasion. [Christians] have before them the appointed symbols of that efficacious offering by which the divine justice was propitiated towards them; and, at the same time,

the signs of the support and solace provided for that spiritual life of which they are all partakers. They look upon the pledges of a Saviour's love to all, and of their love to each other . . .[146]

Baptists were drawn into the discussion. The Northamptonshire Association Circular Letter for 1844, written by A. Burdett, dealt with the subject of Christian Union. Its writer, too, appealed to those 'essential resemblances' of belief which bound Christians of Evangelical persuasion together. Whilst the pursuit of Christian unity was to be characterised by 'a manly adherence to principles, and no fellowship with expediency', there was also to be a 'meeknes of wisdom, in maintaining our own pecularities'. Certainly denominational predilections were not to be allowed to obtrude in relationships between Christians. The prospects for unity with Evangelical Episcopalians would be increased only if 'the piety which now exists within the Church of England [were] released from the fetters of the state', a plea for disestablishment that was to be a recurring theme of many Evangelicals outside the Anglican Church, if not within it. Amongst Baptists, if unity was to become a possibility, then ministers were to strive to be more truly ministers of reconciliation. The letter appeals:

> Aid us brethren in expelling an uncharitable and exclusive spirit from the pulpit, and we will assist in removing it from the pew, and from the table of the Lord.[147]

In 1846, J. Mortlock Daniell, the minister of Cavendish Chapel in Ramsgate, published his book, *The One Church, or Sects Unscriptural*, a work that did not belie its title in the passion with which it defended the case for Christian unity. Daniell, in the same year, attracted the criticism of the *Primitive Church Magazine*, a Strict Baptist journal which had culled from the pages of the *Patriot* magazine a report dealing with Daniell's introduction of a liturgical form of prayer in his Ramsgate church. Daniell confessed that he had introduced such a form but, in view of his intention to establish the Dumpton Hall Educational Society for the 'sons of Baptist and Independent ministers', he had determined to avoid all polemical engagements. His morning and evening services continued to follow a traditional Dissenting pattern, but the afternoon service included responsive readings between minister and congregation. He had introduced this order because he felt that 'three services exactly similar in the form of arrangement, on the Sabbath, are not expedient on many accounts, either for minister or congregation'.[148] Similar side references throughout the century serve to demonstrate that not all Baptists believed that the only response to the growing Catholic influence in the Church of England was to entrench themselves in a Protestantism isolated from other streams within the Christian tradition.

Daniell was, however, sufficiently within the radical tradition to argue against creeds as a basis for communion. Against the proposed doctrinal basis of the Evangelical Alliance, he argued that creeds were causes of division rather than healing agents:

> The introduction of creeds both among Episcopalians and Dissenters, to which subscription has been expected, as a term of communion, has been the fruitful parent of conflicting sects, of which the Word of God knows nothing, unless it be to censure them.[149]

Disunity, he contended, too often centred on 'trifles' such as 'vestments, organs, steeples and pews, and all such appendages'.[150] Christians were also divided by the forms of prayer which they used, instead of being enriched, as they would be were they united. He claimed that

> ... the opinion is growingly obtaining among the most enlightened of our ministers and people, that more of scripture reading, and some active service for the congregation generally, at least on some occasions, would be a decided improvement.[151]

Further, the church was meant to be a nurturing community, assisting people at all stages of their Christian growth, even those who, in the early stages, 'only see men as trees walking'.

Baptist approaches to the question of unity, at least for those most drawn to relationships with other Christians, had moved from the intense theological pre-occupations of the early communion controversy. Perhaps it was true, as Ivimey had claimed, that Baptists had grown weary of the internecine strife it had caused and, whilst not forsaking the church of their first faith, were finding enrichment through relationships with others. Whilst not setting on one side the question of doctrinal differences, they contended that they should be seen in the perspective of a scenario where love was the dominant feature. Theological differences were relative and not absolute, a point argued by John Aldis. In 1846, following the forming of the Evangelical Alliance, he gave six lectures, published under the title, *Christian Union*.[152] He argued that theology, dealing as it did with truth about an eternal being, must always be 'but part of his ways'.[153] The depth and complexity of many religious issues meant that some Christians, lacking the ability to weigh the arguments, had to accept much on trust from others.[154] Interpretation of scripture was itself altered and modified by the passage of time and the situation within which those who sought to interpret it found themselves. All Christians inherited the theological bequest made to them by the denominations to which they belonged. For Aldis, piety was superior to knowledge.[155] The true pursuit of the Christian faith should be faith, hope and charity, the last of which was 'the centre and living heart of Christian union'.[156] The Lord's Supper was the place where that love between God and man, and between Christians, was supremely expressed. For some Baptists, and for many Evangelical Christians, the communion was not so much an abiding sign that gave theological meaning to the church as an unsurpassed opportunity for Christian fellowship. The step from eucharist to love-feast was a short one.

One step towards Christian unity was the formation of 'union' churches with the express purpose of gathering into membership Christians of differing persuasions. One such was the Union Chapel in High Wycombe, opened in 1845 with a celebration of the Lord's Supper that brought together 'about 180 christian brethren and sisters of other denominations - Episcopalians, Independents, Wesleyans, Primitive Methodists, and Baptists, around the table of their common Redeemer'.[157] On this occasion the sermon was preached by Dr Joseph Angus, secretary of the Baptist Missionary Society and later to become Principal of Stepney College. He described the new church as a 'Christian, in distinction from a Baptist church'. Pressed to explain the distinction, he put it thus, 'In a Baptist church, baptism (as we understand the term) is essential to membership. In a christian church the possession of true faith is alone essential'.[158] Baptists had come a long way from the hyper-Calvinism of some of their eighteenth-century forebears. Robert Hall had opened a door to territory in which neither baptism nor the Lord's Supper were central to their concern and certainly not grounds for division amongst Christians of a common Evangelical persuasion.

Not all Baptists were as sanguine at the prospect of closer communion between Christians or as prepared to allow love to cover a multitude of theological differences. Predictably, opposition from the *Primitive Church Magazine* was uncompromising. Founded in 1841 as an organ of closed communionist opinion, it was adopted in 1854 by the Strict Baptist Society. One of its co-editors during the years 1838-1847[159] was William Norton who, a few years later, was to play such an articulate role in the defence of closed communion at St Mary's, Norwich. It found the inclusion of Evangelical Episcopalians in the invitation to the New Year communion service at Surrey Chapel in 1844 almost beyond belief, and derived no comfort from its indiscriminate embrace of Dissenting Christians, either:

> What! - a church which not only numbers infants among its members, but even the ungodly and profane? even infidels and the most abandoned? Is such a church a gospel church? Do not the Methodists, the Presbyterians, the Independents, all speak of infant church membership? And can a Baptist with a clear conscience publicly recognize such churches as evangelical or gospel churches?[160]

Another of the editors of the same magazine, R. W. Overbury, a successor of Ivimey in the pastorate of the Eagle Street church in London, gave a less emotive response in his book, *A Serious Enquiry into Christian Union*.[161] He attacked the movement towards unity on the grounds that, far from healing differences, it would simply hold them in abeyance.

Differences had to be faced honestly, otherwise whatever ground was gained in the cause of unity would soon be lost:

> They have built a wall and daubed it with untempered mortar. And the result will be what it ever is, when things are done improperly ... the wall which has been daubed with untempered mortar, will not be able to withstand the wind and the weather, but will be injured by the slightest shock, and will melt away and disappear before the coming storm.[162]

He did, however, find common ground with the supporters of the Alliance in their distaste for credal tests. In this Baptists seem to have been united. Having resisted the passion for dogma exhibited by the closed communionists of their own denomination, it was unlikely that the open communionists would pliantly accept the imposition of doctrinal tests in the quest for Christian unity. The closed communionist objection arose not from a distaste but an excessive zeal for dogma. Overbury judged the proposed doctrinal basis for the Evangelical Alliance to be 'unscriptural', a 'defective exhibition of divine truth', in danger of usurping living faith with a formal subscription to credal propositions and deficient in its statement of the wholeness of Evangelical truth[163]. He also stated the familiar closed communionist position that there could be no inter-communion between those who were baptized and those considered to be unbaptized.[164]

Opposition to the credal tests coloured the reactions of other Baptists to the moves towards unity. The General Baptist magazine, the *Baptist Reporter*, founded in 1836, welcomed the new movements that had brought Christians together in united action. 'Where there is little or no activity, there will be little or no love. Let there be more activity, and there will be more love', it argued.[165] Creeds, however, were instruments of repression and torture. Christians were to grow closer together by mutual persuasion rather than the 'brute force' of imposing their creeds upon one another.[166] Each denomination was a custodian of some aspect of the truth that might otherwise be swamped in 'some liberal scheme of comprehension'.[167]

The *Baptist Record* gave a welcome to the Evangelical Alliance that was qualified only in its dislike of the doctrinal basis. It argued that there were too many articles and that they would inevitably be received by the participants with 'some latitude of interpretation'.[168] The *Record* saw no need for any credal statement beyond the 'doctrine of justification by faith in the atonement of Christ'.[169] It viewed with some regret the implicit exclusion of the Society of Friends.

The Baptists of the nineteenth century, no less than their successors in the twentieth, were to remain ambivalent in their attitude to the cause of Christian unity. In 1860 the weekly denominational newspaper, the *Freeman*, accused the Baptists of Upper Norwood, who had accepted an invitation to receive communion at the local parish church, of exhibiting 'suburban snobbery' and lacking 'dissenting manliness', a stricture that was delivered, hand on heart, with the bland disclaimer of being 'without a particle, as far as we know ourselves, of unchristian bigotry'.[170] The pastor of the wayward Baptists of Upper Norwood graciously pointed out that they had accepted the invitation from an Anglican clergyman, Dr Lester, who was noted for 'the Catholic spirit [he has] manifested and the fraternal regard for Christians of other denominations'.[171] Twenty-two years later C. H. Spurgeon, whose bruising condemnations of Catholicism in the Church of England had proved that, if he was lacking in anything, it certainly was not Dissenting manliness, gave rein to his imagination in a speech given at the opening of the Woodgrange Baptist Church in London:

> I wonder whether we shall ever one day meet together, all Christian people, and try to pick out all the good of all denominations . . . If so it will be a grand thing, and matters seem running that way. We do not now merely talk about Christian unity. The person that is not kindly disposed towards his Christian brother is rather shunned and looked down upon now. The time was when to break through the narrowness of sect was thought rather a wonderful thing, but now there is nothing wonderful about it, because it is so commonly done by us all.[172]

Perhaps the representatives of other local churches were sitting in the front row . . .

F) BAPTISTS AND SCHISM

The charge of schism was one that closed communionists had laid at the door of the open communionists. Baptists had a single justification for their existence as a separate denomination and that was their unique understanding of the doctrine and practice of baptism. If this was set on one side as non-essential then schism was being perpetuated unnecessarily. In fact, it was the closed communionist position that led more frequently to schism. The stance adopted by each was illustrative of two recurring attitudes towards the church. The first, that of the open communionists, seeks structures that will comprehend rather than exclude. The first object of that search is not the perfection of the church but an accommodation of the various ways in which men and women experience the revelation of God in Christ. It has never been possible to impose conformity upon that experience nor, for those of an 'open' persuasion, has it been possible to deny its validity in others. Any church which accepts a wide range of Christian experience has to sacrifice the notion of perfection as an end that is either attainable or, indeed, desirable. The church may resemble a field of wheat and tares but that is considered preferable to the rooting out of a portion of the wheat in the otherwise commendable enthusiasm to be rid of the tares. The second stance, that of the closed communionists, seeks first the purity of the church. Having identified ways in which that perfection might be safeguarded, it endeavours to bring experience into line with its definitions rather than to frame definitions that will accurately reflect experience. The closed communionists, except in their most exclusive mood, knew that in their fellow-Christians they were faced with evidence of the working of God's grace, even though it did not conform with their own definition of the church. Loyalty to that definition, however, required separation from others. Thus the quest for purity invariably leads to schism, since purity is only sustained by separation from that which is deemed to be impure. The open communionists chose the way of unity and inclusiveness without, perhaps, being aware of the pitfalls into which their otherwise laudable liberality might lead them. The closed communionists chose the way of separation and became much like an ever decreasing army defending an ever diminishing territory.

An example of the incorrigibly schismatic consequences of the closed communionist view of the church is found in the columns of the *Primitive Church Magazine* during the years 1844 and 1845. The readers and editors of the magazine became purveyors of an ecclesial casuistry that provided instant guidance to closed communionists who found themselves victims of population mobility. What was to be their attitude to open communionists living in the vicinity of a closed communionist church? What were the closed communionists to do if they were faced with a choice between a 'live' Independent chapel and a 'dead' closed communion chapel? What was a closed communionist to do if no longer living near enough to a chapel of his persuasion to be able to attend it?

These questions were usually answered in a way that tended to perpetuate or extend schism. For instance, whilst closed communionists limited the Lord's table to baptized believers, a baptized believer who was a member of an open communion Baptist church was reckoned to have associated himself with error and was therefore barred from the table in a closed communion chapel. One correspondent claimed that the reception of a baptized member of an open communion church at a closed communion table was an implicit recognition of infant baptism and that it drew closed brethren nearer to the open Baptists and away from the closed Baptists.[173] Another correspondent claimed that an 'individual who has been immersed upon a profession of faith, but who is still in membership with an unbaptized and unscriptural church, [is] walking disorderly'.[174] The apostolic injunction, it was argued, required that the church dissociate itself from him. Another open communionist had forsaken the church of his own persuasion because the minister wore a gown and the church boasted an organ which he considered to be 'if not the marks something resembling the "marks of the Beast"'. He had, however, been refused communion in the closed communion church. Urged to transfer his membership, he questioned whether such strictness had scriptural authority. The editor assured him that it had.[175]

The magazine opened its columns to those who were clearly not lovers of the closed communionist position. One correspondent accused it of having 'a thousand evil results' and went on to present a case-history. Z, he wrote, is a village with a 'nearly antinominan strict Baptist church'. Nearby is an Independent place of worship 'where the gospel is preached with energy from the pulpit'. A and B 'are the only active christians in the sluggish Baptist mass that encumbers the cause of religion in the village'. They become involved in the work and worship of the Independent chapel 'while they still partake of the eucharist as Strict Baptists' at the Baptist chapel. He asked, 'Are these persons wrong? Ought they, because Strict Baptists, to be spiritually starved themselves, and be accessory to the spiritual starvation of others?' The editors were undismayed by the caustic tone of the letter, nor did they hesitate in prescribing what they believed to be the correct course of action for the hapless A and B. Faced with a strict Baptist church whose ministry was 'essentially defective', they were to resolve the matter, not by turning to an Independent church, but by commencing a 'new church', whose members were 'regularly to meet together on some part of the Lord's Day, for exhortation and prayer'. The Lord's Supper, observed by such an assembly 'would no doubt be scriptural, and a blessing might be expected to attend it'.[176] The schism did not end even with the formation of a closed communion church for, where this was found to be wanting, the remedy was to begin again.

The passion for new beginnings extended to closed communion Baptists who found themselves too far from a strict Baptist chapel to be able to attend. A correspondent, signing herself, 'Sincere Baptist', living thirty miles from the strict Baptist chapel, asked whether it would not be preferable to share in communion at the open communion Baptist church rather than to neglect the Lord's Supper altogether. Again, the magazine's editors were in no doubt as to her painful duty. Attendance at an open membership church would have meant eating the Lord's Supper in a way not instituted by him and also would have involved 'the idolatry of paying homage to the creature instead of the Creator'. Her duty, therefore, was to seek out 'some of like mind' and with them 'unite in church fellowship, and meet in some cottage, as a church of Christ for the observance of his ordinances'.[177]

It would seem that, blanketed in the certainty of their own conviction, closed communionists of the same genre as the editors and readers of the *Primitive Church Magazine* felt no pain in schism. They knew only one cure for all ecclesial diseases - amputation, for which doctrinal certitude provided a more than adequate anaesthetic.

G) SUMMARY

In the communion controversy of the nineteenth century, Baptists were compelled to face perplexing questions. Access to the Lord's table was bound up with the way that they saw their relationship with other Christians. The uniqueness of their doctrinal stance posed what seems to have been an irresolvable dilemma. On neither side of the debate did they come to a satisfactory solution. Their predicament was well described in a perceptive letter, published in the *Primitive Church Magazine*. Looking at both side of the debate, it claimed that:

> Each brother is compelled by the stern necessity of the case to depart from the practice of the primitive churches. The Strict Baptist refuses to receive those whom he knows are christians indeed. This the primitive churches did not. The Open Baptist receives those whom he knows are unbaptized. This the primitive churches did not. Therefore neither can plead exact conformity to apostolic example; both are driven away from the primitive practice:- one sacrifices visible unity, the other ritual uniformity.[178]

Robert Hall saw the Lord's Supper as a sign of the church's unity. He was also a member and spokesman of a denomination whose very existence called into question the validity of baptism as it was almost universally practised by other Christians. The Baptist enterprise, undertaken at the dawn of the seventeenth century, was amongst the most radical attempts to recover the spirit and structure of the early church. In that attempt it laid the axe, as John Smyth put it, at the root of the tree, by rejecting the baptism by which the vast majority of Christians had been initiated into the church. Thus, if their action is left unembellished by theologically sophisticated disclaimers, Baptists unchurched and thereby excommunicated most of their fellow Christians. Hall saw clearly the difficulty. It was, of course, impossible to produce a replica of the first-century church in the vastly changed situation of the nineteenth century. Baptists, any less than other Christians, could not avoid the burden of history. It could not be dismissed like a dream at the dawn of a new day. If baptism and the concept of the church that went with it mattered to Baptists, it mattered no less to their fellow Christians, even though it was differently understood and practised. In endeavouring to recover the New Testament concept of baptism and all its consequences for the church's understanding of itself, Baptists never really came to terms with baptism as others interpreted and practised it. Simple rejection might seem to solve everything but in fact solved nothing.

Hall simply relegated baptism to the status of the non-essential. He refused to recognize any validity in infant baptism, seeing his fellow Christians as unbaptized. He removed the baptismal barrier to inter-communion by claiming that baptism was not of the *esse* of the church. This abdication, in the name of charity, had unhappy consequences for Baptists in succeeding generations. Firstly, his attitude to baptism and his description of it as 'ceremonial' was to be extended, by other Baptists, to the Lord's Supper. If an observance so fundamental to Baptist self-understanding could so easily be dismissed, then it followed that an emphasis on inner attitudes and moral renewal could easily dispatch communion into the realm of the non-essential. Once there, the temptation for Baptists was to neglect that task which is incumbent upon every new generation of Christians, namely to reflect on the nature and purpose of the Christian sacraments. The second consequence of Hall's too easy dismantling of the baptismal barrier was the departure of theological rigour. Any movement towards Christian unity must wrestle with the doctrinal differences that divide Christians. The Baptist response to the formation of the Evangelical Alliance revealed a profound distaste for credal formularies and reluctance to face theological differences.

Given the ethos of the denomination, such distaste was understandable. If the right of individual judgment is highly prized, if the Bible in isolation from Christian tradition is the sole guide to understanding truth, if the checks and balances of an historic understanding of Christian ministry are absent, then creeds can too easily become the province of power-seekers and the rallying cries of witch-hunters. Baptists had suffered a surfeit of doctrine at the hands of the eighteenth-century hyper-Calvinists and, for some, the doctrinal inflexibility of the closed communionists was no less indigestible.

In the wider world of Christian relationships, however, Baptists could not afford to be so fastidious. The wholly laudable desire to be reconciled in love with other Christians had to go hand-in-hand with the rigorous quest for truth. Hall conceded altogether too much. He sought to remove the pain of division by ignoring the reasons for it.

Kinghorn and the closed communionists, on the other hand, conceded too little. They sustained theological rigour and ceased to feel the pain of division. In the communion argument, theirs was the stronger position: the Lord's Supper is a sacrament of the church and admission to the church, as scripture and tradition witness, is through the waters of baptism. They, however, placed consistency before love. They did not accept Hall's argument that the conditions of the first-century church could not be reproduced in the nineteenth. They believed it was possible to establish a church that was in conformity with the New Testament ideal, acted on the same assumptions, enjoyed the same commitment and was ordered by identical rites and practices. To argue in this way was, in the first place, to turn a blind eye to reality. The Baptists, no more than any other denomination, have not succeeded in creating a church marked by a devotion and life-style in stark contrast to its neighbours. It was this that Hall saw so clearly. Baptists were not more pious, more loving, more devoted to Christ, more faithful members of the church than were other Christians. In the second place, the quest for such a church could only result in fresh schisms. Baptists were, and have remained, a minority. The rest of Christendom has not been tempted to disavow its baptism, nor to submit to believer's baptism.

During the nineteenth century, Baptists on both sides of the communion divide were, for the most part, gradually reconciled to each other though both, in the process, sacrificed something valuable which they sought to defend. Hall and Kinghorn needed each other but failed to find each other. They each held two halves of a key that was essential to the Baptists' understanding of themselves and their place in Christ's holy, catholic and apostolic church. It was the challenge of that larger context that they had to face next, in the rise of the Tractarians and the Catholic revival.

NOTES

1. O. C. Robison, 'The Particular Baptists in England 1760-1820', Oxford D.Phil. Dissertation 1963, p.267.
2. B. R. White, 'Open and Closed Membership among English and Welsh Baptists', **Baptist Quarterly** (hereafter **BQ**) 1972, 24, No.7, pp.330-34.
3. See M. J. Walker, 'The Relation of Infants to Church, Baptism and Gospel in Seventeenth Century Baptist Theology', **BQ** 1966, 21, No.6, pp.242-62.
4. W. T. Whitley, ed., **Minutes of the General Assembly of the General Baptists,** Vol.2, 1910, p.293.
5. **General Baptist Repository and Missionary Observer,** New Series 5, 1838 p.377.
6. ibid. p.414.
7. ibid. p.455.
8. Quoted by A. C. Underwood, **A History of the English Baptists,** 1947, p.103.
9. E. A. Payne, **The Baptist Union: A Short History,** 1958, p.86; see also p.41.
10. D. J. Jeremy et.al., **A Century of Grace: The History of Avenue Baptist Church, Southend on Sea 1876-1976,** Southend 1976, p.4.
11. ibid. p.6.
12. Irene Morris, **Three Hundred Years of Baptist Life in Coventry,** 1925, p.59.
13. ibid.
14. White, op.cit. pp.333f.
15. **Freeman** 14 January 1876, p.22.
16. G.Gould, **Open Communion and the Baptists of Norwich,** Norwich 1860, p.liv.
17. ibid. p.lx. See also C. M. Birrell, **Life of William Brock,** 1878, p.121.
18. Gould, op.cit., pp.lxiii.f.
19. ibid. p.lxiv.
20. ibid. p.lxviii.
21. ibid. p.lxix.
22. ibid. p.lxix.
23. ibid. p.lxx.
24. ibid. p.lxx.
25. ibid. p.lxxi.
26. ibid. p.lxxii.
27. ibid. p.lxxiii.
28. ibid. lxxiii.
29. ibid. p.xc.
30. ibid. p.xcii.
31. ibid. p.314.
32. ibid. pp.314-315.
33. ibid. p.317.
34. ibid. pp.318-319.
35. ibid. p.320.
36. ibid. p.322.
37. **Baptist Reporter,** New Series, 6, 1849, p.343.
38. Quoted by Payne, **op.cit.** pp.85f.
39. A. H. MacLeod, 'The Life and Teaching of Robert Hall (1764-1831)', Durham M.Litt. Dissertation 1957, pp.186f.
40. W. R. Ward, 'The Baptists and the Transformation of the Church, 1780-1830', BQ 25, No.4, 1973, pp.168f.
41. Robert Hall, Jnr. 'On Terms of Communion', 1815, in Olinthus Gregory, ed., **The Works of Robert Hall A.M.,** 1832, vol.2, p.9.
42. Joseph Kinghorn, **Baptism a Term of Communion at the Lord's Supper,** Norwich 1816, p.10.
43. J. C. Carlile, **The Story of the English Baptists,** 1905, p.197.
44. Hall, **Works** vol.2, p.14.
45. ibid. p.9.
46. ibid. p.12.
47. ibid. pp.63f.
48. ibid. pp.87f.
49. Christmas Evans, **A Decision of the General Congress Convened to Agree on Terms of Communion,** 1816, p.11f.
50. ibid. p.15.
51. Joseph Ivimey, **Communion at the Lord's Table, Regulated by the Revealed Will of Christ, Not Party, but Christian Communion,** 1826 p.43.
52. Hall, **Works** vol.2, p.254.
53. ibid. p.77.
54. ibid. pp.80f.
55. ibid. pp.109f.
56. ibid. p.119.
57. ibid. p.123.
58. ibid. p.144f.
59. ibid. pp.280f.
60. Thomas Helwys, **A Short Declaration of the Mistery of Iniquity,** 1612, p.69.
61. Hall, **Works** vol.2, p.84.

62 ibid. p.86.
63 Galatians 5.12.
64 Hall, **Works** vol.2, p.90..
65 ibid. p.93.
66 ibid.
67 Edinburgh 1845.
68 Innes, op.cit. pp.17ff.
69 ibid. p.23.
70 ibid.
71 ibid. p.26.
72 ibid. p.29.
73 Robert Hall, **Works** vol.2, p.107.
74 ibid.
75 ibid. p.495.
76 Ivimey, **Baptism the Scriptural and Indispensable Qualification for Communion at the Lord's Table**, 1824, p.57.
77 Kinghorn, op.cit. p.58f.
78 ibid. p.161f.
79 Ivimey, op.cit. p.63.
80 Kinghorn, op.cit. p.43.
81 ibid. p.44.
82 Ivimey, **Communion at the Lord's Table** . . .. p.38.
83 Kinghorn, op.cit. p.68.
84 ibid. p.68.
85 G. Pritchard, **A Plea for Primitive Communion**, 1816, pp.59f.
86 William Button, **An Answer to the Question 'Why Are You a Strict Baptist?'** 1816, p.78.
87 Kinghorn, op.cit. p.75.
88 Ivimey, op.cit. pp.26f.
89 John Stevens, **Thoughts on Sanctification**, 1816, p.59.
90 ibid. pp.67f.
91 W. Palmer, **Free Communion Examined** reviewed in the **Primitive Church Magazine** September 1846, p.329.
92 See above pp.51f.
93 Quoted by Hall, **Works** vol.2, p.136.
94 ibid. p.137.
95 ibid. p.254.
96 ibid. p.281.
97 ibid. p.285.
98 ibid. p.325.
99 ibid. p.367.
100 ibid. p.80.
101 ibid. p.296.
102 ibid. pp.300-29.
103 ibid. p.31.
104 ibid. p.340.
105 ibid. p.346.
106 ibid. p.261.
107 H.Daniel-Rops, **The Church in the Eighteenth Century**, 1964, p.157.
108 Seymour J. Price, 'Narrative of Andrew Leslie 1823', **BQ** 11, Nos.3 & 4, 1942, p.90.
109 Thomas Armitage, **A History of the Baptists**, New York 1887, p.595.
110 see Calvin A. Pater, **Karlstadt as the father of the Baptist movements**, Toronto 1984, pp.15-115.
111 Kinghorn, op.cit. p.165; see also William Newman, **Baptism an Indispensable Pre-Requisite to Communion at the Lord's Table**, 1805, p.10.
112 ibid. pp.104f; cf. John Clifford, **The Ordinances of Jesus and the Sacraments of the Church**, 1887, p.25.
113 Robert Hall, **Works** vol.2, pp.151f.
114 ibid. p.154.
115 ibid. p.155.
116 ibid. p.157.
117 ibid. p.267.
118 ibid. p.272.
119 Quoted in the **Baptist Record** February 1845, p.192.
120 Hall, **Works** vol.2, p.292.
121 ibid. p.296.
122 Walker, op.cit. pp.245f.
123 Kinghorn, op.cit. pp.13f.
124 ibid. p.67.
125 ibid. p.79.
126 ibid. p.67.
127 Ivimey, **Baptism the Scriptural and Indispensable Qualification . . .**, p.60.
128 J. Aldis, **Six Lectures on the Importance and Practicability of Christian Union**, 1846, p.111.
129 Kinghorn, op.cit. p.54.
130 Newman, op.cit. p.14.
131 Kinghorn, op.cit. p.88.
132 Hall, **Works** vol.2, p.31.
133 ibid. p.48.
134 Kinghorn, op.cit. pp.20f.
135 ibid. p.32.
136 ibid. p.90.
137 ibid. p.92.
138 ibid. p.95.
139 Ivimey, op.cit. p.55.
140 Kinghorn, op.cit. p.102.
141 Ivimey, op.cit. p.70.
142 Kinghorn, op.cit. p.129.
143 Ivimey, op.cit. p.63.
144 Ivimey, **Communion at the Lord's Table**, p.44.
145 1844.
146 John Leifchild, **Christian Union**, 1844, p.36.
147 Northants Baptist Circular Letter 1844 p.11.
148 **Primitive Church Magazine**, September 1845, pp.342.
149 J. Mortlock Daniell, **The One Church,**

or Sects unscriptural, Ramsgate 1846, p.14.
150 ibid. p.30.
151 ibid. p.31.
152 J. Aldis, Six Lectures.
153 ibid. p.22.
154 ibid. p.28.
155 ibid. p.118ff.
156 ibid. p.148.
157 **Primitive Church Magazine**, December 1845, p.432.
158 ibid., January 1846, p.14.
159 The other editors were George Pritchard 1838-41 and Robert William Overbury 1838-51.
160 **Primitive Church Magazine** January 1844, p.30.
161 1844.
162 R. W. Overbury, **op.cit.** p.24.
163 ibid. pp.33-8.
164 ibid. p.47f.
165 **Baptist Reporter** May 1846, p.67.
166 ibid. October 1846, p.404.
167 ibid. p.404.
168 **Baptist Record** May 1846, p.323.
169 ibid. p.323.
170 **Freeman** 17 October 1860, p.669.
171 ibid. 24 October 1860, p.682.
172 ibid. 22 September 1882, p.602.
173 **Primitive Church Magazine** February 1844, pp.78f.
174 ibid. May 1844, p.243.
175 ibid. March 1845, p.98.
176 ibid. March 1844, pp.130f.
177 ibid. May 1844, p.245.
178 ibid. April 1844, p.187.

Chapter Three

BAPTISTS AND THE CATHOLIC REVIVAL

The communion debate was largely a domestic affair conducted amongst Baptists. Although it centred around the question of their relationship to Christians of other denominations, it sprang from their particular theological pre-occupations. It was the product of a whole view of faith, the church and the meaning of baptism. With the coming of the Catholic revival, they were compelled to look at questions that otherwise would have been of little concern to them and to examine their own beliefs and practice in the light of the Catholic eucharistic tradition. The rise of the Tractarians and Ritualists in the Church of England and the revival of English Roman Catholicism inevitably focused the attention of all Christians on the Lord's table and what took place there.

Through the eyes of nineteenth-century Baptists, a view shared by most of their Evangelical contemporaries, the precious ground gained by the Protestant Reformation was in danger of being lost to the advancing cause of Catholic Christianity. Amongst Evangelicals as a whole there was, as Geoffrey Best reminds us, a widespread repugnance to Roman doctrine and influence:

> ... feelings about Rome, ranging from cultivated distaste to deep and genuine horror, were shared by most of the Protestant public, and the Church of England Evangelicals ...[1]

Apart from this universal distaste, fuelled no doubt by tribal memories and polemical distortion, the doctrinal priorities of the Evangelicals were totally at variance with those of Catholicism. Evangelicalism stressed conversion rather than baptism as the important occasion of entry into Christ's Church. It stressed the scriptures, rather than tradition or ecclesiastical authority, as the source and test of religious truth. It stressed 'the word' working through preaching and prayer, rather than sacerdotally administered sacraments, as the main channel of grace. It stressed 'faith alone' as the Christian means of salvation: salvation through Christ's atoning sacrifice, not through meritorious works or a mixture of faith and works.[2]

The Baptists' reaction to the Catholic revival was not, then, a single example of an exclusive and aggressive Protestantism. Their feelings on many issues were shared by Evangelicals of all denominational persuasions. Apart from events at home, developments in Rome itself served to heighten their fears. In 1864 Pius IX published the notorious *Syllabus of Errors* which condemned, amongst other things, the propositions that every man was free to choose the religion he wished to profess, that the church should be separate from the state and *vice versa*, and that it was no longer necessary that the Catholic religion should be the only religion of a state to the exclusion of all others.[3] The Vatican Council convened five years later in Rome, carefully reported by both the *Freeman* and the *Baptist Magazine*, declared the doctrine of papal infallibility and confirmed Protestant fears of Roman incorrigibility by the definition of the doctrine of Mary's immaculate conception. It was not a climate conducive to the interment of old quarrels or for a dispassionate appraisal of Dissenting beliefs in response to the undoubtedly renewing influence of the Tractarian movement. Rather Evangelicals felt it essential to widen the already yawning gulf between what they believed and what was coming out of Rome. For some Baptists it became *de rigeur* to measure orthodoxy by its distance from Catholic beliefs. The slide from Zwinglianism into Anabaptist radicalism accelerated as the century wore on.

A) THE BAPTIST RESPONSE TO THE CATHOLIC REVIVAL

Professor Horton Davies claims that the Tractarian movement had a three-fold effect on Evangelical Anglicans and the Free Churches.[4] Firstly, it provoked them to look at their own worship and to value it as something more than simply the preparation for the sermon. Secondly, more Christians began to think in terms of the *ecclesia* instead of the *ecclesiae*. Thirdly, it influenced others in their approach to and use of culture, in music and architecture, for instance. There are hints that the first and the third were true in the case of Baptists. It might be argued that the foundation of the Baptist Union in the nineteenth century pointed to the truth of the second claim, but the Union owed everything to the internal development of Baptist church life and nothing to Catholic concepts of the church. On the contrary, the powerful individualism of Victorian times only re-inforced the innate autonomy of Baptists and their churches.

The Baptists' response to the Tractarian movement was more clearly marked by a negative attitude of anxiety and distrust. A more positive response can be inferred from some of the ideas and practices that were being aired in Baptist churches but nowhere was there a direct acknowledgment of Catholic influence. Indeed, if it could be proved that new ideas were in any way tainted by Catholic sympathies then they were damned from the outset.

The view most widely shared by Baptists was that Tractarianism and Ritualism confirmed their suspicion that the Church of England was incurably biased towards Rome. The Catholic movement could serve only to push faltering Anglicans inexorably in a Rome-ward direction. At the Baptist Union meetings in May 1867, J. H. Hinton moved the resolution that:

> This Union hereby place on record their continued and profound abhorrence of the sacerdotal doctrine and spirit which have for many centuries characterised the apostate Church of Rome, and are now so extensively and vigorously revived in the Established Church of England . . .[5]

Similar fears were still being expressed more than twenty-five years later. An unattributed article signed simply 'W.H.' made what was by then a familiar claim that the Ritualist party was heading towards Rome. Anglicanism was judged to be

> ... the ally of Sacerdotalism, and, consciously or unconsciously, is undoing the work of the Reformation. It tends naturally and inevitably towards Rome, creates a desire for reconciliation with the Pope, and for affiliation with the so-called Catholic community of which he is the head, though affiliation is but another name for absorption.[6]

A few months later, editorial comment returned to the same theme:

> Romish doctrines and practices are gaining a firm footing in that Establishment which was supposed to be a bulwark against them. The Anglican Church is saturated with Romanism...[7]

A theme that constantly recurred was that of sacerdotalism. The Baptists had some justice on their side when they argued that the logical outcome of the Catholic revival was that it took on a new importance. The placing of the eucharist in the centre of the church's life and worship inevitably led to a renewed emphasis on the role of the celebrant in the sacrament. The presence of Christ could be made real only through the ministry of the celebrant, and if that ministry was to be effective then it must be received at episcopal hands. For Baptists this stress on the priestly function of the celebrant only opened the door, as they saw it, to the abuses of priest-craft and the worst features of Catholic subversion. The *Syllabus of Errors* could have done little to allay their fears of what might happen were power to return to the hands of a priestly caste. In his pamphlet replying to Pusey's sermon on the eucharist, delivered in Christ Church, Oxford, in 1843, Dr Benjamin Godwin, the minister of New Road Baptist Church in Oxford, was content to observe that the emphasis on episcopal ordination as an invariable requirement for a valid celebration of the Lord's Supper could only lead to the exclusion of other ministries. Such teaching would give rise to

> ...a spirit of pharisaic exclusiveness, of haughty superiority, and intense bigotry.[8]

An article by T. Pottenger, written fourteen years later, was less restrained in what it saw as the renewed threat of sacerdotal power:

> In the hands of a priesthood, these precious ordinances have been turned into instruments of spiritual tyranny. Sacramental efficacy gives them power over their victims from the cradle to the grave, and even beyond the grave; it begins with the new-born child, and attends the dying man;

it subdues reason, enslaves nations, and ruins souls, fills peasants with terror and princes with alarm; lays the foundation of Papal arrogance, and brings reproach upon the cause of Christ.[9]

Towards the end of the century, Dr Alexander Maclaren still felt it necessary to urge

... all Evangelical Nonconformists to draw their ranks closer together, and to stand shoulder by shoulder in the great fight before them - a fight to the death with encroaching and arrogant Sacerdotalism.[10]

The same note was struck in a review of the nineteenth century published in the *Baptist Magazine* at the turn of the century. Looking back over the century just ended, it pin-pointed the Tractarian movement as a significant step towards sacerdotalism and Rome:

Sacerdotal powers were claimed for the duly ordained clergy; sacraments were exalted into channels of grace; obsolete superstitions were brought from their hiding place ... The Tractarian movement has done much to de-Protestantise the English Church and to furnish recruits for Rome.[11]

None of this served to create an atmosphere in which Baptists might listen to Tractarians and discern whether in what they were saying the Lord might be speaking to the whole of his church. Yet the one did not completely leave the other untouched. There are indications that Baptists, like other Nonconformists, were influenced by what was happening in the Anglican church. In the nature of the case, no trend amongst Baptists would be universally true of all of them: what took place Sunday by Sunday in one Baptist church would be a liturgical world away from what was happening in another Baptist church a few miles away. In 1869 the editor of the *Freeman* might vividly describe a service in a Congregationalist church as an 'aping of the Established Church', with its 'altar' adorned with the sacred monogram *IHS*, its two reading desks, its east wall 'draped with crimson curtains', its minister dressed in 'the rag of Geneva', its use of the Lord's Prayer and *Te Deum*, and even its 'two crimson velvet bags' to receive the offering,[12] yet, by the beginning of the next century, F. B. Meyer, a Baptist minister, was leading a liturgically-structured form of service week by week in the undenominational Christ Church, Westminster Bridge Road, in London. Perhaps the church was untypical, but the fact that Meyer adopted the approach that he did in no way negated his considerable standing within the life of the denomination. That others were engaged in their own experiments is clear from the rather odd warning from a correspondent to the *Freeman* in 1868 that, in addition to speaking of 'church' instead of 'chapel', being married in the parish church and wearing crosses, some

Baptists were 'interposing an anthem in the course of the service, and the choir having it to themselves, the congregation not allowed to join'.[13]

Other signs are evident that Baptists were influenced by the milieu created by the Tractarians, if not by the Tractarians themselves. They can be discerned in the changing pattern of worship, in the architecture of church buildings and in certain 'external' matters. Baptists, like other Nonconformists, became more aware of a lack of balance in their worship. The sermon was central to their act of worship and, in an age populated with gifted preachers and congregations eager to hear them, there is little cause for surprise in that. Yet, as comparatively early as 1857, a writer in the *Freeman* observed:

> Roman Catholicism tends, by all its peculiarities, to strike out of Christian worship the one half - teaching, Protestantism, and especially English Dissenterism, is very apt to reduce to too great unimportance the other half - devotion.[14]

A year later, in the same journal, 'An Old Baptist of the Old School' (an expansive *nom-de-plume* even for those days of literary concealment!) bemoaned the departure of '. . . good, sound, old-fashioned Nonconformity . . . in all its vigour' and wondered whether it was a concession to a younger generation of Dissenters who

> . . . are looking for a genteeler road to heaven; and hence . . . must have a Baptist church, and steeples, with responses, and all the little ornaments and follies attendant upon it.[15]

Others were not so enamoured with the past as not to desire something better. The tendency of prayers to become sermons was bemoaned by a correspondent 'Catholicus', who argued that churches should not be built entirely for the hearing of preaching but for worship, 'a house of prayer'.[16] Another, signing himself 'Sexagenarian', demonstrating that the years had done nothing to dull his appetite for the new and innovative, asked if it was necessary for Baptists to dispense altogether with liturgical forms. If hymns were used as a corporate expression of the people's praise, then why not prayers? He argued:

> . . . both prayers and praises with responses should form a part large enough to give variety to the service, and relief to the occupant of the pew.[17]

Others were being influenced by the pattern of the Christian Year. Admittedly, the influence was minimal, Baptists at this time regarding all festivals as popish devices, and many of them prepared to go on regarding them as such. A simple request by a correspondent of the *Baptist Magazine* in May 1857 to be told why Baptists did not observe Good Friday or Christmas Day, was firmly answered in the following issue:

1st. [Baptists] objected to the authority by which these observances were imposed. 2nd. They objected to the superstitious usages involved.[18]

In the same year one of the General Baptist associations meeting in Loughborough carried a motion designed to introduce a liturgy for the use of ministers in their churches. It was later claimed that the motion was carried by an unrepresentative majority and protests were voiced in the *General Baptist Magazine*.[19]

Clearly, Baptists were asking the same questions as others about the quality and content of their worship. It is doubtful whether those who wanted a change to a liturgical structure gained much, if any, ground, but they were present in the life of the denomination and their presence is evidence that the issues raised by the Catholic renewal were not foreign to many ordinary Baptist church members.

A perhaps more dramatic proof of the Tractarian influence is to be found in the buildings that Baptists were erecting in the second half of the nineteenth century. It was for them, as for other denominations, a great period of church building. Populations were on the move, cities and industrial areas were expanding and, wherever new communities came into existence, new churches were being built. The influence of the Gothic revival is evident to this day in many of the Baptist churches built during the period. Its appearance was greeted with derision by some. S. Wilkin, a resident of Hampstead, writing to the *Baptist Magazine* in 1852, deplored the architecture of some of the new Nonconformist chapels being built at the time

. . . in monkish fashion, and splendidly adorned with painted windows, and provided with magnificent organ.[20]

Fifteen years later a correspondent from Shipley took a more appreciative view of the new chapels and argued for the social significance of the choices made by a church in the erection of its building. A spire was a

. . . picturesque object in country towns, and both in towns and cities a guide to the house of prayer. A standing witness to our existence, and a constant challenge to public attention to our principles and growth. How often are we spoken of as a small and *obscure* body? Again I ask, why should Church people have all the beautiful things? Why should they have a monopoly of bells and spires that keep public attention always directed to them as a body, and add so much to their influence, importance, and *prestige*?[21]

The third and least important area of possible Tractarian influence was in certain 'external' matters. One example was the use of the title 'Reverend' for a minister, bound up as this was with the question of ministerial status. Some Baptist ministers despised and would not accept the title. The *Freeman* argued for its usage claiming that:

> If we give up the name, we shall be understood to confess, either that we doubt that there is such an office, or that we doubt our right to fill it.[22]

If on this occasion the *Freeman* supported a title giving some ministerial status, nine years earlier it had supported 'An Old Baptist', to whom reference has already been made, in his complaint that Baptist ministers could now be seen 'in gown and bands'. The *Freeman* was in no doubt about the matter: it considered 'gowns and bands, and such like frippery ... inexpressibly silly'.[23] That diversity was of the essence, however, is clear from a leader on 'Christmas Candles' written on 24 December 1862, in which the writer recounted the value of candles at the Christmas season because 'we English love to connect the present with the past' and urged his readers to decorate their homes with candles and tell their wondering children:

> ... of mitred bishop, cowled priest, veiled nun, passing, taper in hand, from cathedral aisles along the streets of the city; the crucifix borne aloft, the censer scattering fragrance and the choir sweet sounds, on the still night air.[24]

This enraptured vision of mediaeval Christendom was greeted with no cries of dissent, no angrily penned letters. Perhaps Baptist readers, replete with Christmas fare, were too drowsy to bestir themselves to Protestant anger.

The basic Protestant radicalism of Baptists remained unchanged, then, by the Catholic revival. Rome was still the great enemy and its priestly doctrine suspect. Because the eucharist was closely bound up with questions of ministry, reflection on the nature of the sacrament itself had constantly to be on guard against any taint of Catholic influence. Baptist attitudes were clearly modified, however, by the climate of liturgical renewal created by the Tractarians. On the safer ground of buildings and architectural fashions Baptists were able to follow enthusiastically down the road of Gothic revival. From the splendour of the Vatican Council[25] to the significance of a Christmas candle they held a strangely ambivalent attitude towards the Catholic glories of colour, spectacle and symbolism. They recognized that their own way of worshipping might conceivably not be the only way but, for all that some brave souls were willing to raise the question, it is doubtful whether they were ever as liturgically influenced by what was happening around them as were, for instance, their spiritual cousins, the Congregationalists. Preaching remained central for them. Some, however, rose to the eucharistic challenge posed by the Tractarians.

There were no great Baptist treatises on the subject. Apart from the preachers and their sermons, there was no Baptist who wielded his pen with the skill of a Robert Hall. There were, however, tracts and articles. These reveal that some Baptists thought deeply on the eucharistic questions with which a renewed Catholicism faced them.

B) THE LORD'S SUPPER

On the fourth Sunday after Easter in 1843, E. B. Pusey, Regius Professor of Divinity and canon of Christ Church in the University of Oxford, preached in the University Church on the subject 'The Holy Eucharist, a Comfort to the Penitent'. Following protests his sermon was later examined by the vice-chancellor and six appointed doctors of divinity. The board, having read the sermon, judged that it was not in harmony with the teaching of the church and the vice-chancellor ruled that Pusey should not be allowed to preach within the university for a period of two years. Pusey was to become the natural leader of the Oxford movement following the departure of John Henry Newman for the Roman Catholic Church in 1845. The sermon, whilst not representing the full flowering of Pusey's thought, set down a marker in eucharistic theology and attracted a good deal of attention, not least from Evangelicals. Amongst those who wrote pamphlets setting out to refute Pusey's arguments was the minister of the New Road Baptist Church in Oxford, Benjamin Godwin.

The structure of his pamphlet, *An Examination of the Principles and Tendencies of Dr. Pusey's Sermon on the Eucharist*, was largely determined by the shape of Pusey's sermon. The subjects dealt with were to be themes over which debate was to continue and to which other Baptist writers were to give their attention during the coming decades. Using this basic structure it is possible to examine first what Godwin wrote, and then to trace the ideas of those who followed him. The themes covered by Pusey and his later disputants were the nature of Christ's presence in the sacrament, the exegesis of eucharistic passages in the New Testament, the place of tradition and especially the teaching of the early Fathers on the nature of the eucharist, the sacrament as a means of grace and, finally, the tension between 'personal' and 'ceremonial' religion.

i) The Presence of Christ in the Eucharist

For all its length and erudition Pusey's sermon was intended to serve the pastoral purpose of enabling Christians to find forgiveness for their sins in the holy eucharist. The starting point of his eucharistic doctrine was the incarnation of Christ. It was because Christ had come in our flesh, and that flesh had been joined indissolubly to his divine life, that we now, in the eucharist, receiving that which had been made flesh, receive him:

> ... such is undoubted Catholic teaching, and the most literal import of Holy Scripture, and the mystery of the Sacrament, that the Eternal Word, Who is God, having taken to Him our flesh and joined it indissolubly with Himself, and so, where His Flesh is, there He is, and we receiving it, receive Him, and receiving Him are joined on to Him through His flesh to

the Father, and He dwelling in us, dwell in Him, and with Him in God.[26]

Because Christ was inseparable from the flesh and blood he had taken into heaven, then, his presence in the eucharist could not be merely figurative. To receive bread and wine after consecration was to receive the body and blood of him who was present in the sacrament. Christ was 'truly and really present'. His presence was at once spiritual and substantial.

Godwin, in reply, argued that the 'elements are emblems', they were 'outward and visible signs', adapted to bring before the mind important truths. Where they were received by believers 'the blessings resulting from the Saviour's death' were enjoyed.[27] Pusey, he claimed, had argued for something immensely different from this:

> ... the elements on being consecrated have undergone a stupendous change, and are now literally, though without losing their natural substance, the very body and blood of Christ.[28]

Pusey had fallen short of transubstantiation, his view being probably closer to that of those Caroline divines for whom the incarnation itself was the model of eucharistic presence. Far from destroying the substance of bread and wine, the body and blood of the divine Lord are joined to them in a mystery as profound as the incarnation itself. Two problems stand out to which Pusey did not address himself. The first is that of the location of the risen body of Christ which, whilst seated at the right hand of God is also, it is claimed, present in the consecrated species on the altar. It was at this point that Calvin had parted company with Luther, the latter stressing the ubiquity of Christ's humanity, the former his glorified status at God's right hand. Godwin posed the objection in familiarly Calvinist terms:

> ... the literal sense supposes the body of Christ to be at once in heaven and on earth, at thousands of miles distant, and in thousands of places, at the same moment of time.[29]

The second problem arises from the *reductio ad absurdum* made in Godwin's argument. A heaven which can be located in terms of linear distance from the earth, or a body that can be in one place but not another, cannot be described as spiritual realities. They are locked in space and time and derive their identity from their spatio-temporal location. Despite Calvin's criticism of Luther it can be claimed that the latter had anticipated his objection. Luther argued for the real presence of Christ in the sacrament by deploying the Christological doctrine of the *communicatio idiomatum*. The humanity of Christ is universally present in the sacrament because his humanity shares in his divinity. The humanity is omnipresent because the divinity is, by definition, omnipresent. However, ubiquity is not the core of the problem. The difficulty that stalks the various attempts to relate the humanity of Jesus to his presence in the sacrament is the pressing need for an exact definition of the humanity which he took with him into heaven. Pusey made the incarnation central, laying a scent that Godwin and others followed hungrily. If Christ has taken into heaven the body, blood and bones which were seen and handled in Galilee, then indeed sacramental theology must face an insuperable problem. If, however, the *terminus ad quem* of the incarnation is placed at the ascension of Christ then it can be argued that a change had occurred in Christ's body. It belonged to that order described by Paul in 1 Corinthians 1.15, the order of incorruption, imperishability, glory and strength raised out of corruption, perishability, dishonour and weakness. The post-resurrection body of Jesus was substantial but dispensable, his own but recognized by others only with difficulty. It is this incarnate body, now risen and glorified, that is at the heart of the eucharistic mystery.

If the real presence of Christ in the sacrament is understood in terms of the risen and glorified body of the Lord, then a key is provided to the eucharistic dialectic between substantial and spiritual. Pusey and other Catholics continued to use the notoriously slippery concept of substance in order to signify that what was given in the Lord's Supper was neither simply a projection of the communicant's faith nor a consequence of an exercised imagination. Christ's presence was centred in the bread and wine, not in the pious disposition of the believing communicant. At the same time, this substantial presence is spiritual, in the sense that the risen and glorified body of Jesus is both substantial and spiritual. It is real whilst belonging to another order of reality. Again, to draw on the Pauline analogy, just as material entities have bodies that are compatible with the order of which they are a part, so the resurrection body belongs to the new order of the kingdom of God. The resurrection body of Jesus was really and substantially present in the Upper Room, occupying space and perceived in time; the same Risen Christ who met Paul on the road to Damascus was real and substantial, i.e. he spoke, he was perceived in that moment of time and yet, it would seem, he did not occupy space. It is that risen and glorified body, clearly identifiable with the Incarnate Lord, that provides the model for our understanding of the Lord's presence in the eucharist.

It was the 'localized' presence of Christ, implicit in the belief in his substantial presence in the sacrament, that was a stumbling block for Godwin and those who agreed with him. If the flesh and blood of Christ were given in the eucharist, then Christ's body was on the altar, in the priest's hand, in the communicant's mouth and divided between the chalice and the plate.[30] Godwin was not prepared to be reconciled to the notion of the real presence by recourse to its essential mystery. All Catholic theologians would have claimed that their eucharistic doctrines provided not factual descriptions of what happened at the altar but attempts at unfolding a mystery as profound as the incarnation and resurrection. Godwin discounted the appeal to mystery as if it was nothing more than an excuse to jettison reason:

> Almighty power is never exercised but under the direction of infinite wisdom, that to suppose it capable of doing that which is contradictory or absurd is to impute imperfection to a Being infinitely perfect.[31]

He insisted that Pusey had invested the eucharist with 'awful mystery' which could be maintained only if some 'change' was being argued for. No such mystery existed if it was accepted that

> ... the only change in the elements is their separation from an ordinary to a religious use, that the only sense in which they are the body and blood of Christ is figurative, that the only 'real presence' is 'in the heart and soul' of the communicant, and that the only participation is a reception by faith of the benefits of that death and passion which are there set forth ...[32]

Godwin believed that it was his interpretation, not Pusey's, that carried the authority of the English reformers. When they

> ... speak of a real participation in the body and blood of the Lord, of a real presence, of the body and blood of Christ being 'verily and indeed taken and received'; strong as the terms are, they mean only a spiritual reception of Christ, by faith, as our Saviour, and a participation, in consequence, of the benefits of his death.[33]

He quoted the communion service, averring that it taught there is 'literally no presence of the actual body of Christ in the sacrament', and further supported his argument with quotations from Cranmer, Hooker ('The real presence of Christ's most blessed body and blood, is not therefore to be sought for in the sacrament, but in the worthy receiver of the sacrament'), and Jeremy Taylor.[34]

Although his central purpose was to repudiate what he saw as Pusey's leaning towards transubstantiation, Godwin does not himself emerge as a thoroughgoing memorialist. Given the unresolved problem of the difference between Christ's incarnate humanity prior to the resurrection and his glorified body after it, with the corollary problem of the exact nature of a 'substantial' presence, Godwin affirmed that what was perceived, given and received in the eucharist was 'spiritual'. This, however, did not lessen his conviction that something was given. A Christ who was 'spiritually' present was no less 'truly and really' present, to the eye of faith and contemplation, than was a Christ who was 'substantially' present. Faith was crucial to our knowledge and experience of God, as much at the Lord's table as in the secular paths of daily discipleship. The objection to a 'spiritual' presence of Christ in the sacrament, perceived by faith, is that the anchor-chain of objectivity is broken and the sacrament in danger of drifting into the shallows of subjective states of mind and a greater emphasis on the recipient's experience than on God's salvific activity. The danger is certainly there, just as there is a danger that a belief in the actual body of Christ upon the altar can drift into sacramental magic, divorced from the faith, love and obedience that are asked from all who 'truly and earnestly' come to share in the sacrament. Godwin avoided turning the sacrament into an *aide-memoire* in which the believer's psychological experience was central. Christ was present in the heart. Participation in the sacrament was a participation in the death and passion of the Lord. Earlier he had dealt with the eucharistic teaching of 1 Corinthians 10, and declared that, by partaking of the outward sign,

> ... we participate in the benefits and blessings of [Christ's] death: and, as far as our faith is brought into exercise, this institution becomes the means of our enjoying these benefits, and having actual communion with Christ.[35]

Whether later Baptists were able to refute the eucharistic views of the Tractarians and Ritualists and, at the same time, hold on to as much as Godwin was able to grasp is open to question. Theological debate was too easily overwhelmed by polemical enthusiasm and the desire to deny any 'real' presence of Christ in the sacrament could too easily become a denial of any presence at all. The tension is later seen in John Clifford, for instance, who highly valued the Lord's Supper but was constantly driven to qualify any statement that seemed to lend it objective validity.

The question of the 'real presence' arose again in a series of articles that the *Baptist Magazine* devoted to the study of the Tracts in 1867. Under the general title 'What is Anglican Ritualism?' they came from the pen of J. H. Hinton, who had recently retired from the pastorate of the Devonshire Square Baptist Church in London, a post he had combined with that of joint secretary of the Baptist Union.

The first article dealt with the act of consecration in the eucharist. The belief that, at the words of consecration, Christ became actually present in the bread and wine, Hinton described as 'the root from which the whole tree of Ritualism grows'.[36] The description 'the Real Presence' was appropriate only to the Roman rite of transubstantiation, the Ritualists believing that the body and blood of Christ were 'mystically and spiritually' present in the elements. The following month, Hinton returned to the subject of the real presence, quoting a definition by Mr Mackonochie, the incumbent of St Alban's in Holborn:

> I believe that in the Holy Communion the Body and Blood of Christ are present 'really and spiritually' ... not after material, or local, or corporeal, or earthly mode of existence; but after a fashion supra-local, supernatural, heavenly, and spiritual.[37]

The removal of the word 'substantial' that had caused so much confusion in Godwin's dispute with Pusey should have helped to clarify the discussion that followed. In fact, that was not the case. It was dogged by the same difficulty of defining exactly what was implied in a belief in Christ's glorified body. Hinton began by arguing that the body and blood of Christ must be a material substance:

> If the Body and Blood of Christ be in the Eucharist, it is as material substances they *must* be there; if that which is there is spirit, and not matter, then it is clearly no longer the Body and Blood of Christ.[38]

Having set up what he believed was the inescapable conclusion that the body and blood of Christ must be material, he argued that such a presence could not be 'supra-local':

> ... it is an established maxim of physical philosophy that no substance can exist in more than one place at the same time ... To deprive a substance of its essential property of occupying space cannot be less than to destroy the substance itself.[39]

Hinton had used the term 'substance' as interchangeable currency between 'physical philosophy' and theology, investing it with a material connotation implicit in the usage of the former but not necessarily of the latter. This prevented him from developing the nascent solution to the problem of substance which he himself provided. Quoting 1 Corinthians 15.50, he contended that flesh and blood could not inherit the kingdom of God; therefore the body of the risen Christ was a spiritual body. Instead of exploring further the nature of that risen body and its implications for eucharistic theology, he used it as a counter to any claim that Christ was 'substantially' present in the sacrament. The risen body of Jesus was not a material body, therefore there could be no substantial presence of the body and blood of the Lord in the eucharist.

The same confusion hung unacknowledged in the air when Hinton, in the following edition, went on to deal with 'The Miracle of the Altar'. Any miracle, he claimed, must be 'as a fact, obvious to the senses of mankind'. This was not so in the eucharist:

> Not only does no apparent change take place in the bread and wine, but the closest examination demonstrates that, according to the evidence of the senses, no change of any kind or degree has taken place. The elements are, by all physical tests, as simply bread and wine after the thaumaturgic words as they were before.[40]

The underlying assumption was again that the glorified body of Jesus was subject to the same conditions as the body of his incarnation: in other words it occupied space. Hinton took no cognizance of the Thomist distinction, satisfactory or not as it may be, between substance and accidents. Standing four-square on 'physical philosophy', he could not escape the conclusion that substance had accidents. The spatial stumbling-block got under his feet again when he related the body of Christ in the sacrament to the body of Christ in heaven, raising the Calvinist objection that Godwin had used before him:

> The body and blood of Christ ... (which, if existent anywhere, are in Heaven, and may be assumed to be so for the purpose of this argument), are alleged to be also in the bread and wine, and thus the same thing is affirmed to be in two places at the same time - and not in two only, indeed, but perhaps in two thousand, if in every Eucharist - which in the nature of things is impossible.[41]

His article ended:

> ... here are the body and blood of Christ, held to be in heaven in their natural condition, and affirmed to be in the Eucharist in a spiritual condition; so that the same things are affirmed to be at the same time in two opposite conditions, which is in the nature of things impossible.[42]

The crucial questions went unasked. Given their view of the sacraments it was unlikely that the Baptists, any more than other Evangelicals, would have wrestled with the problem of the nature of the divine 'substance' present in the Lord's Supper. Godwin and Hinton were about the business of refuting incipient Catholicism in the Church of England, not framing a eucharistic theology. Even their maladroit juggling of spatio-temporal categories, however, might well have served to push the notion of substance in the direction of greater clarity. It was a time of confrontation, however, and it is unrealistic to suppose that they could anticipate a dialogue that even one hundred and fifty years later has hardly begun. Abhorrence of the Anglo-Catholics was inspired by fear of the doctrine of transubstantiation more than by any other alleged feature of Catholic teaching. It became increasingly more important to distance oneself from it than to understand it.

ii) The Exegesis of the Eucharistic Texts

Baptists have been happier with what they consider to be the plain word of scripture than with the more philosophical demands of speculative theology. The Bible has been an open book, its riches available to any prepared to explore its pages. In his pamphlet, Godwin gave his attention to those passages of the New Testament currently referred to in eucharistic debate. Others were to give them their attention after him. The classic passages with which Godwin dealt were the gospel eucharistic narratives, the Corinthian passages and the teaching of Jesus in John 6.

a) The Eucharistic Narratives in the Gospels

In handling the narratives, Godwin was concerned with three main points: the meaning of 'blessing', the significance of the word 'is' in our Lord's eucharistic statements, and the purpose of the sacrament. Of the first, he said that blessing was synonymous with thanksgiving. The verb $ευλογειν$ was interchangeable with the verb $ευξαριστειν$. The point of this for Godwin was that the prayer offered in the eucharist was not a prayer of consecration in the Catholic sense. It was simply a prayer of thanksgiving. The object of the 'blessing' was not the bread and wine that thereby were transformed into the body and blood of Christ, but God, whose goodness was acknowledged by his people.

Secondly, when Jesus said, 'This is my body . . . this is my blood', the language was figurative. Godwin illustrated his meaning from daily life. Seeing sketches in a print-shop window, one would say, 'This is Dr Pusey, and that is Mr Newman':

> When our Lord, therefore, taking up the bread, said 'this is my body', the meaning this represents my body, was so perfectly natural, and accordant with those forms of speaking to which [the disciples] had always been accustomed, that it was morally impossible that they should understand the words in any other sense.[43]

The argument was, and is, familiar.

His third concern, was to express what Jesus intended in instituting the sacrament:

> . . . we see the Saviour . . . appointing a standing memorial of his death . . . in the observance of which his faithful followers should have their mutual charity increased, their love to himself quickened, and their faith brought into so lively an exercise, that they should enjoy renewed communication of the rich benefits procured by his death.[44]

There was nothing exceptional in Godwin's exposition. It fairly represented the more Zwinglian wing of Evangelical Christianity. His claim that $εστι$ in the statement, 'This is my body', was to be taken as an analogy was echoed in a letter to the *Baptist Magazine* in 1874. The writer claimed that the verb bore the same significance as in the statements, 'I am the door' and 'You are the salt'.[45] The same journal, a year earlier, carried an article, written by an anonymous layman, under the pseudonym of 'A Deacon', on 'The Lord's Supper Simply Stated'. This writer's interpretation of the dominical statements was similar to those employed in the discussion of the real presence. Our Lord could not have been referring to himself, says the writer, as he was present, whole and undiminished, in the room with them. The writer also denied that the 'blessing' that Jesus pronounced over the cup was a prayer of consecration and, even if it had been, there was no scriptural support for the belief that priests inherited the same right and power.[46]

Another article, by an unnamed writer, appeared in 1883, entitled 'Jesus at the Eucharistic Supper'. It was an examination of the text in Matthew 26.29, 'But I say unto you, I will not drink henceforth of the fruit of the vine, until that day when I drink it new with you in my Father's kingdom.' The writer began with an examination of the rather academic question whether Jesus himself shared in the bread and wine at the Last Supper. Those who argued that he did not, he claimed, were shying away from the implications of their own eucharistic beliefs, namely that 'He must have partaken of himself'. This could not have been the case, as

i) the words 'I will not henceforth do this' implied that he was doing it then

ii) three out of four of the evangelists described Jesus as eating the Passover meal with his disciples

iii) the Passover and Last Supper were 'feasts of love'.

His partaking of these was the natural method by which he showed the sacred and holy joy in the love he had for the disciples; just as the partaking of them was the natural method by which they showed their sacred and holy joy in the love they had for him.[47]

What followed reflected the writer's belief that the Lord's Supper was as much a sharing in the new life of the Kingdom, as the memorial of a death. The Last Supper, he said, was the last time that Jesus shared a meal with his disciples in that particular way. After the passion and resurrection, 'the outward relationship will be changed'.[48] He recognized that the Lord's Supper was not simply a perpetual re-enactment of the Last Supper; with the cross and resurrection a banquet came into existence which was altogether new:

> ... He will be with them spiritually; and in that deeper, closer, more sacred, because more spiritual, union betwixt Himself and them in the new economy, the feast will be spiritualised. The wine will be 'new' - not earthly wine, but heavenly. They will have the earthly wine to symbolise it, and to remind them of it; but of that earthly wine He will not partake with them. The wine of which He and they will drink together in the new economy will be the 'wine of the soul' - the wine of holy, heavenly love. Thus the fellowship will become transcendental.[49]

The language of 'spiritualisation' is familiar in the Baptist vocabulary. At least, however, there was here the recognition that, in the Lord's Supper, the communicants participated in something greater than themselves, their own thoughts and their own mental recollections; there was the germ of an idea that this was more than an 'ordinance' dutifully obeyed, it was a 'feast', it was a transcendental sharing in 'holy, heavenly love'; there was the joy of sitting with Jesus at table in the Father's house.

b) The Corinthian Eucharistic Passages

Godwin was brief in his exposition of the two eucharistic passages in 1 Corinthians 10.16-17 and 11.27. Dealing with the first passage, he repeated his interpretation of the word 'blessing'. By blessing the cup used in the Lord's Supper it was 'set apart to a sacred use'.[50] The participation in the body and blood of Christ of which Paul speaks was a two-fold participation, a communion with other Christians and, through faith, a sharing in the benefits of Christ. It was, he said,

> ... a communion with the followers of Christ, in the emblems of the Saviour's 'body and blood'; and in partaking of them we declare, by an outward sign, that we participate in the benefits and blessings of his death: and, as far as our faith is brought into exercise, this institution becomes the means of our enjoying these benefits, and having actual communion with Christ ...[51]

The second passage, with its words 'guilty of the body and blood of the Lord', he interpreted as:

> ... not discerning or making a difference between food applied to common purposes, and bread and wine used in so sacred a manner, and therefore he profanes these emblems of the Saviour's passion, and makes light of the great sacrifice itself.[52]

In both expositions Godwin betrayed his affinity with Robert Hall and those to the Calvinist side of eucharistic theology. The cup, the bread and the wine were 'emblems', they were important for what they signified, but they could not be dismissed as mere signs. The eucharistic vessels, the earthly symbols of bread and wine laid upon the table, alike were to be treated with reverence in view of the holy purpose for which they existed. The pseudonymous writer of the article, 'The Lord's Supper Simply Stated', dealt with 11.23-29 differently and, one suspects, in a way more characteristic of Baptists later in the century. The references to 'the bread' and 'the cup' indicated that they were 'purely symbolical representatives', whilst 'discerning the Lord's body' was taken to allude to the Corinthian confusion in mistaking their own ordinary social occasion for the solemnities of the Lord's Supper.[53]

c) The Eucharistic Teaching of John 6

Godwin's treatment of this passage was much fuller. A key passage for Pusey in his sermon and one central to later writings on the eucharist, it appeared again in Baptist disputes with the Ritualists. Pusey had argued

BAPTISTS AND THE CATHOLIC REVIVAL 101

that verses 51-58 were to be understood as referring to the eucharist. Godwin disagreed with this and gave five reasons for doing so.

1) The words should be metaphorically interpreted in keeping with scriptural usage. As the body is fed, and animal life is sustained, by natural food, so by the exercise of faith, the soul receives spiritual life and nutriment from 'him who loved us and gave himself for us'.[54] He proceeded to give many scriptural references in which he supported his argument that the imagery of eating and drinking was often used to describe the way in which the soul 'feeds' upon divine truth.

2) The context of Chapter 6 showed that the reference of the later verses was not to the eucharist but to 'spiritual blessings received by the soul'.[55] The Jews had come seeking a repetition of the miraculous feeding of the crowds. Jesus turned their attention from what was 'carnal' to what was 'spiritual'. The request that he should give them something akin to the manna that God had given their fathers in the wilderness was met by the assertion that Christ came 'to unfold to men those sacred truths and doctrines, which, when received by faith, as the food of the soul, impart and sustain spiritual life'.[56] Added to the benefits of Christ's incarnation were the benefits of the sacrifice wrought through his violent death. It was the benefits of both incarnation and sacrifice which were received; as food was taken 'into the system by eating, digestion and assimilation', so the benefits of Christ were 'received and appropriated by faith, so as to be incorporated, as it were, into the spiritual system'.[57] Godwin claimed support for his interpretation from the words of Jesus in verse 63, 'It is the spirit that quickeneth; the flesh profiteth nothing ...', a verse by which Zwingli had set great store in his dispute with Luther at the Marburg Colloquy. If this exposition was correct, claimed Godwin,

> ... our Divine Teacher is speaking throughout his discourse not of a sacramental sign, but of saving truth, not of eating and drinking in the Eucharist, but of the necessity, and the blessed results of receiving Christ by faith, as our sacred Instructor and our only Saviour.[58]

3) A further argument was that the Lord's Supper had not been instituted by the time of the events recorded in John 6. Therefore the passage could have had no sacramental meaning for the hearers.

4) The effects from feeding on 'the bread of life' and on the 'flesh and blood' of the Redeemer were, both in John 6 and elsewhere in the New Testament, 'attributed to believing on Christ'. Godwin drew the following comparisons:

    v.51 = v.47   v.54 = 3.15

v.54 = v.40   v.56 = Eph.3.17
v.57 = Gal.3.11,2.20

Godwin clearly believed that the first half of our Lord's discourse which dealt with hearing and believing the word was given poetic focus in the imagery of eating and drinking the body and blood of Christ. It was through the word that we came to Christ, through belief that we knew him, through knowing him that we shared in his life and the benefits of his sacrifice for us.

5) What was affirmed in John 6 as true of believing in Christ was not true of participating in the eucharist. The benefits of Christ's life and death were received through hearing the word and responding to it in belief, not by sharing in the eucharist. Godwin here stood firmly in the Evangelical tradition. Christ was known by faith. The eucharist was a means of nurturing faith; it did not procure salvation.

J. H. Hinton also dealt with this passage in his series of articles on the Tracts in 1867. Examining the tract on *The Real Presence* by Dr Littledale, he disputed his eucharistic interpretation of John 6. Littledale had argued in support of his claim that:

a) John 6 was universally interpreted in a eucharistic sense until the time of Cardinal Cajetan;[59]

b) if John 6 did not refer to the eucharist then the gospel of John contained no reference to the solemn rite;

c) the account of the changing of the water into wine in John 2.1-12 was followed by a discourse on baptism, so John 6.5-15 was followed by a discourse on the eucharist.

Against this, Hinton argued firstly, and rather oddly, that it could not be proved that the weight of tradition supported the eucharistic interpretation. For good measure he added that even if it could be that was no reason, in itself, why contemporaries should follow down that road. Secondly, John was silent on the matter of the eucharist, his purpose being to write about those things which had been omitted from the first three gospels, all of which contained accounts of the supper. Thirdly, he declared that John 3.1-9 was not about baptism. Hinton then added some points of his own.

i) The Lord's Supper not having been instituted at the time of the events recorded in John 6, 'His hearers must have been totally uninformed. Such a discourse, in such circumstances, could have had no tendency whatever to their instruction'.[60]

ii) v.35 spoke about 'coming' and 'believing' which were different from 'eating' and 'drinking'.

iii) If the discourse had referred to the Lord's Supper, Jesus would have sympathized with his hearers' perplexity. As it was, he 'evidently blamed His hearers for not understanding Him at the time' (6.43,44).[61]

iv) If a eucharistic interpretation be given to vv.53 and 54 it would suggest that those who did not receive the Lord's Supper could not be saved and those who did would be.

Hinton's points are fair and recur to this day in exegesis of this passage. The problem of the inevitable confusion of Jesus' hearers if they were being expected to understand the significance of an event which had not yet taken place is a real one. A modern exegesis would emphasise the role played by the first readers of the gospel who would have been expected to perceive the eucharistic undertones of the passage. This line of interpretation, however, requires a critical understanding of the biblical texts that would not have been accessible to Hinton. The question of the relationship between vv.35-50 and vv.51-58 is still very open, the eucharistic interpretation being by no means universal. A number of New Testament scholars have argued that the whole discourse is 'sapiential', i.e. it refers to the teaching of Jesus.[62]

A contributor to the *Baptist Magazine*, Frank Slater, returned to the theme again in an article entitled 'The Flesh and Blood of the Son of Man in John VI'.[63] Taking verse 53, 'Except ye eat the flesh of the Son of Man, and drink His blood, ye have not life in yourselves', as his starting point, he argued that Jesus was here imposing a spiritual test.[64] The words were shaped in a 'form grossly material', so that only those of a spiritual mind might discern that they were in 'essence sublimely spiritual'.[65] What Jesus asked 'shocks both the natural reason and moral sense'.

> Literally construed, it demands the doing of that which is utterly impossible, and therefore absurd; or else disgustingly gross, and therefore immoral. The logical outcome of such unspiritual treatment of this and kindred sayings is the Romish dogma of Transubstantiation, which, by the very nature of the case, cannot at the same time be true and moral.[66]

The very grossness of the statement compelled his hearers to look for a meaning that would purge it of such descriptions. He quoted Alexander Maclaren, 'The grosser you make the symbol, the more imperative you make the purely spiritual interpretation of it'. Not surprisingly, Slater concluded that 'the statement is not concerned with the observance of the Lord's Supper at all.'[67] If it was, then this would consign men to the powers of an official priesthood:

> The whole burden of His mission and message was in direct and irreconcilable antagonism to mechanical ideas of religion

in any shape or form, substituting in their place the only true idea that religion is, from first to last, a matter between the spirit of man and the Spirit of God.[68]

Putting the text in the context of the rest of the chapter, Slater argued that the miracle of feeding introduced the idea of 'eating'. The crowd, eager for another miracle, needed far more 'that which would nourish and sustain the soul'. The idea of 'drinking' was added simply by association of ideas. The idea of 'bread' sprang from the Passover, the celebration of which was drawing near. Jesus substituted the word 'flesh' for 'bread' and thus set

> ... forth His claim to be to the spiritual life of the world what the Passover was to the national life of the Jews.[69]

The addition of 'blood', however, was 'something more than the mere filling up of an idea'. Jesus was on his way to Jerusalem to be crucified, where in the shedding of his blood he would lay down his life for the world. The 'flesh and blood' were the gift of Christ; 'eating and drinking' signified the human response. We must discover, if we can, the spiritual equivalents of the Saviour's material flesh and blood, and of the physical actions of eating and drinking by which these are received. In other words, we have to consider the divine gift and its human appropriation.[70]

The 'flesh and blood' stood for 'the living personality of the Saviour in its entirety'. The flesh was his life and the blood his sacrifice. The one could not be separated from the other. Slater inferred that there could not be an incarnational Christianity that sat loose to Christ's death upon the cross, nor yet an acceptance of remission of sins that was not also concerned with the sanctification of every part of life. The means of appropriation, the 'eating and drinking', were equivalent to the 'coming and believing' that were found in the first part of our Lord's discourse. It was by faith that we received the life that he gave - not faith which was 'an act, once done, done for ever', but a 'doing protracted into habit; a perennially present feasting of the soul upon Christ'.[71] Slater did not, at this point, refer to the Lord's Supper as a means of perennial 'feasting of the soul upon Christ'. Having denied any connection between John 6 and the eucharist he saw no need to explore its role in the ongoing life of the Christian.

Slater wrote his article at the turn of the century. It reflects two developments that had taken place in the previous hundred years. The first, to which we shall return, was the growing enthusiasm for separating matter from spirit. The germ of the idea was present even in that ardent realist, Robert Hall, who had opened up the fatal distinction between the 'spiritual' and the 'ceremonial'. The wedge between spirit and matter and thus between sign and thing signified was a legacy of Zwinglianism and the radical Anabaptists, but in the nineteenth century it was overlaid with a peculiarly Victorian high-mindedness that cherished 'natural reason and moral sense' as the antithesis of the 'grossly material'. The repugnance against 'material religion' was directed, in Slater's article, against the Roman doctrine of the Mass.

This illustrates the second development, which was an increasing tendency to construe doctrine in the interests of anti-Catholicism. This completely coloured Slater's view of our Lord's words in John 6. The Roman doctrine of transubstantiation and its allied stress on the role of the priest were totally alien to the 'sublimely spiritual' view that Slater took of the Christian faith. Therefore, if the words of Jesus were to be used in any way to support such an offensive belief, they could be viewed as nothing other than 'disgustingly gross' and 'immoral'. For all that Evangelicals claimed adherence to the plain word of scripture, the words of Jesus in John 6 aroused a deep aversion in late Victorians such as Slater. There was more at stake than simply loyal adherence to Baptist beliefs or even the radical dichotomy of matter and spirit. After all, Slater's Baptist forebears had happily sung of that body 'torn with rudest hands' which had become the 'finest Bread' and the blood which ran in purple torrents from 'each opening Vein' to fill the 'Cup with gen'rous Wine'.[72] Slater, like others, shared the Victorian vision of man struggling from the crudities of his spiritual adolescence into the clear air of true religion which was 'a matter between the spirit of man and the Spirit of God'. The Catholic revival was nothing less than a regression into crude mediaevalism, deeply insulting to modern men who had witnessed a century of change largely brought about by human ingenuity and invention. Seen through those spectacles, the words of Jesus were 'grossly material' and could be made acceptable only by elevation to another, higher plain upon which 'spiritual' men and women walked in the congenial company of 'natural reason and moral sense'. Godwin, Hinton and Slater all took the 'sapiential' view of John 6, the first two being largely content with careful exegetical support for their view, the latter speaking from a wider set of presuppositions. All of them shared the view that the various interpretations of the passage revealed two contrasting views of the Christian faith, the one sacramental, the other Evangelical. To choose the latter left no room at all for the former.

iii) The Place of Christian Tradition

The Tractarians believed that they were restoring the liturgy of the church to its primitive and uncluttered splendour. The development of liturgy in the first five centuries of the church's history, in particular, was held to be germane to the understanding of liturgy for the church in every age. Their conviction led to a renewed interest in patristic studies. Baptist reaction to this was similar to Evangelical reaction generally. Evangelicals stood uncompromisingly by the principle of *sola scriptura:* no other authority for Christian belief was to be sought or accepted. The Catholic tradition had always placed far more store by the traditions of the church, believing that what was in harmony with scriptural revelation and acceptable to the mind of the church carried a confirmatory authority that could be placed by the side of scripture. Evangelicals, whilst holding firmly to their conviction that scripture carried priority in everything relating to faith and practice, were at variance amongst themselves in their attitudes to tradition. Some accepted that the Christian tradition was helpful in understanding the biblical tradition as long as the priority of scripture was in no way compromised. Some Evangelicals, amongst them Baptists like Godwin himself, displayed a commendable knowledge of patristic texts, indeed a knowledge that would rarely be found amongst ministers in pastoral charge in most present-day Baptist churches. Others placed the early Fathers in a quite different historical scenario. The closing of the New Testament era was seen as the closing of the era of authentic truth. What followed was the decline of the church, a slow descent into pagan ways that reached its nadir in the grim darkness of the mediaeval church. The living fellowship of the New Testament church became the petrified institution of later ages, priest-ridden and tyrannical, its pristine experience of faith, hope and love replaced by sacramental systems, formal rites and gaudy ceremonies. This monstrous regime had been over-thrown by the great reformers, though some believed that even they had not had complete success in pulling themselves out of the slough of Catholic error. It was Dissent that had done what the Reformation had left undone. It was the mission of the Dissenting churches to restore the original purity of New Testament Christianity, to establish again Christian communities under the rule of faith, founded upon the personal commitment of each person to Jesus Christ.

In his sermon, Pusey had quoted the Fathers in support of his view of the eucharist. In his reply, Godwin weighed the value of the evidence that Pusey had adduced, then the usefulness of the patristic tradition in general. He went on next to claim support from the reformers for his repudiation of Pusey's ideas. Godwin began by weighing the value of the evidence. The Fathers were, first of all, not to be regarded as 'inspired writers' but men who had 'their prejudices and their party predilections'.[73] Their witness was not to be deprecated as they were, after all, men willing to suffer and die for the faith in which they believed. They were, nevertheless, influenced both by 'Pagan philosophy and Jewish fables', and they 'laid an inordinate stress on the ritual of Christianity', evincing 'a tendency to credulity and superstition'. Further, in arguing against the errors that appeared in the early centuries they had tended to over-react and had themselves fallen into opposite errors. In spite of these cautionary observations, Godwin argued that Pusey and his followers could be confounded on their own ground. Giving chapter and verse, he quoted from Clement of Alexandria, Tertullian, Origen, Basil, Athanasius, Jerome, Eusebius and Augustine to prove that 'by the Fathers the Eucharist is called a sign, figure, type, antitype, and image, of the body and blood of Christ'.[74] But what was meant figuratively had gradually come to be understood literally. By degrees, and through constant employment of such language, the figurative sense was gradually lost sight of, and the literal meaning adopted.[75]

Passing to the reformers, Godwin argued that they did not dispute 'the divine presence of the Saviour' in the eucharist, but meant something different from what Catholics held to be 'the real presence'. Luther, Zwingli and Calvin all rejected the explanation of Christ's presence in terms of transubstantiation. Protestants, he argued, used language similar to that employed by Rome whilst giving it a quite different meaning. Leaving the continental reformers, he passed to the English reformers who were, he said, greatly influenced by the Swiss divines during their periods of exile in Geneva in the reign of Queen Mary. He quoted Bishop Jewel as maintaining that the eucharist was not 'a naked figure, and a bare sign and token only', but also denying that Christ's presence was to be understood in corporeal terms. Thus

> ... when [the English reformers] speak of a real participation in the body and blood of the Lord, of a real presence, of the body and blood of Christ being 'verily and indeed taken and received', strong as the terms are, they mean only a spiritual reception of Christ, by faith, as our Saviour, and a participation, in consequence, of the benefits of his death.[76]

In support he quoted the communion service itself, and a telling sentence from Cranmer:

> And therefore I say that Christ giveth himself truly to be eaten, chawed, and digested; but all is spiritually with faith, not with mouth.[77]

Whilst arguing that the reformers' understanding of Christ's presence in the sacrament was different from the Roman, he does not make clear whether his own view was identical with theirs. It was one thing to commend their clear rejection of transubstantiation, another to believe that they had provided an alternative that was true to scripture. The language of the reformers was compatible with the eighteenth-century Baptist hymns and the realist language of Baptists such as Robert Hall, but it signified something more than an appropriation of Christ in the way that Godwin had conceived it in his exegesis of John 6. He might appeal to it with approval because it seemed to place Pusey outside the reformed tradition. The question remains whether, at this point, he saw himself inside that same tradition.

A few Baptist writers endeavoured to handle the problem of tradition with the same judicial impartiality as Godwin; for most, however, tradition was the target of their most vitriolic attacks. Typical of the cautious approach was an article by John Stock on 'The Apostolic Fathers', published in the *Baptist Magazine* in 1857. He began with the unpromising observation:

> Between the Word of God and the writings of the earliest and best of the Fathers, there is an impassable gulf - a line of

demarcation, which at once proves the essential difference between the one and the others.[78]

He then went on, however, to point to the value that a study of the Fathers had for contemporary Christians. They showed the development of opinion in the professing church, they also verified the genuineness of the inspired books: they indicated those books which came to be included in the canon and they could be usefully read to throw light on the meaning of scripture. From what Stock wrote, it might be argued that a church possessing the spiritual discernment so to divine the word of truth as to recognize what was and what was not inspired scripture might be equally trusted to throw some light upon the meaning of the church's ongoing life in ministry and sacrament. If there was an impassable gulf between what the Fathers wrote and what the New Testament writers wrote, does it follow that there was an impassable gulf between the life and worship of the church of the Fathers and that of its New Testament predecessor?

Another example of interest in the Fathers is to be found in the same journal in 1888 where H. C. Leonard wrote on 'The Lord's Supper in the Writings of the Apostolic Fathers'.[79] In view of the title Leonard makes the rather odd selection of Clement, Ignatius, the Didache, Quadratus, the Epistle to Diognetus, Barnabas, Hermas and Polycarp, odd in that only two of these, he claimed, mentioned the Lord's Supper. Taking two quotations from Ignatius, in which the eucharist had been referred to as 'the medicine of immortality', the other as 'the flesh of our Saviour Jesus Christ', transubstantiation, he claimed, was implied in neither of them. They pointed, nevertheless, to 'the beginning of confusion between the sign and that which was signified by it'.[80] The problem was always one of language, inseparable from verbal imagery of any sort. He dealt scantly with the Didache, simply observing the use of the title eucharist, the absence of any reference to the atoning blood of Jesus in the thanksgiving and a reference to the Lord's Day - 'a festival, the resurrection day, the queen and chief of all days'.[81] The article fell far short of the claim implied in the title, seeming to have little more purpose than to reassure his fellow-Baptists, by a cursory glance at the patristic sources, that they had nothing to fear from such quarters.

Articles such as these were, however, the exception. Most other Baptists moved away from the spirit in which Godwin debated with Pusey. They were more concerned than he to discredit the Fathers and, in the matter of the eucharist, the reformers as well. A leader in the *Freeman* for 20 July 1860 compared the tradition of the Fathers to the tradition of the elders in New Testament times, and the Puseyites as nothing more than latter-day Pharisees. Their appeal to tradition was in clear contrast to the authority on which Baptists rested their beliefs. Puseyites sought justification

> ... on the ground of Church authority, or the practice of men in the earlier centuries of Christian history. Very few,

if any, venture to maintain their views by an appeal to Bible teaching and authority exclusively.

The Baptists, on the contrary, strenuously contend for a strict adherence to the spirit and letter of Scripture.

George Gould, speaking at the autumn session of the Baptist Union in October 1867, devoted his paper to a study of the Bishop of Salisbury's theory of 'the sacerdotal function in the administration of the sacrament of the Lord's Supper'. In the course of his address he described the Church of England as 'that miserable compromise between Evangelical truth and Patristic error'. He moved far from Godwin's claim that the Tractarians received little support for their ideas in the Fathers: as far as Gould was concerned, any sacerdotalist who searched the Fathers would only too readily find

> ... no good grounds upon which to reject Sacerdotalism, or to deny the Real Presence of Christ in the Lord's Supper, or to refuse submission to other and similarly unscriptural absurdities received by tradition from the Fathers.[82]

In 1891, the *Baptist Magazine*, in an article by Edward Medley, commenting on the findings of the Lincoln judgment,[83] saw tradition as the root of all prevailing errors in the Church of England. The appeal to development brings us to the root of the whole business. Few men are competent to say what may have been the prevailing practice of Christian bodies in the past, for the voices of bygone ages are not harmonious: Fathers of the Church often fell foul of one another with a hearty virulence, more suited to the senate than the Christian assembly; they still carried about with them the stigmata of the heathenism and the imperialism in which they had been bred. Councils, in which the Church was supposed to speak decisively, were not free from the taint of chicanery, intrigue and violence.[84] The charge that the early Fathers were only half-converted from their former 'heathen' ways was echoed by W. T. Whitley who, as we have seen, saw developments in the early church stemming from 'partly heathen sources'.[85]

At some hands, the reformers came to fare no better. An article on what it describes as the 'gross tenet' of the Real Presence in the *Freeman* for 28 December 1866 stated:

> The Romanist has continued true to his colours, the Protestant has yielded. The incomprehensible dogma of LUTHER, real presence without transubstantiation; the mystical tenet of CALVIN, that there is no change, yet the elements become the body and blood of Christ; the long-winded metaphysical deliverance of the Confession of Augsburg: all show the peculiar difficulties which surround the least attempt to establish sacramental efficacy.[86]

In reference to a correspondence currently appearing in the pages of the *Guardian*, dealing with the Real Presence, the *Freeman* referred in 1869 to the 'ludicrous obstinacy of . . . Luther'[87] in endeavouring to attribute sacramental significance to the bread and the wine.

The post-Tractarian generation of Baptists was increasingly prone to be manoeuvred into a theological isolation that would have been unacceptable to an earlier generation. For all that their doctrine of baptism placed them at the farther reaches of Dissent, Baptists such as Hall, Kinghorn and Godwin consciously wrote within the context of the Christian tradition. In certain crucial areas they dissented from it but were never contemptuous of it. Those who followed them grew shrill in their denunciations of Catholic doctrine and cavalier in their willingness to dismiss anything that remotely resembled it. The particular myth through which they chose to view Christian history required the belief that the sub-apostolic church had gone into rapid spiritual decline, vitiated by pagan influences, had half revived at the Protestant Reformation but regained its early simplicity and integrity only with the coming of Dissent. Their anti-Catholicism and their zeal for their own cause exacted a heavy price.

iv) The Lord's Supper as Means of Grace

Apart from the efficacy of Christ's presence in the sacrament, Pusey had emphasised its role as a means of conveying forgiveness to the penitent. Godwin challenged this and the concept of gradual forgiveness that flowed from it. Forgiveness was through faith in Christ, said Godwin:

> All who believe in Him . . . are forgiven, whether they have received the Eucharist or not; none who have not believed in Him are pardoned, however often they may have received it.[88]

Pusey, concerned to make the sacrament central to the nurture and growth of the Christian life had applied a similar principle of gradualness to the forgiveness of sins.

It is easy to see how understanding broke down between Pusey and the Evangelicals. His portrayal of the central experience of forgiveness as a gradual release from the burden of sin, with the attendent agonies of doubts, uncertainties, unstilled conscience and guilty memories was in stark contrast to that experience of mercy that lay at the heart of the Protestant encounter with God. In Evangelical theology, whatever failure there may have been to take full account of the sacramental nourishment by which the soul was brought to maturity in Christ, the central experience of forgiveness was beyond doubt. Forgiveness was not part of a process, slowly realized, it was a *fait accompli*, an irreversible gesture of merciful acceptance on the part of a loving and just God. To an Evangelical, there was something almost obsessional in Pusey's notion of cleansing by slow degrees:

... as the loving kindness of God admits [the penitent] again and again to that Body and that Blood, the stains which his soul had contracted, are more and more effaced, the guilt more and more purged, the wounds more and more healed, that atoning Blood more and more interposed between him and his sins.[89]

Godwin accepted that the sacrament was a means of grace in which we continue to grow, but:

... this removal of guilt by slow gradations, this pardon by degrees, this forgiveness by instalments, is a doctrine altogether foreign to the scriptures.[90]

Godwin argued that faith was central and it was in the context of faith that 'this ordinance [has] all its value as a means of grace'.[91]

In the discussion that followed, there was further evidence of the failure of the theological worlds of Pusey and Godwin to meet. By making the eucharist the means of forgiveness, and gradual forgiveness at that, Pusey had supplanted the liberating, renewing merciful truth at the heart of Evangelical theology. Acceptance through faith, with the forgiveness of all our sins, was the starting point of the Evangelicals' pilgrimage, the heart of their experience of God. So, in reply, Godwin emphasised the centrality of the word in that experience. It was the word that declared the sinner forgiven. What followed was a less clear appreciation of the sacrament as a means of Christian nurture. Godwin disagreed with Pusey's assertion that the eucharist was 'the means by which spiritual life is imparted and maintained in the soul, and the work of sanctification carried on.'[92] On the contrary,

... the great and chosen instrument by which the Divine Spirit works in renovating and sanctifying the human soul, is, according to the sacred writers, THE TRUTH OF GOD, as revealed in the gospel, and received by faith.[93]

The 'ordinances of religion, duly administered' might be employed with other means 'accessory and subordinate', but it was the gospel itself which was basic. It was the gospel that called and the gospel that sustained the spiritual life:

The Lord's Supper may, as a means of grace, greatly aid this spiritual process; but it is not by any mysterious and invisible virtue, contained in the bread and wine, or connected with them, but as this institution serves, under God's blessing, to bring the truth vividly before our minds, and in an affecting manner home to our hearts, so that we feel and enjoy the saving benefits of the redeeming work of Christ.[94]

The sacrament was subordinate to the word. It was the word of the gospel that effected the saving experience by which men were forgiven in Christ. The sacrament served to remind believers of that central experience, it held it ever before their minds, but it was not itself a channel of saving grace.

Earlier Godwin had testified to the nurturing benefits of the Lord's Supper. Pressed, however, to define the sense in which it was a 'means of grace', he fell back on a partially Zwinglian view of its role. The sacrament brought the truth 'vividly before our minds'. The Lord's Supper was didactic and commemorative. This definition was filled out some years later in an article by J. T. Gale of Putney in the *Baptist Magazine*.[95] He described the present significance of the supper in the experience of Christian believers. At the Last Supper Jesus saw that two needs should be met for his disciples. The first was that their communion with him and their sense of his presence should be sustained, the second that they should be constantly reminded that they belonged also to one another. To serve these twin purposes he left them the ordinance, a sign at once of their union with him and of their unity in Christian fellowship. Of the first, he wrote:

> By eating the bread as the symbol of the body, by drinking the wine as the symbol of the blood of Christ, we understand simply the believer's appropriation of the atoning work of Christ.[96]

It was through that appropriation that the Christian was bound as one to his Lord. 'There is a union of the believer's spirit to his Lord - they are one - the Christian is in Christ . . .'. The relationship of the sacrament to this experience was that of 'outward and visible sign':

> As often, then as we eat this bread and drink this cup, we not only show the Lord's death till He come - we proclaim also to ourselves and to one another the great truth of our present living union with Christ. We show forth that which is secret and invisible. We embody in an act of greatest simplicity a reality of inexpressible grandeur and worth. The deed is only the clothing of the holiest and most blessed convictions our spirits possess. The sacrament itself is but the outward and visible sign of an inward, invisible and inexpressible spiritual consciousness.[97]

Further, the 'one loaf' used in communion was a sign of the unity of all Christians. It was

> . . . in the truest sense, a communion of the body and blood of Christ - a joint participation of the merits and virtues of His sacrifice and spirit . . . The act of a joint participation in one symbol is designed to keep in clearest possible distinctness the fact of oneness in Christ.[98]

Gale offered an undiluted Zwinglianism in describing the benefits of the sacrament to those who received it. He linked it, in a living way, with the two most personal of Christian experiences, the union of the believer with Christ and with his fellow believers. Here was more than didacticism or a prod to the memory. In Gale's language, the sacrament did more than teach the communicants what Christ had done for them. It was itself part of their experience of him and of one another. Gale echoed the Augustinian definition of a sacrament, an outward and visible sign of 'inward, invisible and inexpressible spiritual consciousness', the outward 'clothing' of the inner experience. Baptist attitudes swung like a pendulum from radical rejection of any sacramental efficacy to brave attempts to put into words exactly how the sacrament was a 'means of grace' without selling the pass to the Catholics. If, on the one hand, Godwin could find no role for the sacrament in the central Evangelical experience of forgiveness, Gale placed it as central to the believer's continuing experience of union with Christ and his church.

Nearer the end of the century, Edward Alden could speak in similar terms in his article on 'Baptism and the Lord's Supper'.[99] The Lord's Supper

> ... sets forth ... the Saviour's Body given and His Blood shed, not only ... for the remission of sins and the gift of a new and eternal life, but for the perpetual sustenance of that life.[100]

On the human side, the Lord's Supper

> ... exhibits the ... perpetual need of the soul – the need of sustenance in the New Life – a need only to be supplied by the continual feeding of our faith on the Bread of Life.[101]

The sacrament was still 'an object lesson', but powerful in its reminder that Christ was the continuous source of sustenance in the Christian life and the need of the believer to turn constantly to him, the Bread of Life.

The didactic view of W. T. Whitley and J. Hunt Cooke's rejection of the elements as no more than *inania symbola* have already been observed.[102] Baptists were torn between the difficulties of theological definition and adequately describing the experience that was actually theirs at their communion tables. There was no clear agreement amongst them. The *Baptist Magazine* in 1896 reported a conference of Baptist ministers held in New York at which J. M. Whiton had read a paper on 'The Meaning of Communion'. He had argued that 'the view of Zwingli was not adequate. The ordinance was a memorial, but it was more'. A discussion followed in which all the brethren were not of one mind. The reporter was right in his conclusion:

> The subject needs discussion in England also. Even Baptists are not entirely of one mind about it.[103]

Like Whiton himself, there were clearly those, even at the end of the century, who held 'the ordinance was a memorial, but it was more'.

v) The Conflict between 'Spiritual' and 'Ceremonial' Religion

At the conclusion of his pamphlet, Godwin levelled a charge at Pusey that we have already encountered, and whose origins we have endeavoured to trace, in the writings of Robert Hall.[104] It was that a religion that set too great store by the observance of sacraments or 'ceremonies', of which Tractarianism was, to Baptist eyes, a prime example, devalued true 'spiritual' religion. Rites and ceremonies had their roots in the old covenant that had been swept away by Christ who called for obedience from the heart, an inner and 'spiritual' response of faith. It was as if the very elements of the sacraments, the earthly bread and wine, and the significance that was attached to them rooted man's religious experience in the earthy and the 'carnal'. It turned what belonged to man's soul and the inner perception of faith in the direction of things that could be seen, handled, tasted: substances that, by due performance of certain rites, became the means of God's presence. The move away from this into a more 'spiritual' religion was shared by members of Free Churches other than the Baptists. J. W. Grant believes that the later decades of the nineteenth century were marked by an increasing 'spiritualization' on the part of Free Churchmen: there was 'an inclination to depreciate forms and institution, to contrast the spiritual with the material and formal'.[105] What Pusey taught, claimed Godwin, 'militates against the simplicity and spirituality of the gospel'.[106] As a result of Pusey's emphasis upon the eucharist,

> ... everything ceremonial has risen in importance, and there seems great reason to fear the spiritual nature of Christianity will be lost sight of, and its evangelical and saving truths be superseded by a religion of outward forms and delusive hopes.[107]

In part, the Baptist emphasis reflected the increasing importance that was being attached to the personal character of religious experience during the nineteenth century, an emphasis that was intrinsic to the Evangelical view of man's relationship with God.

Rites and sacraments were helpful, but if elevated too much in their importance they acted as a barrier rather than a bridge between God and man. What was true of the sacraments was also true of the church. The church could not proffer faith on behalf of its members, it could not stand proxy for the commitment of the individual, or his own experience of death and resurrection in Christ. The assent of the individual to Christ, in faith and commitment, was central and crucial to the Evangelical understanding of the Christian experience.

This contrast of the individual against the corporate, as well as of the 'spiritual' against the 'material' was illustrated in a leader on 'The Individual and Personal Nature of Religious Profession' in the *Freeman* of 9 October 1861. The article was concerned with the sacrament of baptism and argued that it was not to be administered with the sponsorship or by the authority of the church, but purely as a personal and individual declaration of faith, an astonishing departure from earlier Baptist views of the sacrament, apart from its incompatibility with main-line Christian teaching:

> Baptism ought to be so observed that it shall be clearly understood to be an individual and personal act and not an act administered in the name, or by the authority, of any church whatever.

In a later letter, written by an anonymous layman, this same detachment of the church and sacrament was applied to the Lord's Supper itself. Writing to the *Freeman* of 12 June 1868, he drew on his 'oriental experience' to recount how there the breaking of bread was a daily occurrence and that it bound those who shared it in a covenant relationship. He then, strangely, drew a conclusion from the first observation that seemed to cut clean across the second. It should be possible, he said, to celebrate communion often, even daily, and it was not therefore to be tied to the church. He argued that the Acts provided evidence that the ordinance was observed 'independently of the church'.[108]

This exalted sense of the individual's responsibility in the matter of his religion was underlined in a paper on the subject of 'Ritualism', read by C. Room to the Baptist Board, a London fraternal of Baptist ministers, in 1867.[109] The Nonconformist churches, he claimed, placed their emphasis upon the 'personal character of New Testament religion'. His definition of what he meant by this suggested that the role of the church and its rites was secondary in matters of faith:

> By the personal character of New Testament religion we mean the performance of all religious exercises and acts by each individual for himself, and the impossibility of any one of them being performed for him by another consistently with the Christian system.[110]

The setting of this claim was Room's vivid rescription of the Passiontide and Easter liturgy of which he had been a witness at the Anglo-Catholic church of St Alban's in Holborn. What was evident in those services, as far as Room was concerned, was a retrograde step, a retreat from the spiritual responsibilities of the individual into a less worthy and 'material' form of the Christian faith:

> What then; are we mistaken in the progressive character of religion - in its advancement from a lower to a higher standard - from a material to a spiritual form; is the Church to retrograde from its majority to its nonage, from its manhood of intelligence and insight to its childhood of symbol, picture and type; are we, for example, to learn the two natures of the Saviour, not from the lips of the preacher,

but from the candles on either side of the communion table; are we to become acquainted with the crucifixion and the atonement, not from scripture lesson and doctrine, but from a material crucifix or cross?[111]

The growing use of sign and symbol by the Ritualists was clearly far removed from the more cerebral modes of apprehension favoured by the radical Nonconformists. Room's rhetorical questions ricocheted about the heads of his no doubt appreciative listeners, but they displayed an acute failure to understand his adversaries and, indeed, the ways in which humankind comes to the knowledge of God. All entrances to the heart of man, sight, touch, smell, all, save the ears, were blocked and discounted. Victorian individualism combined with a quite worldly view of the power of man's intellect to betroth faith to rationalism, religion to the upward evolutionary march of man. The judgment of J. H. Newman carried a great deal of truth:

> A system of Christian doctrine has risen up during the last three centuries in which faith or spiritual mindedness is contemplated and rested on as the end of religion, instead of Christ . . . Stress is laid rather on the believing than on the Object of belief, on the comfort and persuasiveness of the doctrine rather than on the doctrine itself.[112]

The emphasis on the 'subjective' nature of faith returned in an article by J. H. Hinton in which he examined a paper by William.Humphrey of St Mary Magdalene, Dundee.[113] What, he asked, was the nature of true religion?

> Two divergent and widely dissimilar views are held. The one that religion is in its nature subjective, consisting wholly and exclusively in affections of the mind, with (of course) such practical results as flow from them; the other, that religion is in its nature sacramental, essentially requiring the use of sacraments, and effectually generated and perfected by the employment of them. The former view is, I may presume, that held by ourselves; the latter appears to be held by the Ritualists . . .[114]

Hinton, in his dispute with Humphrey, traced the consequence of this for the doctrines of man, of Christ and of the sacrament. Humphrey held that God sought the co-operation of his creatures. Hinton denied that man was able to co-operate with God. Underlying the dispute was the Reformation gulf between the Catholic view of man called to share with his maker in his own redemption and that of the world in which he lived, by the obedient response of faith and prayer; and the Protestant view of man as standing as a helpless sinner before God. The one led to an emphasis upon the incarnation, a *theologia gloriae*, in which man was 'divinized' by grace, the other to an emphasis upon the cross, a *theologia*

BAPTISTS AND THE CATHOLIC REVIVAL 117

crucis, in which man, through faith and repentance, threw himself upon the mercy of God. Hinton denied that the root of man's relationship with God was one in which there had simply been a rupture of the divine and the human, but rather

> ... a disobedience under a system of moral government, a system based upon righteous authority, and issuing in solemn retribution.[115]

The divergence between the two men extended to their Christology and, through that, to their view of the sacrament. Humphrey's sacramental theology was clearly in sight as he embarked on the subject of Christ's person and the truths he wished to draw from it. Through the union of the divine and human in Jesus, the human had been 'divinized', it was adorable, 'not with an inferior and relative worship, but, in virtue of its personal union with divinity, adorable with, and entitled to, the supreme worship which is due to the uncreated essence of the Eternal Trinity'.[116] Hinton replied that, if the human nature of Christ had been 'divinized', there could no longer be two natures in him:

> It may be added that the divine nature, as essentially uncreated, infinite and eternal, is one into which it is not possible that an essentially finite and created nature should be converted.[117]

Again, the shadow of the unresolved question that had constantly dogged similar discussions fell bleakly across the landscape. Again, the glorified humanity of Jesus, the prize of his death and resurrection, remained undefined. Again, there was confusion between the humanity of Jesus incarnate and glorified. From his person, Humphrey passed to Christ's union with humanity. God desired union with all humanity through Christ, but how was such union to be achieved?

> In Jesus are united two things - Divinity and Humanity ... There is in Jesus something which is outward and visible and something also which is inward and spiritual. In man are united two things - a body and a soul. In him ... is something which is outward and visible, and something also which is inward and spiritual.[118]

By his choice of language, Humphrey had clearly indicated his destination. The sacrament was, by definition, an outward and visible sign of an inward and spiritual grace. Thus the sacraments were the means of effecting the union between God and man.

Hinton denied both the argument and its sacramental conclusion. The two elements, joined together, needed no intervention to unite them. Further, unlike Gale, who had paraphrased the classic definition of a sacrament and accepted it,[119] Hinton rejected it:

> It is quietly assumed as a fact, that Sacraments are at once outward and visible and inward and spiritual - an assumption which we altogether deny.[120]

He finally returned to Humphrey's basic premise, that 'there is an interruption of [man's] physical union with God which, accordingly, it is the object of God, through the Incarnation, to restore'. Hinton restated his own conviction that man was

> ... by a voluntary estrangement ... morally separated from God, and, by transgression of His law, subject to the penalty enacted by God's government.[121]

This was the ground upon which reconciliation with God was to be effected, in the inward being of man:

> We revert, therefore, to the alternative position that Religion is subjective - wholly and exclusively subjective, in strict accordance with man's position under the moral government of God ... Pure and undefiled religion is neither less nor more than a change of man's heart from enmity towards God to friendship, and from the love of sin to the love of holiness.[122]

The language that Hinton used did less than justice to what he intended. Protestant orthodoxy had always strongly emphasised the objective reality of saving grace in the experience of those who, in repentance and faith, threw themselves upon the mercy of God. Salvation rested upon the divine initiative that had acted in Christ and was proclaimed in the word. Hinton stressed the response as against the deed, the inner, 'subjective' state of the believer as against the objective reality of that in which he believed. Humphrey had stressed the ontological nature of salvation: Christ had transformed the human situation by uniting his divinity with our humanity. The sacraments were objective acts that incorporated men and women into that new humanity, salvation was a being and a becoming more than simply a believing. The danger of distortion threatened both sides. Only in the worst Catholic theology can the sacraments be separated from the consenting faith of those who receive them, just as only in the worst Protestant theology can the inner consent of the convert be sundered from the prior acts of God in saving grace. There was failure to understand on both sides. Dr Peter Toon has argued that, although the controversy with the Tractarians had the effect, on the one side, of confirming Anglican Evangelicals in the position they held before the contest began, on the other the 'Tractarians virtually denied the Evangelical emphases by their sacramental theology'.[123] He claims

> ... in terms of their differing systems what mattered was that for Evangelicals the individual sinner approached God directly through Jesus Christ the Mediator, in faith and

prayer, while for Tractarians this direct route through Jesus Christ involved a detour through the visible Church with her apostolic ministry and efficacious sacraments.[124]

In fact, what both sides held as exclusive emphases rightly belonged together. The individual sinner needed the church and sacraments and the recipient of the sacraments needed the inner consent of faith. When sundered from each other the role of the individual was made too self-sufficient and the role of the sacraments too mechanical.

Baptists were tempted to lean too far in the direction of the individual and his subjective experience. Hinton, Room and the thunderer of the *Freeman* internalized saving grace to the extent of isolating the individual from the church and sacraments and making him the master of his fate and the captain of his soul. In doing so they struck a responsive chord amongst their Victorian contemporaries whose innate individualism contributed so much to the strengths and weaknesses of the age. All disputes are locked into the times in which they take place. In spite of the undoubted spiritual stature of the leading Tractarians, nineteenth-century Catholicism in general did little to allay the justifiable fears of the Protestants. Thus the tentative efforts of individual Baptists to go beyond didacticism or memorialism were frustrated by their overwhelming need to distance themselves from a resurgent Catholicism.

NOTES

1. Geoffrey Best, 'Evangelicalism and the Victorians', in Anthony Symondson, ed., **The Victorian Crisis of Faith**, 1970, p.47.
2. ibid. p.38.
3. J. Derek Holmes, **The Triumph of the Holy See: a short history of the papacy in the nineteenth century**, 1978, p.146.
4. Horton Davies, **Worship and Theology in England 1690-1850**, 1961, pp.245f.
5. Freeman 24 May 1867, p.415.
6. **Baptist Magazine** (hereafter **BM**) 86, 1894, p.353.
7. ibid. p.518.
8. Benjamin Godwin, **An Examination of the Principles and Tendencies of Dr Pusey's Sermon on the Eucharist**, 1843, p.79.
9. T. Pottenger, 'On the Constitution and Working of our Churches', **BM** 49, 1857, p.211f.
10. BM 90, 1898, p.145.
11. BM 93, 1901, p.26.
12. **Freeman**, 16 April 1869, p.302.
13. ibid. 25 September 1868, p.768.
14. ibid. 10 June 1857, p.327.
15. ibid. 17 November 1858, p.702.
16. ibid. 8 February 1867, p.107.
17. ibid. 2 October 1868, p.766.
18. BM 49, 1857, p.373.
19. **General Baptist Magazine** New Series, 1857, p.310.
20. BM 44, 1852, p.637.
21. **Freeman**, 1 February 1867, p.87.
22. ibid. 25 January 1867, p.62.
23. ibid. 15 December 1858, p.763.
24. ibid. 24 December 1862, p.831.
25. ibid. 28 January 1870, p.78.
26. E. B. Pusey, **The Holy Eucharist a Comfort to the Penitent**, Oxford 1843, p.14.
27. Godwin, op.cit. p.9.
28. ibid. p.9.
29. ibid. p.11.
30. ibid. p.12.
31. ibid. p.14.
32. ibid. p.58.
33. ibid. p.50.
34. ibid. pp.50-5.
35. ibid. p.24.
36. BM 59, 1867, p.86.
37. ibid. p.153.
38. ibid. p.153f.
39. ibid. p.154.
40. ibid. p.216.
41. ibid. p.217. 42. ibid. p.217.
43. Godwin, **op.cit.** p.21.

44. ibid.
45. **BM** 66, 1874, p.631.
46. **BM** 65, 1873, p.259.
47. **BM** 76, 1888, p.264.
48. ibid. p.264.
49. ibid. p.264f.
50. Godwin, **op.cit.** p.23.
51. ibid. p.24.
52. ibid. p.25.
53. **BM** 65, 1873, p.259.
54. Godwin, **op.cit.** pp.28ff.
55. ibid. p.30.
56. ibid. p.31.
57. ibid. p.32.
58. ibid. p.34.
59. Cajetan rejected it on the grounds that a eucharistic interpretation would seem to require communion in both kinds.
60. **BM** 59, 1867, p.446.
61. ibid. p.446.
62. R. Brown, **The Gospel According to St John**, 1971, 1, p.272, cites Godet, B. Weiss, Bornhauser, Odeberg, Schlatter and Strathmann as examples of the 'sapiential' interpretation.
63. **BM** 94, 1902, pp.97-104.
64. ibid. p.97.
65. ibid. p.98.
66. ibid.
67. ibid. p.99.
68. ibid.
69. ibid. p.101.
70. ibid. p.102.
71. ibid. p.104.
72. See p.22.
73. Godwin, **op.cit.** p.38.
74. ibid. p.43.
75. ibid. p.45.
76. ibid. p.50.
77. ibid. p.53.
78. **BM** 49, 1857, p.619.
79. **BM** 80, 1888, pp.437-441.
80. ibid. p.438.
81. ibid. p.440.
82. **BM** 59, 1867, p.702.
83. See J. Bentley, **Ritualism and Politics in Victorian Britain**, Oxford 1978, pp.117ff.
84. **BM** 83, 1891, p.27.
85. See p.8.
86. **Freeman** 28 December 1866, p.582.
87. ibid. 26 February 1869, p.161.
88. Godwin, **op.cit.** p.68.
89. Godwin, **op.cit.**, p.69.
90. ibid.
91. ibid. p.70.
92. ibid. p.71.
93. ibid. p.71.
94. ibid. p.73.
95. J. T. Gale, 'The Lord's Supper', **BM** 56, 1864, pp.596ff.
96. ibid. p.600.
97. ibid. p.600.
98. ibid. p.601.
99. **BM** 83, 1891, pp.397-405.
100. ibid. p.398.
101. ibid. p.399.
102. See pp.15f.
103. **BM** vol.88, 1896, p.286.
104. See pp.58-62.
105. J. W. Grant, **Free Churchmanship in England 1870-1940**, n.d., p.74.
106. Godwin, **op.cit.** p.74.
107. ibid. p.77.
108. **Freeman** 12 June 1868, p.474.
109. **BM** 59, 1867, p.281..
110. ibid. p.281.
111. ibid. p.280.
112. J. H. Newman, **Lectures on Justification**, pp.324f, quoted by Horton Davies, **op.cit.** p.263.
113. **BM** 60, 1868, p.143.
114. ibid. p.143.
115. ibid. p.144.
116. Quoted by Hinton, **ibid.** p.146.
117. ibid. p.147.
118. ibid.
119. See above, pp.112f.
120. Hinton, **op.cit.** p.148.
121. ibid. p.149.
122. ibid. p.149.
123. Peter Toon, **Evangelical Theology 1833-1856**, 1979, p.209.
124. ibid. pp.209f.

Chapter Four

Order and Discipline at the Lord's Table

At the same time as repudiating the new Catholic emphases within the Church of England, Baptists had to contend with one another over a number of questions concerning the right administration of the Lord's Supper within their own ranks. In the main, none of these aroused the bitter and divisive attitudes of the open and closed communion debate. Like that issue, however, the questions owed something to the inherited tensions within Baptist practice and theology, and something to the theological and social pressures of the nineteenth century. Five such questions may be identified.

First, there was the question of who should properly preside at the Lord's table. It was a problem that stemmed, in part, from a diversity of practice inherited from the seventeenth and eighteenth centuries and, in part, from the challenge posed by the Catholic revival and the desire on the part of Baptists and other Evangelicals to distance themselves as far as possible from any association with sacerdotalism.

Secondly, Baptists asked themselves whether it was right to celebrate the Lord's Supper in any context apart from that of the gathered church met for worship on Sunday. Could communion be taken to those who were sick or aged and unable to attend the services in chapel? Was it right that meetings of area associations and of the Baptist Union itself be marked by observance of the supper?

Thirdly, there was the question of frequency of celebration in the local churches. There were those who argued for a weekly communion, wheras others felt that the proper course was that of less frequent observance.

Fourthly, in common with other Free Churches, Baptists gradually introduced the use of unfermented wine in the Lord's Supper. This almost universal change was brought about by the growth of the temperance reform movement in the latter half of the nineteenth century and the firm footing it found in the life and convictions of the Free Churches.

Fifthly, Baptists continued to observe the connection between communion and church discipline that had been characteristic of them since their earliest days.

A) THE PRESIDENCY OF THE LORD'S TABLE

The attitude of Baptists towards their ordained ministry underwent a radical change in the nineteenth century from what it had been in the seventeenth and eighteenth.[1] Two over-simplifications in assessing this development need, however, to be avoided. The first is that prior to the nineteenth century there had been universal agreement amongst Baptists concerning the nature of the ordained ministry and its role in relationship to the Lord's Supper; the second, that change came about solely in reaction to the Catholic revival. In the case of the first, there is evidence that Baptists held differing views about the ministry prior to the nineteenth century and, in the case of the second, differences were already being debated before the emergence of the Tractarians. In a study of the presidency of the Lord's table amongst Baptists in the seventeenth century, E. P. Winter has argued that, whereas opinions differed as to whether only an ordained minister might preside at the Lord's table, there was universal agreement that only a person recognized by the church might do so. This would normally be the minister but in his absence, through illness or, in times of persecution, imprisonment, another officer of the church might be delegated to preside. Not all churches agreed in this practice, however, and some went without communion in the absence of the minister.[2] This latter practice was not uncommon in the eighteenth century.[3]

Certainly, the Baptists of the eighteenth century were agreed on the seriousness with which they viewed the ordained ministry and its necessity for the maintenance of proper order in the life of the churches. It was on these grounds that Daniel Turner argued for a recognized ministry of word and sacrament in 1758.[4] The influential Calvinist, John Gill, was even more specific in his description of the ordained ministry. He argued that the ordinand was to be a member of the church to which he was called to minister before being ordained, that he was not to preside at the Lord's table in any other church than his own and that he was not to move on to another church to exercise his ministry there.[5] Gill lent his theological weight to the Baptist practice of inviting ordained ministers from a wide area to be present and responsible for the laying on of hands at the ordination of a new minister, but the presidency of the Lord's table was the sole prerogative of the minister in the church to which he was ordained and the church was not at liberty to depute a private member to preside in his place. Clearly, Gill based his view of the ministry on the local church and gave no encouragement to the idea of an ordained ministry which was universally recognized, though his insistence on the presence of other ordained ministers and their role in the ordination does concede a degree of recognition beyond the boundaries of the local church. Within the church, the function of the minister was that of, in the classic Calvinist sense, minister of word and sacrament.

Features of this pattern survived well into the nineteenth century. The extent to which it was to be discarded is evidenced by a leader in the *Freeman* on 5 February 1869. Even allowing for that journal's contempt for nuance and subtlety in theological matters, and for the Victorian predilection for making pronouncements, the length of the stride taken from the views held at the turn of the century can hardly be exaggerated:

> It was once a notion common in our churches that any one could pray in a prayer meeting, but that only an 'ordained minister' ought to 'administer', as it was most inappropriately expressed, the Lord's Supper. Churches used to send for such

a one, if their pastor was absent, or even defer the service till his return, as if we too had some slight belief in the magic of consecration by ordained men! That superstition, we presume, is now wholly gone. When the usual president of the church is present he of course presides; but we suppose no Baptist now thinks that Christian brethren meeting together are incompetent to break bread in memory of their Lord, and that without an official administrator His presence would be wanting.

Reaction to Catholicism had become the starting point from which definitions were framed and theologies worked out. Indeed, the Baptist practice was vulnerable to misunderstanding, but instead of clarifying the minister's role later Baptists were content to minimise it, if not dispense with any traditional understanding of it altogether. The sole right of the ordained pastor to preside at the Lord's table, or for someone recognized by the church to do so, had been defended on the grounds of right order. Faced with the challenge of the Catholic revival that same insistence upon the role of the ordained minister as the only proper president of the Lord's table could be construed as sacerdotalism by those who had forgotten its original intention. Further, the renewed emphasis on apostolic succession amongst Anglo-Catholics cast its shadow on the Baptist practice of placing ordination in the hands of already ordained ministers. The Catholic revival, however, simply gave impetus to a process of reshaping that was already under way in the earlier years of the century. In 1838, J. H. Hinton complained that:

> ... on [ordination] great differences of opinion prevail among Nonconformists; that many, even of our ministers, have scarcely a definite idea about it of any kind, and that it has of late been all but abandoned, as by common consent, to an almost helpless obscurity.[6]

That the malaise over ordination was something shared by all Nonconformist churches was true. By the end of the century the Dissenting churches had all downgraded their concept of the ministry in reaction to the Catholics.[7] That the situation was quite as parlous as Hinton portrayed it is more open to question, though its shortcomings as a statement of historic fact are more than compensated by its accuracy as prophetic utterance.

i) A Question of Right Order

It is clear that the controversies about ordination came before the Catholic revival and that they dealt with questions of order, not whether or not ordination imparted some special character to the ordinand. The discussions were engaged in, not at the level of weighty theological writing, but through the correspondence columns of Baptist magazines. The November 1815 edition of the *Baptist Magazine* featured a letter deploring the fact that younger ministers, who had yet to be ordained, were administering the Lord's Supper. The magazine clearly shared its correspondent's unease and quoted a letter of Andrew Fuller in which he had expressed his objections to the practice. He wrote:

> I must say, it appears to me very wrong, to administer the Lord's Supper without ordination, as it goes to render void that ordinance.[8]

The reason he gave for the voiding of the ordinance was not that it depended for its efficacy upon the priestly character of the president, but that right order had been set on one side. The purpose of ordination was 'to keep out unworthy characters from the churches'. The service of ordination required the presence of those already ordained and thus was a sign of their consent and approval of the one whom the church had called to be pastor. He cited the case of the ministers in a particular area refusing to attend an ordination because they had considered the prospective ordinand as unworthy, in consequence of which the ordination had been cancelled and the man had left the vicinity.[9] Where a person administered the Lord's Supper before ordination, there ordination itself was set aside, a practice that Fuller believed would be 'a source of many mischiefs in the churches'.[10] He cited the case of another church that had 'fallen prey to a designing man'. The local ministers had refused to attend the ordination, but the church had proceeded none the less. 'The consequence, I doubt not', wrote Fuller, 'will be mischiefs incalculable'. Fuller saw ordination as a means of safeguarding the health and integrity of the churches. To admit someone as president of the Lord's table without ordination was to bypass that safeguard and therefore to expose the church to the risk of exploitation by pastoral hirelings.

The question of church order also appeared in a church dispute in which the Baptist Board, a fraternal of London Baptist ministers, was asked to intervene. In the autumn of 1811 a group of members seceded from the Prescot Street Church and met together in Artillery Street. They requested that the Baptist Board give them its 'countenance and support' as they sought 'the great head of the church . . . [to] direct one to us whom he has qualified for the office, and who shall prove a blessing to us'.[11] Before responding to the request, the Board approached the Prescot Street church and asked the members whether they were disposed to recognize the Artillery Street seceders as 'a church of Christ'.[12] The question of ministry lay at the heart of the reply they received:

> We think it our duty under present circumstances to pause on this matter, Because we think it admits of considerable doubt, whether persons withdrawing themselves from a regular Church, and saying, they have formed themselves into a distinct church, is sufficient to constitute them such,

in conformity with the prevailing and approved practice of Christian Society. A church having been regularly organized, and settled under the care of a pastor, may still be considered a church, if it be deprived of its pastor, but whether that distinction is justly applicable to a body of persons, where the organization has never been complete, we are not fully satisfied of.[13]

The concept of order underlying this reply is not easy to tease out. That it is a question of order can hardly be challenged. It would seem that the Prescot Street members argued that a rightly ordered church consisted of people and pastor. An interregnum did not disturb that order whereas a secession did, since the seceding group had no pastor and therefore was irregularly constituted. The argument is difficult to maintain in the light of Baptist history, since Baptist churches had themselves seceded from other churches and, having seceded, had appointed ministers from their own ranks. Except where the secession was led by leaders such as John Smyth, who was pastor of the people who gathered about him, the order of events was first the community and then the pastor. The pastor derived his call from the community. It would appear that the members of the Baptist Board either found themselves faced with a theological conundrum or were unprepared to involve themselves in other people's squabbles. In the event, the Artillery Street church, whatever its propensity for secession, was charitable enough to release the Board from any further involvement in the matter:

> We lately made application to you for assistance in preaching, and administering the ordinance among us ... but lest a further consideration of our case should in the smallest degree interrupt that peace and harmony so desirable should continue amongst you, we wish to withdraw our request ...[14]

The *Baptist Magazine* in 1828 provides evidence that the need for order as it was embodied in ordination was not universally felt amongst Baptists. The magazine published an interchange of letters between two pastors who, in the fashion of the times, amply concealed themselves under the pseudonyms of 'Publicly Recognized Minister' and 'Country Minister'. The first of these initiated a correspondence with a letter deploring the fact that 'two young men who studied at one of our academies, have lately settled as pastors, without ordination'. He was not alone in his misgivings since 'some excellent men are pained with the fact. They think it a departure from the order of the New Testament'.[15] The rise of this departure from what he believed to be accepted practice he attributed to the growing tendency of men to move from one pastorate to another and to have no service of 'public recognition' in their new sphere of service. The reply of 'A Country Minister' throws interesting light on the diversity of practice that was already occurring in Baptist church life. Not only was it wrong to impugn the motives of the young, he wrote, but it also had to be observed that some 'rather elderly ministers' had not received ordination.[16] He then went on to attack the notion of ordination implicit in his adversary's letter. The scriptural word for 'ordain', he argued, referred to 'appoint' and carried no sense of a public ceremony. It also implied 'a power and authority in the church which not even the most obstinate stickler for ordination, at least among us, ever pretends to'.[17] It is noteworthy that the correspondent was prepared to argue that a New Testament practice should not be followed because it did not match what was done in Baptist churches, rather than that the latter should be modified to fit the former. He instead warned that the danger of the common form of ordination was that it should 'beget an idea that ordination (in our, not the scriptural sense of the term) is a divine ordinance; and that it and not the choice of the church, bestows the right to act as a pastor'.[18] The mistake, he believed, was best corrected by omitting the ceremony altogether.

The depth of the gulf separating the adherents of each opinion was illustrated in a further letter from 'Publicly Recognized Minister'. Scripturally understood, he wrote, 'ordination is a divinely instituted ordinance' and it 'can only be scripturally performed by Christian ministers themselves previously ordained'.[19] He challenged his opponent's view that ministry was validated by the call of the church and not by the act of ordination. There was a distinction between choice and appointment: ' ... I contend that the choice of the people is not ordination, but that the appointment or separation to the office to which they are thus chosen is the work of those previously in office'. He concluded, 'I deeply regret the introduction into our Denomination, of what I consider a very unscriptural practice'.[20] The interchange ended with a letter from 'A Country Minister', making the exegetical point that the Greek word $\chi\epsilon\iota\rho\sigma\tau\sigma\nu\eta\sigma\alpha\nu\tau\epsilon\varsigma$ in Acts 14.23 meant 'the stretching out of the hand in voting' and not 'appointment',[21] reflecting the Baptist method of reaching decisions in Church Meeting by the casting of votes.

ii) The Laying on of Hands

Baptist uncertainties with regard to ordination were sometimes focused on the issues of laying on of hands and the presence at ordinations of other ordained ministers. In the first of these, they found themselves in a dilemma, torn between what they believed to be loyalty to apostolic practice and the desire to avoid any erroneous interpretation that might be placed upon the act. The traditional practice of Baptists had been to ordain by prayer and the laying on of hands. The accounts of ordination services carried in the *Baptist Magazine* invariably record this procedure until the middle of the century where ordinations begin to appear that omit the laying on of hands. Disagreement on the matter had already appeared in the correspondence columns of that journal earlier in the century. A dispute between two contestants who identified themselves simply as 'T.T. of Peckham' and 'W.N. of Stepney' may, in fact, have reflected a discussion taking place in Stepney College, if 'T.T.' is identified with Thomas Thomas, College Secretary 1813-19, and 'W.N.' as William Newman, Principal 1811-26. Writing on the subject in 1814, Thomas contended that the mode of ordination 'has generally been by prayer and the imposition of hands'.[22] To depart from this practice would be a 'deviation from primitive example, and a violation of the divinely established order'. The correspondent was aware that objections had already been raised against the practice on the grounds that, in the New Testament, it implied 'the conveyance of extraordinary gifts', an argument which Thomas rejected, citing the appointment of the seven deacons in Acts 6.6. Others had contended that the laying on of hands was no more than 'a trivial ceremony and matter of indifference', an argument similar to that used by Robert Hall with reference to baptism and encountered again in the debate with the Catholics. Both objections were swept aside, on the grounds of apostolic order, for

> ... it is a very dangerous thing for us to make comparisons between one duty and another, especially with a view of dispensing with any of them, or altering their order.[23]

Thomas received a reply to his letter from Newman in the September edition. Whilst supporting the necessity of setting apart those who were to 'sustain the character of public teachers', Newman challenged the use of the laying on of hands. He took up the cry of those for whom the rite was no more than a ceremony and what it signified more important than the sign itself. 'Economy is unallied to ceremony', he wrote, 'simplicity and spirituality are its prominent features'.[24] He also questioned whether the practice could be supported on the grounds of apostolic example. The fact that members of the early church practised the laying on of hands was not sufficient, since they also washed each others' feet and saluted with a holy kiss:

> In such things I apprehend they are to be considered as men conforming to the customs of the country in which they lived; and these customs were sanctioned and sanctified by their religion ... Nor will it suffice to shew that the practice was in use among the Apostles ... In various particulars they must be regarded as acting in their apostolic character, in which they can have no successors, to the end of the world.[25]

The significance of the apostolic example inevitably gave rise to conflicting claims in a church polity which, whilst striving to translate eldership into contemporary terms, had left apostolicity either unobserved or ill-defined. In his reply in the October issue, Thomas was not prepared to accept Newman's limitation of various rites to the social norms of the first century or the duration of the apostles' lives. Apostolic example, he asserted, rendered 'any rite of a religious nature ... of perpetual obligation'.[26] The imposition of hands was 'a rite, accompanied with prayer, used in the designation of persons to any sacred work or office, in the exercise of which a divine blessing was implored'.[27] In the continuing practice of the church, such a rite was given added solemnity 'when it receives the concurrence of several persons', that is, when a number of ministers were present at ordination.

The continuing practice of the imposition of hands was again called into question in a dispute between J. H. Hinton and Joseph Angus. The setting of the dispute was extraordinary. Hinton had preached at Angus' ordination and, in view of the confusion that he believed to exist amongst Nonconformists on the question of ordination,[28] offered a résumé of his sermon to the columns of the *Baptist Magazine*. This appeared in March 1838. In April, a letter from Angus revealed that he had disagreed with Hinton's views on the occasion of the ordination, and had told him so. He then proceeded to give his own opinion in the matter. One can only applaud Hinton's imperturbability in offering to clarify the thinking of a wider audience when he had so singularly failed to persuade the man he was ordaining at the time. Not that either of them could make undisputed claims to clarity since both their contributions leave the reader in some doubt as to their exact theological intentions. Hinton claimed that 'the laying on of hands in ordination had no necessary or ordinary connexion with the communication of supernatural gifts'.[29] What it signified, in his view, was the allocation of certain tasks. Amongst these was administration of the word and ordinance, though only in a qualified way:

> I cannot admit . . . that ordination ever was intended to confer the right of administering the word and ordinances of the gospel. Every disciple of Christ has a right so to do, if endowed with gifts, and moved by love'.

It is difficult to see what function ordination entrusted to the few that love had not already entrusted to all. He nevertheless regarded the office of the ministry as of sufficient importance for great care to be taken in recognizing those who felt called to it. For those so called, ordination was to be 'in the primitive manner, by prayer and laying on of hands'.[30]

The challenge advanced in reply by Angus dealt with the question of the imposition of hands. If, in scripture, he argued, the laying on of hands was used to impart a miraculous gift, divine approbation or full permission to enter upon the duties of office, in the sense that a master delegated trust and authority to his servant (Matthew 24.45, Acts 7.10, Daniel 2.24), then it should be discontinued, since there was only one Master, Christ himself. If, on the other hand, no such intentions were attached to the laying on of hands and it was simply a 'form of salutation, or a dignified expression of fraternal love', then it should be set aside as 'nothing else than an eastern custom . . . liable to misrepresentation and abuse'.[31] Further, if ordination was to be administered by 'inspired men only', then it could not 'consistently be practised by those that deny apostolic succession'. What was handed down from the apostles, he argued, were the truths they taught and not the authority with which they taught them.[32] As far as ordination was concerned, though it might mark the entrustment of qualification and duties of office, those should never be entrusted 'through the intervention of any third person, or class of persons'.[33] He concluded:

> I cannot but wish that the solemn assumptions of a modern ordination service were exchanged for the affectionate greetings of public recognition.[34]

Between them, Hinton and Angus left little intact in the theory and practice of ordination that Baptists had inherited from the earlier centuries. Hinton, whilst arguing for public recognition of ministers, had nevertheless emphasised the inner constraints of love which required only the response of the individual. Though he stressed the importance of wider recognition of the individual's call by his claim that the ministry of word and sacrament had its origin in a right conferred upon all believers, if endowed with gifts and motivated by love, he had undermined the role of the church in its custody of the Lord's table and in its responsibility, under Christ, solemnly to delegate those who were to preside at it. Similarly, Angus had reduced the church to the role of an intrusive third party in the rite of ordination. Indeed, the rite itself was redundant where the emphasis was to be placed upon the individual's response to his Master and his personal submission to his authority, and upon the church's fraternal interest, as opposed to its authority, under Christ, to appoint those called to solemn office. Thus, with the Catholic revival barely begun, some Baptists had moved from the concern for right order and apostolic precedent that characterised earlier generations to an emphasis on the 'rights' of individuals and only the vaguest generalisations when describing the role of the church. The significance of this shift is heightened when it is recalled that the combatants in this case were not an anonymous T.T. of Peckham or W.N. of Stepney, but two men who were both to hold high office in the the denomination, Hinton being secretary of the Union from 1841 to 1866, and Angus, first the secretary of the Missionary Society and then president of Stepney College. The changes that were taking place could not but be given added impetus by the advocacy of those who led the denomination and, presumably, rose to positions of leadership because of an increasingly widespread assent to the views they represented. An anonymous writer in the *Baptist Reporter* probably spoke for a declining minority:

> I have attended many ordinations, and have found them most solemn and impressive services, leaving a savour on the minds of multitudes for many days to come; . . . I have no wish to retain unscriptural usages, or relics of popery in the church of God; but in our rage for change we must be careful not to remove the ancient land-marks of the divine word.[35]

iii) Ordination by Ordained Ministers

Another issue over which there was growing uncertainty concerned the presence of other ministers and their role in the service of ordination. We have already examined the testimony of Andrew Fuller. For him the presence of other ministers signified the recognition and approval of the wider church and safeguarded individual churches against errors of judgment that would lead to exploitation by unworthy characters. Earlier, John Gill had argued for the presence of ministers from a wide area who were to be responsible for the act of ordination. As far as Robert Hall was concerned, a correspondent in the *Baptist Reporter* claimed that Hall, amongst others, did not accept the practice of ordination.[36] A. H. MacLeod argues that Hall was opposed to large numbers of ministers being present at ordination on grounds similar to those later stated by Joseph Angus, namely that ministers were appointed to their office by Christ.[37] Hall was concerned, however, that there should be 'a wholesome check on the abuse of the popular suffrage'. Invited to share in an ordination at Salisbury, after his removal to Bristol, he declined on the grounds that ordinations were best conducted 'by the presbyters or elders of the immediate vicinity of the party'. Stepping beyond that circle meant that its chief benefit was impaired, which was to make it impossible for 'a minister to establish himself at the head of a congregation, without the approbation and sanction of the circle of pastors with whom he is to act'.[38] MacLeod claims that at Hall's own ordination at the Baptist church in Cambridge no neighbouring ministers were invited to attend.[39] Perhaps on this occasion Hall felt that there was no need for a wholesome check on any abuse of the popular suffrage! Others were emphatic that ordination should be conducted by already ordained ministers. As we have seen, the 1828 correspondence in the *Baptist Magazine* had stated clearly that ordination was a divinely instituted ordinance which could only be scripturally performed by Christian ministers, themselves previously ordained.[40] Similarly, in the 1814 correspondence in the same magazine, it had been argued that it was 'the province of pastors of other churches to ordain, or set [the ordinand] apart for his office'.[41]

The early advocates of ordination by prayer and the laying on of hands, administered by already ordained ministers from a wide area, believed they were defending a scriptural view of ordination and one that was jealous for the right order and integrity of the church. The practices associated with ordination were being questioned before the coming of the Catholic revival. Attitudes that played their part in the communion debate spilled over into the question of ordination. The nineteenth century was the century of the individual and the voluntary society and some Baptists in the early years of the century saw themselves as pioneers breaking away from the old ways. Impatience with forms and ceremonies and emphasis upon the inner and spiritual forces at work in the life of the individual were to be the hallmark of a new breed of

Christian men, a breed that was to find its most eloquent spokesman amongst the Baptists in John Clifford. The church too, believed that it was discovering a new freedom, liberated from the restraints of the past, the concern for right order and what was viewed as the theological bickering that went with it. This process could only have greatly accelerated with the coming of the Catholic revival. To the existing case against rites such as the laying on of hands and the presence of other ordained ministers at ordination could be added far more telling arguments. The laying on of hands could be misconstrued as a priestly act, especially when it was used to delegate men to the ministry of word and sacrament. Did not the priest alone celebrate the holy mysteries within Catholicism? Were Baptists to be infected with the same poison? Did their ministers, also, have sole right to preside at the Lord's table? Was not the ministry of word and sacrament one that was entrusted to every believer? And did not priests receive their ministry at the hands of bishops in the belief that this placed them in direct succession to the apostles? And did it not seem that Baptists were of a similar persuasion when they limited the act of ordination to the hands of those already ordained? An already unsteady doctrinal edifice could not hope to stand intact against the ubiquitous challenge of a renewed Catholicism which had now found a voice within the established church. For Baptists, distance from present error was valued more highly than identity with past practice.

iv) The Presidency of the Lord's Table

The question of the presidency of the Lord's table moved with the ebb and flow of the ordination debate. Chiefly concerned with right order within the church, it inevitably involved discussion of the presidency of the Lord's table. Gill had contended that only the person ordained to the ministry within a particular church might preside at the table, the church not being at liberty to depute someone else in his absence.[42] Similarly, Andrew Fuller had deplored the practice of some churches in allowing men to preside at the table without ordination.[43] The rigour with which his stand was shared by those of similar persuasion is illustrated in the the situation that arose, following his death, at the Baptist church in Kettering of which he had been minister. Fuller was taken ill during April 1815 and died early in May. A diary kept by George Wallis, a member of the Kettering church, recorded that on the 'Ordinance days', held on Sundays, 28 May, 25 June, 30 July, 27 August, and 24 September, there was no celebration of the Lord's Supper. In June, Wallis reflected:

> Ordinance day at Kettering; but no Minister to preside at it -
> O Lord may the absence of these means make us prize them more highly.[44]

The rigorous withholding of the Lord's Supper is further highlighted by the fact that Fuller had an assistant, John Keen Hall, who had served with him for three years. Hall, however, had never been ordained. In the autumn of 1815, he was given a by no means unanimous call to become minister of the Kettering church and was ordained there on 12 November. Then, and only then, did the church believe it permissible to celebrate the sacrament, and this they did on 26 November.[45] Some churches, such as the church at Melbourne in Derbyshire, followed Gill in requiring that a man be a member of a church for a period prior to his ordination to its ministry and that the administration of the Lord's Supper should be restricted to the one ordained. The Melbourne church invited a Scot, named J. Gilchrist, to preach and subsequently received him into membership in August 1809. The church minutes recall that he was to serve the church on trial for an unlimited period in the hope that this would result in 'a unanimous call to the ministry among them'. As only 'regular' ministers were allowed to serve at communion, it needed a special ruling to allow Gilchrist to preside, a step that was taken only after he had been amongst them for a year.[46]

Amongst the General Baptists, right order maintained a generally stronger hold well into the nineteenth century. This may owe something to their concept of the church and ministry. The church was more central to their understanding of baptism than had been the case amongst the Particular Baptists, for whom the death-burial-resurrection motif had provided the dominant theme of believer's baptism. Since the seventeenth century the General Baptists had also recognized a three-tier ministry, apostolic ministry being embodied in the messengers who were responsible for planting new churches and encouraging existing congregations, whilst care of the local churches lay in the hands of ministers and deacons. The district associations played a significant role in their church life, presenting opportunities for discussion of matters of discipline and church order and providing guide-lines for individual churches. Examples of the way this related to the presidency of the Lord's table can be seen in the minutes of the Midland Association meetings. In 1794 it was ruled that a minister who was not ordained might administer the Lord's Supper only in cases of necessity. In 1810, the assembly made clear its belief that ordination to the office of deacon did not qualify a person to administer the Lord's Supper, whilst in 1815 the practice of men taking upon themselves the office of minister without being ordained was rejected 'with the affectionate request that those who have followed this practice should seriously reconsider'.[47]

The issue of ordination appeared in the pages of the *General Baptist Repository* in 1836, where the question was raised as to what works ordination qualified a minister to perform. The reply limited itself to the question of presidency at the Lord's table and endeavoured to make clear what it considered to be the General Baptist position in the matter. The notion of moral or intellectual qualification was rejected. However,

> When it is said to be irregular for an unordained minister to administer the Lord's supper, the meaning is, we suppose,

that such a practice does not accord with Scripture precedent.[48]

The article went on to warn of the unfortunate consequences of departure from right order in this matter:

> Experience has also shown, that when the apostolic constitution has been departed from on this point, serious mischiefs have ensued: ordination itself has been neglected, contentions have, we believe, risen among leading members who should be the administrator, and Churches have been split up into small parties, each having its own separate table.[49]

Whilst unwilling to rule that churches should in no circumstances allow an unordained person to administer the Lord's Supper, the writer nevertheless claimed that:

> We view the practice as an irregularity which Churches ought to prevent when they are able, and which it is proper to check in the use of scriptural means.[50]

The magazine's successor, the *General Baptist Magazine*, returned to the question in 1852, when reporting an address on 'Church Order' by John Wallis, prefaced by an editorial dissociating the magazine from the views put forward in the address. Wallis argued that only the local church had the authority to appoint a minister and that only a minister so appointed had the authority to administer the Lord's Supper. The local church, however, was not under necessity to appoint a pastor and could, presumably, appoint someone from amongst its own members to administer the sacrament.[51] It is not clear from which of these views the magazine dissented. In a later edition, however, Thomas W. Matthews identified the editor's hesitancy with Wallis' contention that if a church were to choose not to call a pastor it might appoint anyone to preside at the table. He himself expressed agreement with Wallis that anyone might be appointed and continued:

> ... might he not have added, that any one by appointment may perform this act; because this ordinance above all others exhibits the entire equality of all the members. In baptism the administrator confers something on the recipient; in the Lord's supper both are recipients ...[52]

Clearly, the General Baptists were liberalising their practice with greater reluctance than the Particular Baptists. A small contribution to the colourful variety of practice amongst English Baptist churches was added by the appearance of a handful of churches known as Scotch Baptists. Founded through the influence of Archibald McLean, they were to be found in parts of the North of England and North Wales.[53] McLean's Presbyterian background was evident in the resemblances with presbyteral church order amongst the churches which he founded. No ministers were ordained in these churches, but there was a plurality of elders who, amongst other functions, were responsible for the administration of the Lord's Supper. If no elder was available, then the Supper was not observed.[54] The Scotch Baptists had a minimal influence on other Baptist churches but some survived into the twentieth century. The Baptist church in Haggate, near Burnley, for instance, founded on Scotch Baptist principles, was administered by elders who alone could preside at the Lord's table until the church made a break with tradition in 1953 and called its first minister.[55]

The attitude of the strict Baptists to the question of the ministry was increasingly shaped by the difficulty they faced in finding ministers of strict communionist persuasion to preside at their communion tables. This shortage of ministers led some strict churches to invite ministers of the opposite persuasion to conduct the Lord's Supper for them. Their action would suggest that for some, at least, the need to observe order in the matter of administration outweighed in importance the question of who might attend. For the *Primitive Church Magazine* the shortage of strict communion ministers was a problem that deserved better solutions than the expediency, as they viewed it, of calling open communion ministers to preside at the Lord's table with 'all the evils which ensue'.[56] Correspondents were quick to support the editorial stand, arguing that this practice simply 'fed the flame that is destroying the denomination' and would lead to its 'annihilation'.[57]

The 'non-theological' factor of ministerial shortage evoked two reactions. The first was a growing attitude of mistrust towards a trained ministry. The movement amongst Baptists generally to secure an educated ministry had gathered momentum from the establishment of dissenting academies for the training of ministers throughout the nineteenth century. No attempt was made to conceal the contempt that one contributor to the *Primitive Church Magazine* felt for the syllabus that was customarily followed in the colleges:

> It is no direct recommendation that a person has read the heathen classics, or studied natural, mental or moral philosophy, or gone through a course of logic, rhetoric or mathematics; the grand end being the simple inculcation of the truths and precepts of the New Testament 'not with wisdom of words', but 'with great plainness of speech'; confidence of success being placed, not in the power of men, but in 'the demonstration of the Spirit,' and of the power of God. No 'degree' will be available but that of 'minister of the word of God' and this is not as attached to the name, but engraved in deep characters on the broad tablet of the life.[58]

In every generation since, there have doubtless been reluctant Baptist theological students who would have given such rhetoric their unqualified agreement.

The second reaction was more theological and called into question the idea of a separate ministry of word and sacrament. The magazine's leading article for November 1845 saw the restriction of ministerial functions to the few as a reflection of Roman Catholic practice:

> Instead . . . of enjoining it as every brother's duty to preach and teach Christ to the world in every way possible, many of our churches regard it as sin for any person to do so without special licence from the church. Can anything be more injurious to the spread of christianity?[59]

The theme was to be taken up again in the leader of August 1846, but this time it was challenged by a reader who contended that there was a distinction to be observed between the duty of every Christian to preach the gospel and the appointment of men to a public office for that purpose:

> There is, in the church of Christ, a divinely appointed order, and a rule and authority established, which, whenever violated, confusion and disorder follow.[60]

The editor attacked the views expressed in his correspondent's letter, seeing in them evidence of 'a tinge of Puseyism in the constitution of dissenting churches, which, in some measure, may tend to mar the progress of the gospel'.[61] Both these reactions of the strict Baptists, suspicion of learning and the claim that all were equally called, with their attendant erosion of any distinction between the calling of a minister and the calling of other Christians within the church, were to be taken up from time to time by some in the wider fellowship of the Baptist churches.

The problem of ministerial shortage led the strict Baptists to what was, in effect, a downgrading of the ministry. Similar problems led others to a wider concept of the ministry of word and sacrament. Gill had argued that only a minister, ordained to the pastoral oversight of a particular church, might administer the communion within that church. Furthermore, his ordination did not grant him the right to administer it beyond his own church.[62] Inevitably, adherence to this opinion could only lead to difficulties. There would be times when a church was without pastoral oversight, either through a temporary indisposition of its minister or during an interregnum. Some solved this problem by rejecting Gill's restriction of the presidency of the table to the church's pastor and inviting a minister from another church to preside for them. A correspondent in the *Baptist Magazine* of May 1815 examined two reasons why some churches withheld the observance of the Lord's Supper during a pastor's absence because of illness. The first was that the communion was a feast of joy and therefore inappropriate in view of the pastor's condition, and the second, that only the pastor of the church might preside. In reply to the second objection, the correspondent distinguished between the authority that a pastor exercised within the congregation to which he was called and his calling as a minister of the word and sacrament. The first could not be extended beyond his own congregation; however:

> I do not conceive therefore that a church violates any engagement to a pastor, who, in case of his absence, or incapacity, invite the pastor of another church to preach, or administer ordinances to them; nor that the pastor violates any engagement to a church, who performs such services, when invited to another church.[63]

The same distinction was drawn by a correspondent in the November edition of the same year, taking issue with Gill's restricting statute. Whatever ruling function a pastor might perform in the congregation to which he had been called, the administration of the Lord's Supper was a pastoral act and equally valid in whatever church a pastor presided. To invite another pastor to preside at the Lord's table was far preferable to the congregation going without communion. The dangers could not be ignored:

> The neglect of any duty must have a serious effect on the mind; and it will be owing to irresistible grace, if the importance of the ordinance is not undervalued in consequence; and it may be feared, that our gracious Lord, who is jealous of his honour, may resent such inattention to his commands, and withdraw the smiles of his face.[64]

It could be argued that the recognition that a minister was called to an office and function which could be exercised within the wider church, as well as the church of which he was pastor, was implicit in his recognition by other ministers at his service of ordination. So, whereas the Catholic revival rang alarm bells for many Baptists, who took the defensive action of almost obliterating altogether any distinction between minister and people, at other levels the wider recognition of ministerial calling, allowing ministers to administer the word and sacrament in churches other than their own, led to a wider concept of the Christian ministry as the servant of all the churches and not just of one.

v) Conclusion

The warning, given at the outset, that over-simplifications need to be avoided in assessing Baptist attitudes to the ministry during this period, is adequately confirmed by the evidence we have examined. It is not a question of tracing the earlier Baptist doctrine of the ministry and identifying the changes it underwent with any one historical development in the nineteenth century. In the first place, it is clear that there was no single concept of the ministry to which universal Baptist assent was given during the seventeenth and eighteenth centuries. Secondly, it would be inaccurate to claim that there was a Baptist doctrine of the ministry. The one underlying concern that held together Baptist churches until the end of the eighteenth century, despite a limited diversity of practice, was that of church order. Their understanding of the ministry has to be related to that concern. Baptist attitudes to the ministry, like Baptist beliefs about baptism, can be understood only in relation to their view of the church. The communion controversy represented a challenge to that concept of order. Hall's willingness to admit 'sincere' Christians to the Lord's table whether, by his own presuppositions, erroneously baptized or not baptized at all, and his insistence that 'ceremonies' were secondary to the inner, spiritual reality of personal experience, meant that the church abdicated its role of guardian, under Christ, of the Lord's table and threw the onus of responsibility on the shoulders of the individual. There followed a growing decay of interest in matters of church order, a devaluation of the role of the church and a contempt for 'ceremonies' and forms in favour of an inner, more spiritual, religion.

Given that the Baptist understanding of the ministry was shaped entirely by a concern for church order and that there was no real doctrine of the ministry that had been biblically and theologically defined, the growing impatience with the restraints of church order and 'ceremonies' meant that practices associated with the ministry fell into disarray. If baptism could be seen as a 'ceremony' of less importance than the inner sincerity of the individual Christian, then what hope was there for ordination, with its rite of laying on of hands and the acknowledgment of the role of the wider church expressed in the crucial involvement of other ordained ministers, unsustained as it was by a coherent theology of the ministry *per se*? The Baptist churches at the turn of the century followed previous custom in the matter of ordination and made little attempt to discover why things had been done in this way. Gill's teaching on the subject continued to influence the practice of some, but his works were not given everyone's unqualified admiration. Hall, who can fairly be said to represent the new attitudes that were to gather momentum during the nineteenth century, considered Gill's theological works to be a 'continent of mud'.[65] The correspondence columns of the various Baptist journals reveal a changing situation in which some believed that custom reflected apostolic order and should be upheld, while others saw no need for custom, including a few for whom even the evidence of apostolic order could no longer claim to be binding in the changed circumstances of the nineteenth century. None, either the advocates of ministerial order or its detractors, made any sustained attempt to define a theology of ministry, with its attendant questions of ordination, laying on of hands, ministerial 'succession' and the presidency of the Lord's table.

The challenge posed by the Catholic revival sent the majority of Baptists scurrying away even further from the faith and practice of their fathers. To a growing impatience with forms was added a deep distrust of what they represented. If ordination granted an exclusive right to preside at the Lord's table, then it was but a short step from sacerdotalism and the priestly pretensions of the Catholics. If only ordained ministers were to administer the laying on of hands at ordination, then Baptists could be accused of practising a form of apostolic succession, a notion that became increasingly obnoxious the more it was re-affirmed by the Catholics. As with much else, Baptists distanced themselves from Catholics at the cost of distancing themselves from their own heritage. A sober concern for order within the body of Christ stood little chance against the ringing summons to individual freedom and the strong, Victorian manliness of prophetic religion.

B) THE LORD'S SUPPER IN SUNDRY TIMES AND PLACES

The second issue associated with the relationship of the Lord's Supper to church order was that of celebration on occasions other than the gathering of the local church for worship on Sunday. These occasions were of two sorts. The first was created by the unavoidable absence of individuals from the sacrament either through illness or age or the more distressing and rare instance of a Baptist being immured in the workhouse. The second was created by the growing desire of Baptists meeting together in the wider groupings of local associations and national assemblies, or in fellowship with other Christians under the aegis of one of the many voluntary societies formed during the nineteenth century, to celebrate together the Lord's Supper. The discussion as to the rightness of celebrating on any of these occasions was to centre on the nature of the sacrament in relation to the church. Those who opposed all celebrations other than those which took place within the context of the Sunday worship of the local church, argued that the Supper was a 'church ordinance' and therefore to be celebrated nowhere other than within the fellowship of the church. Clearly this objection was based upon a view that limited the church to the local community. Only a community of men and women bound together in faith and based on a particular locality could claim to be the church. When Christians from such local assemblies met together in wider groupings, such as associations or assembly meetings, they thereby formed a fraternal but not a churchly gathering. Similar reasons were advanced for not administering 'sick' communion, with the added objection that it carried sinister associations with Catholic practice.

i) The Lord's Supper and the Sick

Two views of the administration of the Lord's Supper to the sick appear in the pages of the *General Baptist Repository* for 1838. An anonymous letter appeared in the November edition of the former in reply to a question, published in July, asking whether there was 'any valid objection to the administration of ordinance of the Lord's Supper to members of our churches in their sick chambers'.[66] The writer argued against the practice on two grounds. The first was that communion was a 'church ordinance':

> One principal design of the ordinance appears to be, to intimate that the Church, as a united family, have communion with their common Lord, and with each other.[67]

To this was added a second objection which reveals the depth of the writer's fear that the administration of the Lord's Supper to the sick would elevate the sacrament to a status commonly accorded it only by Catholics, giving it a 'peculiar sanctity and importance'. It is probable that he included at least a few Baptists in his strictures on those who had allowed themselves to be unduly influenced by Roman and Anglican attitudes:

> But if they can have the Lord's Supper, some Christians seem as if they could almost be content to give up everything else. The superstitious reverence attached to this ordinance by the usage of the Church of Rome, and that of England, has perhaps created, and certainly done much to cherish such a feeling; and persons, who in the general may have been delivered from the undue influence of those communions, may still retain somewhat of that disproportionate reverence for the eucharist.[68]

A second view was provided by J. T. Heath of Beeston, who replied in the January 1839 edition of the magazine. Heath argued for the presence of the pastor, deacons and two or three individuals at a sick communion. Given that, then the sick chamber would become 'a visible representation of a Church of Christ'[69] and the status of the Lord's Supper as a 'church ordinance' would not be compromised. He also recognized that sick communion might well reinforce a false conception of its meaning, but that did not mean that Baptists could 'neglect the legitimate use of any good because of its abuse'. His argument was prompted by the fact that he still held something of that reverence for the sacrament which the previous writer had so decried:

> ... if [the Lord's Supper] has a tendency to inspire faith, humble pride, excite love, increase hope, subdue murmurings, and to fix the soul more intently upon that great atonement represented by the memorials of our Saviour's death; surely, these inestimable joys are not to be withheld in the hour of man's proper weakness.[70]

Apart from his eloquent reminder of the power of the sacrament in the spiritual experience of Baptists no less than other Christians, Heath performed the charitable service of focusing attention on the plight of those precluded from the table because of sickness or infirmity. By underplaying the importance of the Lord's Supper, the previous correspondent could argue that it was not a necessity in the Christian life and therefore the sick were in no way being deprived if the sacrament was not administered to them. Given Heath's description of the benefits of the sacrament, it was inconceivable that, within those terms, the supper should be withheld from people in the time of their deepest need.

The Particular Baptist approach to the question was illustrated by an exchange of letters in the *Freeman* thirty years later, in 1868. A letter, simply signed 'INQUIRER', from one 'but young in ministry', asked whether it was consistent with Baptist orthodoxy for the minister, with two or three others, to take the Lord's Supper to someone prevented from receiving it at church because of illness.[71] The two replies illustrate the theological preoccupations that now coloured the Baptist response to all such questions. The first correspondent challenged the description of the minister's role in the sacrament as 'administering'. The word, he claimed, had sacerdotal connotations and, further, even to refer to the minister in this context was to imply that his presence was necessary, which it was not. However, such verbal niceties apart, he reminded 'Inquirer' that the communion was a 'church ordinance' and therefore its observance in the sick chamber was 'inscriptural and inexpedient'. The writer concluded, 'I believe we have no warrant for private communion at the Lord's table independently of the church'.[72] The plight of the sick was not completely overlooked, however, as, in the second letter, J. H. Hinton gave them the dubious benefit of his theological acumen. The now retired general secretary of the Baptist Union[73] gave it as his opinion that communion might be taken to the sick on the grounds that the Lord's Suppper was not instituted in a church, but at a 'social gathering'. Further, it was celebrated amongst the first Christians (Acts 2.46) before the church had been formed, 'that is in private houses . . . the word church is not applied to Christians, till in Acts 8.1 we read of "the church which was at Jerusalem"'.[74] A further letter from Hinton the following week, retracting the *faux pas*, acknowledged his mistake in overlooking the fact that the word church was used in Acts 2.47. Hinton's discovery that the church was founded on the day of Pentecost, and not some considerable time later, left him unabashed, however, and certainly not inclined to amend his views. The plight of the sick, for whom there was the possibility of recovery and restoration to the fellowship of the Lord's table, could be said to be less distressing than that of the inmates of the workhouses for whom there could be no release except death itself. A letter in the *Baptist Magazine* seemed more mindful of the writer's dilemma than theirs, however. In the workhouses, ministers could minister only to those of their own denomination. The writer was concerned that this would lead to ministers administering the ordinance to one person only. It being 'a church ordinance . . ., is it right to carry it to an individual who is precluded Church fellowship . . .?'[75]

The Baptists were right to safeguard themselves against schismatic communion. The Lord's Supper has always been a sign of the church's unity, its proper context being the worshipping community and not *ad hoc* groups of Christians. Baptist fear of Catholic practice, however, seemed to blind them to the needs of their own most vulnerable members. Even the local church could claim a reality beyond the circumscribed limits of venerated times and places. The fact that a minister (even in company with representatives of the church), when taking communion to the sick, could be compared to a Catholic priest bearing the reserved sacrament on the same errand of mercy, was accorded a greater importance than the pastoral duty to make available the resources of grace to those most in need of them.

ii) The Lord's Supper and Association and Assembly Meetings

Similar arguments were employed when the question of celebration of the Lord's Supper at association and assembly meetings was raised. The associations had held, and continued to hold, an honourable and important place within the life of the Baptist churches. They provided a counter against the isolationism that constantly threatened churches which cherished their independence from outside control. They also provided opportunities for fellowship and, occasionally, concerted action. In the case of the General Baptist assemblies, they fulfilled an advisory role in matters of faith and conduct, providing guide-lines for member churches in the administration of their affairs. The question of association communions was raised in the pages of the *General Baptist Repository* in 1833. The matter was dealt with by Joseph Jarrom of Wisbech, who argued strongly against the observance of the Lord's Supper on these occasions. He gave four reasons in support of his argument:

a) The familiar one that the Lord's Supper was a 'church ordinance'. Jarrom believed that celebration at association meetings would open the door to other irregular observances. If observed at an association:

> Then why may not a few friends in the same church agree to partake of it among themselves, without the concurrence and presence of their brethren? And why may not a Christian pastor administer it in a private room to the sick, as is the custom in the Establishment, or in the Church of Rome, and the oriental churches?[76]

b) If charity allowed that communion at association meetings was not forbidden by scripture, neither was it enjoined. There was no clear command: therefore it should not be observed.

c) Its observance was 'not expedient, and would not be profitable' because delegates had travelled far and were not at their best spiritually and therefore in no fit frame of mind to observe the ordinance; because divisions of opinion 'of a painful nature' sometimes arose and therefore communion would ill accord with such encounters; and because the timetable allowed no adequate time for observance.

d) The purpose of an association gathering was

> to learn the state of the churches, to deliberate on questions of importance, submitted by the churches for consideration; to consult on the best means of advancing the interests of religion; to give Ministers and representatives an opportunity for personal interview . . .[77]

The concern for physical and spiritual well-being as a necessary precondition for attendance at the Lord's Supper, seen in some measure in the arguments against communion for the sick, is an interesting feature of Jarrom's arguments. Communion was not for the travel-weary. Neither was the Lord's table a place where conflict could be recognized, handled and resolved.

Five months later Thomas Rogers, another contributor to the same magazine, argued in favour of association communions. If other Christians, such as the Methodists, celebrated the Lord's Supper on major occasions then why should not Baptists do the same? he asked.[78] He also addressed himself to the more theological questions raised by the belief that the sacrament should be celebrated only in the local church. Though the association could not claim to be a church, nevertheless:

> . . . it cannot be unlawful for such a body composed of members of individual churches, though not in a church capacity, to celebrate the Lord's supper together, as belonging to the one body; the church of which Jesus is the Lord and Head.[79]

In limiting the celebration to the separate churches,

> . . . it is a making the parts greater and of more importance than the whole, and destroying the unity of the body of Christ.[80]

A little less than thirty years later the celebration of the Lord's Supper at the annual meeting of the assembly was agreed and held for the first time in 1863. There was some satisfaction with the event, over 1500 communicants attending. 'It was the first instance of such a service. It will certainly not be the last'.[81]

The situation amongst the Particular Baptists was similar. Where the Lord's Supper was celebrated by the associations at their meetings it appears to have been well received, but there remained those opposed to such celebrations on the grounds that the sacrament was a 'church ordinance'. A correspondent in the *Freeman* of 14 February 1868 added the further objection that celebration at associations opened a gulf between those representing closed churches and open churches who, in all other respects, were able to work happily and unitedly.

ORDER AND DISCIPLINE AT THE LORD'S TABLE

iii) Conclusion

The discussion on the question of 'irregular' communion raises three interesting points:

a) The now familiar need for Baptists to distance themselves from Catholic beliefs and practices associated with the eucharist. Sick communions raised the spectre of reserved sacrament, extreme unction and communion for the dying, whilst the celebration of the eucharist at association meetings placed it in a setting that challenged their view of the church as a collection of locally based communities.

b) Closely allied with their reaction against Catholicism was their unwillingness to see communion as a means of grace. The Lord's Supper was an 'observance' properly to be celebrated by the local church only within its Sunday worship, emphasis being placed on fellowship and on the state of preparedness of those who together shared it. The question of communion taken to the sick, or to people in other ways disadvantaged, was seen more in terms of proper observance than the grace it gave to those who received it. To withhold from the sick a communion viewed in that light would not have been seen as a deprivation. In the context of the sick room the sacrament gave nothing that could not equally be experienced by reading the scriptures and pastoral prayer.

c) The third question raised by this particular communion issue was that of the relationship of the local to the wider church. The Baptists could rightly argue that the occasional gatherings of the associations did not constitute them as a church. The associations, however, did play an ongoing role in the life of the churches and were representative, if not the actual embodiment, of the wholeness of the wider church. To define the church in terms of the local community was not to exhaust all that could be said of it. As one writer had pointed out, there was a sense in which the local church was a part of the whole. The associations at least provided a glimpse of that wholeness.

C) WEEKLY CELEBRATION OF THE LORD'S SUPPER

During the nineteenth century, a number of Baptists applied themselves to the question, by no means peculiar to Baptists, with what frequency the Lord's Supper was to be celebrated. Many have argued that the New Testament sets a pattern of weekly communion, a practice followed by the church in the earliest centuries. John Calvin believed that the weekly worship of the church should follow a structure based on word and sacrament, but was unsuccessful in persuading the city fathers in Geneva to legislate along those lines. Those in favour of weekly communion have argued on the basis of scriptural precedent and the benefit to the church of frequent access to the Lord's table. Those who have opposed it have argued that familiarity breeds contempt and that the table should be a place whose importance is heightened by the infrequency of celebration and the due preparation of the congregation. Baptist arguments tended to move along similar lines. Amongst the Baptists of Scotland, weekly communion became a widespread practice, in spite of differences on other matters which divided followers of John Glas, Archibald McLean and the Haldane brothers.[82] It has remained the practice amongst the majority of Scottish Baptist churches to this day, despite the tradition of much more infrequent communion followed by the dominant Church of Scotland. James Haldane, an 'unrepentant' Calvinist[83], defended the practice of weekly communion in his book, *A View of the Social Worship and Ordinances Observed by the First Christians.*[84] Haldane made the connection between the death of Jesus, remembered in the Lord's Supper, and the resurrection of Jesus, celebrated on the first day of the week.[85] It was a connection that was to be made by others and it could have been the starting point for fruitful reflection on the nature of the sacrament, had it been pursued. Regrettably it was not, but it at least suggested a relationship between cross and resurrection not always recognized at the Lord's table. Haldane also argued for the weekly celebration of the Supper on the grounds that it represented the union of Christians with one another and was therefore a fitting expression of their fellowship when they gathered Sunday by Sunday.[86] To those who stayed away because they considered themselves unworthy, he quoted the words of the steward in the parable of our Lord, 'I knew that thou art an hard man'. To absent oneself from the Lord's Supper was to betray an unwillingness to submit to the righteousness of God and to receive mercy as guilty sinners, totally independent of one's worthiness.[87]

A fuller defence of weekly communion was advanced by J. M. Cramp, a minister and a Baptist historian, who was later to emigrate to Canada. In his book, *An Essay on the Obligation of Christians to Observe the Lord's Supper Every Lord's Day,*[88] Cramp confessed that his own attempts to persuade his congregation to adopt the practice of weekly communion had proved unsuccessful. He argued that it could be supported from the evidence of scripture, from which he cited Acts 2.42, 20.7 and 1 Cor. 10.14-21. He also appealed to the teaching of outstanding church leaders in the early centuries of the church's existence, tracing the practice of weekly communion through Pliny, Justin Martyr and Chrysostom, its decline following the Constantinian settlement and its re-emergence amongst the Reformers. He appealed to the authority of such 'learned and good men' as Cranmer, Calvin, Richard Baxter, Thomas Goodwin, John Owen, Isaac Watts, William Ames, Philip Doddridge and Jonathan Edwards. The practice of monthly, quarterly or annual communion, he believed, was based upon expediency, which was always a bad principle for any practice. He then repeated the argument made by Haldane, that a weekly celebration established 'a beautiful harmony between the death and the resurrection of Jesus'.[89] Further, as well as being tests of allegiance, the institutions of Christianity were to be seen as 'means of grace and sources of profit',[90] the Lord's Supper being 'a perpetual memento of the death of the Lord Jesus, and a standing declaration of his atonement'.[91] Christians needed constant incentives to godliness as well as that undergirding of fellowship provided by the sacrament which was 'admirably suited to remind the people of God of their union to one another, and their separation from the world'.[92] The most important objection to weekly communion was that it would be 'inconsistent with the solemnity of the ordinance'.[93] To this he replied that, if the sacrament was a duty, then the argument that frequent celebration might lessen its advantage to the communicants did not diminish its obligation as a duty. In any case, the conjectured effects of weekly communion had to be set against experience which had proved that infrequent communion lessened its value in the eyes of communicants, whilst frequent communion increased it. Further, the Bible spoke of the solemnity of prayer but Christians had not presumed from that that they were to pray only infrequently.[94] No one would argue that frequent prayer and hearing of the word of God in any way diminished their value to Christians.

Both Haldane and Cramp, by setting the Supper as the remembrance of Christ's death in juxtaposition with the Lord's Day as the celebration of his resurrection served to remind their fellow Baptists, and other Dissenters, of that which they were too frequently inclined to minimise: that there had to be a relationship between the death and resurrection of Jesus within the Supper if there was truly to be a communion with the risen Lord. Cramp also emphasised what had been sometimes overlooked in the matter of communions for the sick, that the sacrament was a means of grace. However loosely that phrase was defined, it might have safeguarded Baptists and others against totally selling out to their growing anti-Catholicism by emptying the sacrament of all divine activity.

Other voices were to give their support to the idea of weekly communion. The Northamptonshire Circular Letter for 1845 was written by T. T. Gough on the subject of Christian Worship. Like others, he appealed to the existence of two Sunday services as an opportunity for diversity, especially if one of them were reserved for the weekly celebration of the Lord's Supper to be attended by 'those whose religious character is already formed'.[95] In another part of the country, the Western Association at its annual meeting in 1847 agreed on the following resolution:

> That the churches of the association be requested to consider the propriety of adopting the practice of weekly communion at the table of the Lord.[96]

The idea received the support of at least one correspondent in the pages of the *Baptist Magazine*. Spencer Murch argued that every meeting of the church should include a proclamation of the gospel for the sake of any unconverted sinner who might be present. In this March was of a different opinion from those who limited the celebration of the sacrament to those occasions when only the godly were present. Like John Wesley, Murch believed that the Lord's Supper was a 'converting ordinance':

> ... there is an admirable wisdom in the appointment of Jesus in the observance of the Lord's supper every first day of the week. In this ordinance, 'Jesus Christ is evidently set forth as crucified for us'. Here the gospel is presented to the eyes as well as to the ears; would it be any loss to them, if all the churches of Christ were to return to this primitive practice?[97]

In 1866, the plea for weekly communion was addressed to the delegates to the annual meetings of the Baptist Union. An address on 'Public Worship' by S. H. Green was largely taken up with attacks on the ritualist controversies in the Church of England, leading Green to be cautious in his references to the Lord's Supper. Nevertheless, he was prepared to argue for one of the weekly Sunday services to be devoted exclusively to the needs of believers and to be marked by a more frequent observance of the Supper. This, he believed, would recapture the practice of the early church:

> This was their holy service, their Lord's day festival, repeated every week with a faith and gladness ever fresh. Our modern Nonconformist churches have for the most part changed it to a monthly celebration. Is it amiss to ask whether the alteration, however sanctioned by custom, is wise? ... The recommendation to observe it may sometimes come from suspicious quarters; but it is all the more important to consider it upon its own merits; and what defence have we to make against the 'Plymouth Brother' on the one hand, who points us to the New Testament pattern; or the 'Anglo-Catholic' on the other, who pleads the example of the ancient churches? If literalists are narrow, and ritualists are superstitious, should Baptists, therefore, not be scriptural?[98]

A leader in the *Freeman* a week later took up Green's suggestion and urged that weekly communion should be made a subject of discussion. The practice may have been discredited by its association with 'High Church superstition and with Plymouth Brethren crotchitiness', but this did not alter the fact that 'the New Testament evidence for [weekly communion] is quite as strong, to say the least, as for the observance of the first day of the week at all'.[99] Not everyone was to agree, however, and a letter from one correspondent was probably more representative of where the denomination stood and was to continue to stand into the twentieth century. Weekly communion, he argued, became a 'mere formalism'. He himself celebrated the Lord's Supper once a month, preceded by a prayer meeting for preparation on the Friday or Saturday evening:

> To do much more might lead to Sacramentalism, to do much less is to neglect a means of grace . . .

A valuable insight into Baptist practice at the time was provided by the same correspondent:

> The ordinance is tacked to the close of a public service and if in the morning hurried over, or if in the evening languidly attended to at the close of an exhausting day's labour.[100]

That, rather than a universal turning to a weekly celebration, was to become more characteristic of Baptist churches and was to remain so until they were caught up in the movement for liturgical renewal in the 1950s and 1960s when many churches moved from the practice of communion services 'tacked' to the 'main' service and, instead, brought word and sacrament into one integral act of worship. Weekly communion, however, was, and has remained, the practice of the minority. The fears of falling into the 'sacramentalism' of others may have decreased, but the argument that too frequent celebration would lead to familiarity and formalism would probably still carry weight amongst many Baptists. Surprisingly, the unfailing practice of their most outstanding preacher failed to influence Baptist practice. C. H. Spurgeon regarded no Sunday as complete without a celebration of the ordinance, a practice which he observed even when on holiday in his beloved Mentone. A guest at his home there in 1882 recorded:

> In the afternoon, in accordance with Mr. Spurgeon's regular practice when away from home, we observed the ordinance of the Lord's Supper in his sitting room. Five ministers and six other believers completed the assembly . . .[101]

D) THE USE OF UNFERMENTED WINE IN THE LORD'S SUPPER

Throughout the nineteenth century Baptists, in common with other Nonconformist churches, gradually abandoned the use of fermented wine in the Lord's Supper in favour of unfermented. The reasons for the change were social and ethical rather than theological, though some attempt at theological justification was made as an afterthought. The change took place only slowly in the years between 1820 and 1880, but thereafter gathered rapid momentum so that the majority of Baptist churches in London by the end of the century were using unfermented wine.[102] In view of the widespread activity of the temperance movement amongst Baptists in other parts of the country throughout the period under scrutiny, it is probable that London was not untypical.

The temperance movement, with its emphasis on total abstinence, began as a secular movement in the 1820s. Its earliest advocates included many who were renowned for their atheism as well as their abstinence,[103] men with no religious axe to grind who acted out of high moral principle. The transformation of social structures in Victorian times, brought about by urban expansion, rapid industrialisation, with attendant poverty and squalid housing in the growing cities, provided an environment in which alcohol acted as a 'witches' brew', creating grave social problems, especially for those already disadvantaged by the inequalities of nineteenth-century society. It was a cause that drew together secularists as well as Christians from a variety of denominations. By the 1870s, however, the temperance movement was almost exclusively Christian, drawing its fervour and manpower from the churches.[104]

Despite the massive commitment of the churches, the temperance movement was essentially a secular crusade. Brian Harrison argues that it acted as a secularising agent in the thinking of the churches. Teetotalism held before people the prospect of self-improvement, the possibility of a better and healthier life, an emphasis congenial to the Victorian enthusiasm for self-sufficiency, but one that sat ill at ease with the Protestant emphasis upon justification by faith. The great Congregationalist minister, R. W. Dale, complained that it was a doctrine mentioned only rarely in sermons.[105] Further, the teetotal movement provided a subtle challenge to the position of the holy scriptures as the sole guide to belief and behaviour in the life of the church and the Christian individual. Christians had to perform dexterous feats of wordmanship to prove that biblical allusions to wine were, invariably, or at least usually, meant to refer to unfermented wine, pure grape juice unadulterated by the devil's work of fermentation. These verbal exercises demanded not only a working knowledge of Hebrew and Greek, but also a more than casual acquaintance with the scientific principles of fermentation. Alternatively, there were those who accepted that when the scripture referred to wine it meant what people from time immemorial had usually meant by the word wine, but who argued that the changed social conditions of the nineteenth century furnished adequate reasons for refusing to drink it under any circumstances and for substituting fruit juice where scripture decreed wine, as in the Lord's Supper.[106]

The temperance movement amongst Christians also established the priority of 'practical' religion over the theoretical and doctrinal.[107] The accuracy of Harrison's description of the secularising tendencies of the temperance movement is confirmed by the example of one of the outstanding leaders of teetotalism amongst Baptists, John Clifford. Clifford, in his pursuit of a society peopled by the good, the upright and the equal, fired as it was by the enthusiasms of prophetic religion and socialist politics, quickly identified drink as one of the enemies of social harmony. It was an enemy close at hand, one which he was able to confront eyeball to eyeball, and thus a worthy adversary for Clifford's crusading passion. Further, Clifford was influenced by the new critical and historical approach to biblical exegesis and therefore more amenable to making the necessary allowances when translating the norms operative in the societies portrayed in the Bible into the changed circumstances of the nineteenth century. Lastly, he was a man who found the practical aspects of religious faith more congenial than the rigours of doctrinal debate and theological reflection.

Although Clifford's advocacy of the temperance movement did much to hasten Baptists along that road in the last two decades of the nineteenth century, before that their progress had been slow and, in a number of instances, clearly reluctant. The *Freeman* was prepared to carry regular advertisements for Kilnahan's Irish whisky from its earliest days into the 1870s. With the increase of enthusiasm for the teetotal movement amongst an increasing number of Baptists, it tacked its sails to the prevailing wind, accepting advertisements now embellished with testimonials to Kilnahan's medicinal qualities before finally waving goodbye to that longstanding source of revenue. As late as 1880, the London Baptist Association debated whether it should supply intoxicating beverages at the annual dinner for ministerial and lay delegates at the following spring assembly of the Baptist Union, as had been its custom. It was proposed that, were London Baptists to do so, it should be from a separate fund. One non-teetotaller saw this as an infringement of the delegates' liberties, whilst Vincent Tymms (1842-1921), a leading minister who was later to be principal of Rawdon College, claimed that he had been advised by his doctor that it would be unwise for him to become a teetotaller and he, too, argued that to deny the delegates their customary beverages would be an infringement of liberty. It was finally agreed that the association should make its annual grant to the dinner but that the supply of intoxicating liquor should be left to private arrangements.[108] The association doubtless resisted the temptation to charge 'corkage'.

Baptists figured amongst the teetotallers of the early days and, from the outset, turned their newfound zeal to the Lord's table. They were particuarly vocal in the north of England. In 1832 Roger Livesey, a Baptist, together with six others, their trades described as cheesemonger, carder, clogger, rollermaker, plasterer, shoemaker and tailor,[109] signed a pledge not to drink alcoholic liquor for the experimental period of one year. Known as the 'Preston Seven', their example of pledge-signing was to be enthusiastically taken up in the heyday of the temperance movement later in the century. In 1835, Francis Beardsall, minister of Oak Street General Baptist church in Manchester, was able to persuade his congregation to change from fermented wine to unfermented in the Lord's Supper. In 1836, the *General Baptist Repository* carried a criticism of the practice from J. Jarrom:

> To suppose that wine, in the proper acceptation of the term, is hurtful, and that the use of it [wine in the Lord's supper] is to be laid aside, and something else substituted in its place, is a wild and absurd delusion, bordering on impiety, and in a high degree dangerous in its consequences.[110]

Beardsall rose swiftly to the bait. His replies are an instructive guide to teetotal arguments and attitudes at the time. There was the vehemence with which he championed the teetotal cause. Alcohol faced Christians with nothing less than a mortal enemy:

> Why does not the christian world rise up in arms at once when the trumpet of alarm is sounded, and come up to the help of the Lord against the mighty, and banish strong drink from the abodes of men, and especially from the table of the Lord? Thanks be to God the tide is turning. A great number of Churches have resolved to drink no more of the drunkard's drink at the Lord's table.[111]

The passion with which Beardsall viewed the temperance issue coloured his interpretation of holy scripture, giving some substance to Harrison's claim that the temperance advocates were prone to secular presuppositions in their interpretation of certain scriptural passages relating to wine. Beardsall seemed to be more of the opinion that his teetotalism should determine what he found in scripture than that scripture should be the ground and inspiration of his teetotalism:

> Under existing circumstances, particularly the prevalence of intemperate habits, all must agree that it is most desirable we should be able to prove that intoxicating drink was neither made, used, nor commended by the Saviour; and, for the above reason, if any passage of Scripture on this subject is doubtful, the advantage ought to be given on our side, because it is the safe and harmless side.[112]

Two examples of this mode of exegesis followed, one with remarkable consequences. First, he argued that Jesus would not have used fermented wine at the Passover meal which initiated the eucharist since all leaven was banned from the house during Passover. Secondly, he claimed that in our Lord's use of the analogy of the old and new wineskins, the new wineskins were to be seen as resisting 'the fermenting principle', and thus ensuring that its operation was interrupted.[113] Sobriety, it would seem, required that the kingdom be kept within acceptable bounds!

Not surprisingly, Beardsall's immoderate enthusiasm for the cause of teetotalism attracted the criticism of some of his fellow Baptists. The General Baptist Home Missionary Committee censured him for introducing unfermented wine into the communion service and eventually withdrew its support from his church.[114] Jarrom, who had originally provoked the correspondence in the *Repository*, produced a lengthy discussion on the nature of fermentation in which he claimed that the wine used at the Last Supper was undoubtedly fermented, ending his letter with the plea:

> ... my prayer in reference to myself and all my christian friends is, that we may be directed into the truth, and

preserved in the truth as it is in Jesus; and that we may keep the ordinances as they were delivered to the Apostles and first Christians.[115]

Another opponent of Beardsall concealed himself under the *nom-de-plume* of 'Dissenter', airing the rhetorical question:

> ... does it not rise to the true sublime to discover that article, hitherto so neglected, but so essentially important to the stability of the christian creed, the 'tee-total wine'? Had we heard from any other man that such an invention was necessary to protect the moral character of the Saviour, our minds would have instinctively reverted to the idea of blasphemy.[116]

A letter from John Green summed up what many probably felt when faced with the new enthusiasms of the teetotallers. Rebuking Beardsall for his 'overweening self-satisfaction and a rudeness of remark', he attributed the ill-will generated in the issue to the 'intemperance of temperance men'.[117]

There are signs that the change from fermented to unfermented wine continued gradually to take place. In 1841, a Baptist minister, Jabez Burns, introduced unfermented wine into the communion service in his own chapel. He and his son, Dawson Burns, were to be leading advocates of the temperance movement, the latter describing his father as 'the highest and brightest name on the roll of Temperance pioneers and champions'.[118] In 1843, the West Midland Association lent its weight to the cause of total abstinence.[119] The strict Baptists seem to have taken steps towards the use of unfermented wine, judging from a letter of complaint in the *Primitive Church Magazine* in 1847. The writer argued that the New Testament taught that plain bread should be used in the Lord's Supper and wine, possibly mixed with water in order to dilute it, but that certainly 'raisin water' which was without any scriptural justification should never be used.[120] A correspondent two issues later complained at the lack of forbearance shown in this insistence on fermented wine and revealed the writer's opposition to the 'intoxicating cup' over a period of twenty-five years.[121] The increasing use of unfermented wine amongst Nonconformists is further evidenced by the establishment in 1862 of a company to produce it for use by churches in their communion services. The Baptist Total Abstinence movement was founded in 1874 and from then the teetotal movement gathered increasing momentum in the denomination until it became, as with other Nonconformists, the predominant position amongst Baptists. In 1887 and 1888 respectively, Dawson Burns and John Clifford rose to a spirited defence of the use of unfermented wine at the Lord's Supper. The latter's contribution is particularly useful in our understanding of Baptist attitudes in view of the correspondence that it provoked in the pages of the *Freeman*.

Dawson Burns' contribution to the subject came in a lecture on communion wine which he delivered and published in 1887. He recorded that the earliest temperance pledges carried exception clauses recognizing the right of the signatory to continue to use alcohol 'as a medical prescription, or in a religious ordinance'.[122] The exception invited the taunt that what was not good enough for a gentleman's table was good enough for the Lord's table, stinging Dawson's father, Jabez, into introducing unfermented wine at the Lord's table in his own chapel. Burns then went on to examine objections to the use of unfermented wine:

> i) That the Lord's Supper should be celebrated with wine: unfermented juice was not and ought not to be used. Against this, Burns argued in the first place that the word wine did not appear in the Supper narratives, only 'the fruit of the vine' or the 'cup' and, in the second place that, in the biblical record, the word wine often referred to the grape in its unfermented state.[123]

> ii) That Jesus used fermented wine and therefore we should do the same. Burns' response was to argue that we do not, in fact, literally do what Jesus did, otherwise unleavened bread would be used in communion. Further, the purpose in using unleavened bread was that nothing fermented or subject to the action of yeast should be used in the passover. The fact that the Jews, including those of Jesus' time, continued to do so was a departure from tradition. Burns tried to cover his tracks at every point. Either the wine used at the Last Supper was unfermented or, if fermented, its use was a departure from tradition.

He then went on to advance his own reasons in support of unfermented wine:

> a) Bread and wine were to be taken in 'their most natural and innocent form'.[124] Flour, subjected to the fermenting process of yeast, remained essentially the same. Grapes, however, became something different, having acquired 'the most terrible power'.[125]

> b) The value of the Lord's Supper lay in its meaning, in what was signified by the emblems, but they themselves ought to coincide with what they represented, 'the things that are to represent the highest truths ought to be themselves of the truest order'.[126] In the case of bread, there was a beautiful 'analogy between bread as the outward form and that inward sustenance that comes to the soul through Jesus Christ'. Wine, however, had 'changed its nature in passing through a chemical process'; therefore, would 'anyone say that it [was] a fitting symbol of the pure Blood of Jesus Christ?'[127]

> c) 'Of all the places in the world, the safest place for any human soul ought to be the Lord's Table; but if you have intoxicating wine there it is not the safest place - it is a place of possibly great temptation'.[128]

The argument that the wine represented a constant source of temptation to drunkards was a familiar one amongst temperance advocates.

d) 'The Lord's table ought to be in most perfect harmony with the whole design of the Temperance movement'.[129] It should share its aims and, by using unfermented wine, further them.

e) The church should not patronise the liquor trade at a time when others were turning away from it.[130]

Burns' arguments illustrate how both scriptural exegesis and church practice were subject to the pressures of a secular issue. He had argued that the example of Jesus was to be modified in the light of changing social conditions and, further, that justification could be found for doing so by appealing to an earlier Jewish tradition from which our Lord himself had departed, if, in fact, the wine at the Last Supper was fermented. Whatever the passionate protestations of unswerving loyalty to the word of holy scripture amongst Evangelical temperance advocates, it was their unblushing contention that what was done at the Lord's table should serve the needs of the temperance movement, rather than those of exegesis and theology. They convey the impression that, if the scriptures did not wholeheartedly support the temperance case, they should have done and, had they been written in the changed social conditions of the nineteenth century, they would have done. Burns' strongest arguments were that the plight of drunkards should be recognized and that the emblems should comply as closely as possible with what they represented. His argument that wine was unacceptable because it had undergone chemical change was less persuasive than a simple rejection on the grounds of social abuse. Arguing the wickedness of wine *per se* only opened the door to convoluted scriptural exegesis that sought to establish that scriptural wine was not wine.

John Clifford's defence of unfermented communion wine came in an address given at the Band of Hope annual meeting in Exeter Hall on 9 May 1888. The Band of Hope had been founded in Leeds in 1847 as a movement to advocate teetotalism amongst the young. Its chief instrument in the achievement of this end was the pledge not to drink alcoholic liquor, a promise of lifelong abstinence that children were urged to make as early as possible. Harrison argues that the movement represented a change in direction, from the reformation of adult drunkards to temperance education of the young, from an ideal committed to the renewal and reformation of the whole of society to the withdrawal of a teetotal élite concerned to protect its children from the temptations that abounded in the world.[131] For the Nonconformist churches, Baptists amongst them, it was part of a growing enchantment with the young, evidenced also in the Sunday School movement and to be nurtured by numerous other movements for young people that were to emerge in the early years of the twentieth century.

This commitment to the young was to be yet one more influence on the Lord's Supper, shaping it in harmony with the social and ethical preoccupations of Victorian Nonconformity. In his address to his young listeners, Clifford added nothing to what Burns had already written in his lecture the previous year, apart from his claim that it was incongruous to face young people with fermented wine at their first communion when successful efforts had already been made to persuade them to sign the pledge. Apart from that, he repeated the argument that unfermented wine had been used at the Last Supper, based on the injunction forbidding leaven in the house at Passover, and Burns' argument that wine, which Clifford described as a 'curse', was an inappropriate symbol for our Lord's blood. The address, reported in the *Freeman*, gave rise to a correspondence that reveals that Baptists were far from agreed on the matter of unfermented wine, even at this stage of the century. One correspondent did nothing to conceal the depth of his feelings on the temperance movement:

> ... the indiscriminating crusade known as teetotalism I hold to be itself the 'accursed thing' ... and not the God-given wine which it would banish.[132]

The correspondence covered four main areas: the question of young people and the influence that fermented communion wine might have upon them, the schisms that the issue had caused in a number of churches, the resort to the 'two-cup' solution, and the question of scriptural authority and interpretation. Baptists shared the enthusiasm of other Nonconformists for the cause of the young and were prepared to gear their practice and church organizations to their needs. The wisdom of this policy has only come to be questioned in the late 1970s and 80s. One of its victims was the Lord's Supper. Given the commitment of many Nonconformists to a policy of educating the young in temperance principles, especially through the Band of Hope, the Lord's Supper was felt to cut across that education by providing them with their first introduction to alcoholic liquor. 'Why should we be obliged,' asked one correspondent, 'to take at the Lord's Supper what we believe and teach our children to be a great evil?'[133] Another argued that unfermented wine should be used to protect children trained in teetotal principles from the danger of alcoholic liquor.[134] One correspondent suggested that, in some churches, there was a clash between young people trained in teetotal principles and those who held authority in the church and stood by the tradition of fermented wine. The new young converts were refusing to take communion because they could not conscientiously partake of 'the intoxicating wine used at Communion'. Those who continued to pass the cup undrunk were watched and 'threatened with expulsion'.[135] The incident reveals an educational emphasis that prized a worthy commitment to a secular cause above the religious duty and privilege of sharing in communion. It also suggests that the continuing use of fermented communion wine was dependent upon innate Baptist conservatism and could hope to survive only until the time when unfermented wine represented the new orthodoxy.

Many of the correspondents recorded the schismatic effect that the issue had upon some Baptist churches. One correspondent recalled that it had already been having its effect in churches of an earlier generation, recalling that the church of which his father was minister had been 'rent by the question of unfermented wine at the Lord's Supper'. The experience had left him convinced that the issue was not of central importance to the understanding of the sacrament:

> Members do not gather at the Lord's Table for the purpose of drinking wine, but to 'show forth Christ's death'. It is very questionable if any harm would follow celebrating this ordinance with ordinary wine; but there is no question that immense harm has followed the making a schism in the Christian church.[136]

Another correspondent suggested that the issue had been introduced in churches 'by one or two of the most unspiritual and useless members',[137] another that it had given rise to 'unseemly squabbling',[138] causing some people to stay away from the Lord's Supper. If some stayed away because of their aversion to controversy, others did so because their conscience could not be reconciled to the use of unfermented or fermented wine, depending upon which side of the teetotal divide they stood. A correspondent, describing himself as 'Country Deacon', cautioned that care should be taken when the issue was raised, lest churches should find themselves torn by division:

> In a church I know some stay away from the Lord's Table because alcoholic wine was used, in another some stay away because non-alcoholic wine has been introduced.[139]

Even within the councils of the Metropolitan Tabernacle there seem to have been differences of opinion, some deacons favouring the temperance cause and others not. Spurgeon himself went some way to meet the enthusiasm of his sons on the issue but was still very much inclined 'to show indulgence' to non-teetotallers.[140]

Some churches endeavoured to avoid controversy by introducing the 'two-cup' solution. One correspondent suggested this had had unhappy results.[141] An example of this practice is recorded in the history of the Claremont Baptist Church in Bolton. In the 1870s a number of members expressed the desire to have unfermented wine at the Lord's Supper. It was decided that they should sit together in one part of the church where a chalice containing such wine would be circulated amongst them.[142] Other churches followed a similar practice.[143]

The last matter that arises out of this sequence of letters is that of biblical authority and an allied question of traditional usage. There were those who felt that the teetotallers' insistence on unfermented wine in the Lord's Supper represented an assault on a scriptural and historic usage.

One correspondent, having rebutted the argument that the wine used in scriptural times was unfermented, pleaded with his fellow Baptists that they should stand by the faith once delivered to the saints and not be carried about by strange and diverse doctrines.[144] Another recognized the threat that fermented communion wine might present to a few communicants who at some time had fallen prey to the evils of drunkenness. These few were to forego the sacrament until the lordship of Christ in their lives was such that they could put the lust for drink beneath their feet. The fact that some faced this problem, however, provided no reason 'why the Lord's Supper should be tampered with'.[145] The argument that the narratives of the Last Supper spoke of 'fruit of the vine', rather than wine, were redeployed.[146] Another, in his teetotal enthusiasm, addressed the rhetorical question that seemed to invite a negative answer:

> Can we believe that Jesus, the world's Redeemer, would sanction that which robs the Church of its converts and packs prisons with convicts . . .?[147]

Again, it was presumed that the social conditions of the nineteenth century rendered it unlikely that Jesus would have used wine, regardless of scriptural evidence to the contrary. Another correspondent was even more daring, arguing that the contemporary church could rise above 'doubtful texts and bygone usages'.[148] He was in no doubt as to the superiority of the Victorian church, revealing a refreshing candour in his estimation of its qualities, together with a rare unwillingness to romanticize the virtues of the New Testament church. The contemporary church was:

> . . . in a better position to realize the fulness of the law of liberty than were the early churches, and I believe that our churches are many of them doing better work and entering more fully into the Spirit of Christ than were those churches just redeemed out of heathenism.[149]

Clearly, the defenders of fermented communion wine saw themselves as conservatives, safeguarding the biblical testimony and the usages of the church throughout the centuries. The ambivalence of the teetotallers' attitude towards the scriptural witness to the use of wine put them in an extraordinarily vulnerable position for people who belonged to a denomination whose belief in the inspiration and authority of holy scripture was paramount. The dilemma was to be resolved by the establishment of a new orthodoxy based upon accepted practice rather than scriptural principles. The orthodoxy of unfermented communion wine took a firm hold on all the Nonconformist churches and not least the Baptists. The abiding strength of that hold in the latter part of the twentieth century would quickly become apparent to anyone who had the temerity to propose to the average Baptist congregation that it might return to the scriptural practice of celebrating the Lord's Supper with wine.

E) THE LORD'S SUPPER AND CHURCH DISCIPLINE

In common with other Christians, Baptists made the Lord's table the chief agent of discipline within the church. Their separatist theology of the church inevitably led to a concern for the moral and spiritual rectitude of their members. The Church Meeting regularly gave itself to examinations of its more recalcitrant members, those whose guilt was established being excluded from receiving communion for specified periods of time. This practice of scrutinising the lives of church members continued into the nineteenth century. At the Queen's Road Church in Coventry, discipline was administered against those believed to be guilty of inconsistency in their Christian profession. The charges that appeared most often were in connection with excessive drinking of alcoholic beverages and sexual misdemeanours, usually of the premarital variety. The penalty for proven misconduct was exclusion from the Lord's table for a period of six months, in some cases of complete excommunication.[150] The charge of indulging in 'excess of liquor' was also brought against certain members of the church in Tetley Street, Bradford. Other misdemeanours included visiting the theatre, a pursuit frowned upon by nineteenth-century Baptists and one which was partly responsible for Spurgeon's public dissociation from his erstwhile friend, Dr Joseph Parker, the minister of the City Temple in London. The Tetley Street church saw its disciplinary procedures as a means of guarding the good name of the church and leading erring members to penitence. The offenders were given the right of reply, being summoned before the Church Meeting that was to examine the charges brought against them.[151] Some churches recognized the pain that was involved in disciplinary procedures against fellow members. At the church in Hinckley, prior to 1839, the celebration of the Lord's Supper was suspended whilst any member was under investigation.[152]

A common reason for disciplinary proceedings was the declared bankruptcy of a church member. This reflected various features of Victorian society. It was a time of capital expansion and speculative commercial enterprise with all the high financial risk involved. It was also a time that looked unkindly upon the Mr Micawbers who stretched themselves beyond their financial resources and paid the penalty in collapsed businesses and dishonoured debts. As late as 1880 the church at Sparkbrook in Birmingham ruled that members who had become insolvent were to be the subject of disciplinary investigation by the deacons of the church.[155] At the Queen's Road Church culpable bankruptcy was concealed under the blanket of 'Immorality'.[156] The question of the churches' attitude to bankrupts was the subject of an exchange in the *Freeman* in 1879. A letter asked what the attitude of the church was to be to members who had become insolvent 'in consequence of the depression in trade'. Were they to be asked to refrain from attendance at the Lord's table? When could an insolvent be judged to be 'unfortunate' and when dishonest?[157] A week later the questioner was answered with advice that the ministers and deacons should investigate the matter and, if it was discovered that the insolvency had been caused by 'reckless trading or dishonest practices', then the member should be suspended. If, on the other hand, the misfortune had come about by the breaking of banks or other causes beyond his control, then he was to be treated with Christian sympathy.[158] The correspondence was added to a week later by someone, clearly of more radical political sympathies, who questioned the attitude of the church to those whose sharp practices resulted not in bankruptcy but in the acquisition of a fortune.[159] In one famous case, at least, Baptists certainly could not be accused of having double standards. One of their most eminent and generous sons, Sir Samuel Morton Peto, was the victim of the financial collapse of 1866-1867. He had given much of his energies and his fortune to Baptist projects, including the Bloomsbury Chapel which he had built at his own expense. After his bankruptcy, he was able to rebuild his assets but he was never again able to occupy quite the same place amongst Baptists because of their attitude to bankrupts, whether or not they were the innocent victims of circumstance.[160]

As the century wore on there was one failure of Christian duty for which exclusion from the Lord's table was no effective punishment, and this was infrequent attendance at the Lord's Supper. As early as 1836 the General Baptist, Joseph Jarrom, had warned his fellow Baptists against irregular attendance at the sacrament. Absence brought the church into disrepute, dismayed fellow Christians and proved a discouragement to the minister. Those who absented themselves were to be admonished:

> While habitually neglecting the ordinance, their membership is only nominal; and while it answers no valuable end, it is productive of numerous evils.[161]

Some churches introduced a ticket system. Members were allocated a book of tickets, one for each communion service throughout the year. The tickets, duly marked with each member's number, were gathered in during the service and a register marked. This enabled the officers of the church to keep a reliable record of members' attendance. In the Avenue Church, in Southend, the ticket system was introduced in 1878. Whatever its merits as a device for recording attendance, at Southend it apparently failed to act as a spur to regular attendance. In January 1884, the pastor and deacons had to address themselves to the problems caused by the rate of absence from the Lord's Supper and resolved that members guilty of unexplained absence for a period of six months were to be suspended from church membership, the only sanction that remained once the table itself had become a cause rather than an instrument of discipline.[162] In 1878 the members of Ebenezer Church in Ewyas Harold agreed that any member absent from communion without excuse for a period of three months was to be suspended from membership.[163] The ticket system was introduced in Hinckley in 1834. By 1873, however, the church came to the decision that any member absenting himself or herself from the Lord's Supper after a given date and without satisfactory reason would be considered no longer a member.[164] The decision suggests a deteriorating situation calling for drastic remedies. Poor attendance at the Lord's Supper, as well as the weekly prayer meeting, was a constant problem to Ernest Edginton during his ministry at Ashley Baptist Church in New Milton during the period 1892-1909.[165]

Isolated examples culled from the stories of individual Baptist churches such as these lend support to Horton Davies' wider claim that attendance at the Lord's Supper in Nonconformist churches, including Baptist, was markedly poor in the early years of the nineteenth century. Presumably the tendency in this direction was evident in the closing years of the century as well.[166] It must have been sufficiently widespread for the *Freeman* to focus the attention of one of its leading articles upon it in 1886. Entitled 'Attendance at Communion',[167] it distanced itself as far as possible from Catholic eucharistic beliefs and practices and expressed regret that such a simple and scriptural interpretation of the rite as that held by Baptists did not seem to possess the motive power to draw them to the table. On the one hand,

> Perhaps, among denominations that observe the Lord's Supper, not one is to be found whose views of the ordinance are more simple, more the antipodes of sacramentalism and superstition, than our own.[168]

On the other, the writer recognized that those very views had sometimes led to infrequent attendance at communion. This resulted in a two-fold wrong:

> It will be felt a wrong is done to ourselves, as well as a slight offence to our Heavenly Father, if we suffer lax attendance and permit it to continue.

The article concluded:

> We are no mystics. Ours is the religion of the New Testament interpreted, under God, by common-sense, but we are sure there will be less spiritual loss and more spiritual gain, better satisfaction and less self-recrimination, if fidelity to Christ's appointment be maintained in conscientious obedience.

The very blandness of the author's description of the Lord's Supper, his regret at the 'slight offence' caused to the Heavenly Father, and his appeal to 'common-sense' rather than theological principle, went far to provide some explanation of the problem he had himself raised. Decline in attendance at the Lord's Supper marked a decline in the exercise of discipline within the church. Recorders of local history such as the authors of the history of Zion English Baptist Church in Pentre, writing in 1965, were to express astonishment at the discipline of earlier days.[169]

The Lord's table had been a natural and universally recognized means of reinforcing the standards by which the church might expect its members to live. Exclusion from that table had traditionally been, amongst all Christians, the way in which the church expressed its displeasure at those who blatantly violated those standards. With changing attitudes to the Lord's Supper itself, however, suspension from communion proved an increasingly ineffective means of discipline. Exclusion from the table simply compounded the growing problem of infrequent attendance at the Lord's Supper. The remedy for such a lapse had to be enforced attendance, not excommunication. Persistent absence left the church with no other sanction apart from exclusion from membership.

The reason for the growing phenomenon of infrequent attendance, given the theological story of the nineteenth century, is not difficult to find. Each communion dispute took its own toll. The combination of population mobility and the practice of a closed table meant that some Baptists of 'open' persuasion either had to seek the spiritual succour of the Lord's Supper at the hands of other denominations or learn to live without it. Were they to choose the second alternative, time and the non-sacramentalist legacy of the radical Reformation would have led them to the conclusion that the sacrament was essential neither to a living faith nor to the survival of Christian commitment. Further, the lack of charity with which the issue was sometimes debated would have led some to weary of the sacrament in the very act of wearying of the polemics associated with it. Close on the heels of the earliest communion controversy came the Catholic revival and the widespread tendency amongst some Baptists to counteract it by presenting a less than Zwinglian alternative to the high sacramentalism of the Tractarians, the Ritualists and the Roman Catholics. Whatever claims may have been made for the Baptist alternative to sacramentalism, it clearly did not motivate men and women to come eagerly and with expectancy to the table. It was the pulpit that became their chief source of succour and words that fired their deepest imaginings. The further controversy over the use of unfermented wine in the sacrament weakened even further its importance for Baptists. The solemn division of the congregation into those who were to drink from the fermented cup and those from the unfermented cup, the conscientious objections of those who, given no option, refused to drink from a fermented cup, preferring to forego communion, or those of an opposite persuasion who did the same when faced with an unfermented cup, did nothing to enhance the role of the Supper in the spiritual nurture of believers. Passion was used in debating the issues of teetotalism, not in investing with meaning the table over which the debate took place. To the communion controversies themselves must be added the changing attitudes of later Victorians to ecclesial authority. It was inevitable that a people who were so taught to value their independence and the judgment of the individual would no longer willingly continue to appear before ministers, deacons or Church

ORDER AND DISCIPLINE AT THE LORD'S TABLE

Meetings to answer for the moral failings with which others charged them. The changes in society occasioned a growing reluctance on the part of the church to act as prosecution, judge and jury in the private affairs of their fellow members.

NOTES

1 See E. A. Payne, 'The Ministry in Historical Perspective', **Baptist Quarterly** 17, No.6, 1958, p.264.
2 E. P. Winter, 'Who May Administer the Lord's Supper?' **Baptist Quarterly** 16, No.3, 1955, pp.129f.
3 F. M. W. Harrison, 'The Life and Thought of the Baptists of Nottinghamshire (1770-1914)', Nottingham M.Phil. Dissertation, 1972, pp.334-9.
4 Daniel Turner, **Compendium of Social Religion**, 1758, pp.49f, cited by E. A. Payne, **The Fellowship of Believers**, 1944, p.48.
5 John Gill, **Body of Practical Divinity**, 1770, cited by Payne, **op.cit.** pp.48ff.
6 **Baptist Magazine** (hereafter **BM**), 30, 1838, p.100.
7 J. W. Grant, **Free Churchmanship in England 1870-1914**, n.d., pp.80f.
8 BM 7, 1815, pp.454f.
9 ibid. p.455.
10 ibid.
11 'The Minutes of the Baptist Board', **Transactions of the Baptist Historical Society** 6, 1918-19, p.101.
12 ibid. p.102.
13 ibid. pp.103f.
14 ibid. p.105.
15 BM, vol.20 (vol.III 3rd series), 1828, p.63 (rest of correspondence, pp.150-2, 250-2, 492-5, 545-7).
16 ibid. p.151.
17 ibid. p.151.
18 ibid. p.152.
19 ibid. p.251.
20 ibid. p.252.
21 ibid. p.493.
22 ibid. 7, p.269.
23 ibid. pp.269f.
24 ibid. p.364.
25 ibid. p.366.
26 ibid. p.415.
27 ibid. p.416.
28 See above p.123.
29 ibid. 30, 1838, p.102.
30 ibid.
31 ibid. p.147.
32 ibid. p.148.
33 ibid.
34 ibid.
35 **Baptist Reporter** 1848, p.107.
36 ibid. p.68.
37 BM 30, 1838, p.147.
38 Olinthus Gregory, ed., **The Works of Robert Hall AM**, Vol.1, 1858, Robert Hall to Revd P. J. Saffery of Salisbury, 16 January 1826.
39 A. H. MacLeod, 'The Life and Teaching of Robert Hall (1764-1831)', Durham M. Litt. Dissertation, 1957, p.379.
40 see above p.126.
41 see above p.127.
42 see above p.122.
43 see above p.124.
44 The diary of George Wallis is now kept in the Fuller Baptist Church in Kettering.
45 The entry for 12 November in Wallis' diary gives a detailed account of Hall's ordination.
46 Thomas J. Budge, **Melbourne Baptists**, 1951, p.29.
47 Cited by S. C. Osborne, **The First Two Hundred Years**, Hinckley 1966, pp.37f.
48 **General Baptist Repository**, vol.3, New Series 1836, p.100.
49 ibid.
50 **General Baptist Repository**, vol.3, 1836, p.100.
51 **General Baptist Repository** 14, 1852, p.225. (NB **Repository** erroneously prints this as p.235).
52 ibid., p.292.
53 D. B. Murray, 'The Scotch Baptist Tradition in Great Britain', **Baptist Quarterly** 33, No.4, 1989, 186-198.
54 ibid. p.190.
55 ibid. p.196.
56 **Primitive Church Magazine** vol.3, March 1846, p.83.
57 ibid. April 1846, p.130.
58 ibid. vol.4, February 1847, p.47; see also vol.2, November 1845, p.390.
59 ibid. vol.2, November 1845, p.390.
60 ibid. vol.3, September 1846, p.319f.
61 ibid. p.321.
62 see above p.122.
63 BM vol.7, 1815, p.194.
64 ibid. 1815, pp.460f.

65 Cited by A. C. Underwood, **A History of the English Baptists**, 1947, p.170.
66 **General Baptist Repository**, vol.5, 1838, p.257..
67 ibid. p.412.
68 ibid. p.412f.
69 ibid. vol.1, New Series, 1839, p.13.
70 ibid.
71 **Freeman** 29 May 1868, p.426.
72 ibid. 5 June 1868, p.453.
73 Hinton's term of office ended in 1866.
74 **Freeman**, 5 June 1868, p.453.
75 **BM** 30, 1838, p.356.
76 **General Baptist Repository** 1833, pp.361f.
77 ibid. pp.363f.
78 ibid. 1834, pp.81-3.
79 ibid. p.82.
80 ibid. p.83.
81 **General Baptist Magazine**, 1863, p.285.
82 D. B. Murray, 'Baptists in Scotland before 1869', **Baptist Quarterly**, 23, No.6, 1970, pp.255ff.
83 ibid. p.263.
84 Published Edinburgh 1805.
85 ibid. p.299.
86 ibid. pp.299f.
87 ibid. pp.300f.
88 1824.
89 ibid. p.50.
90 ibid. p.51.
91 ibid.
92 ibid. p.53.
93 ibid. p.58.
94 ibid. p.60.
95 **Northamptonshire Circular Letter** 1845, p.10.
96 Western Association, Circular Letter... at 24th Annual Meeting... 1847, Reported in **Baptist Magazine** 39, 1847, p.774.
97 ibid. 40, 1848, p.43.
98 **Freeman** 19 October 1866, p.384.
99 ibid. 26 October 1866, p.401.
100 ibid. 2 November 1866, p.427.
101 ibid. 24 November 1882, p.771.
102 W. Charles Johnson, **Encounter in London 1865-1965**, 1965, p.54.
103 Brian Harrison, **Drink and the Victorians**, 1971, p.184.
104 ibid.
105 ibid. p.185.
106 ibid. p.186.
107 ibid. p.188.
108 **Freeman** 30 January 1880, p.51.
109 Harrison, **op.cit.** p.125.
110 **General Baptist Repository** vol.3, New Series, 1836, p.368.
111 ibid. vol.4, New Series, 1837, p.57.
112 ibid. vol.3, New Series, 1836, p.416.
113 ibid. p.418.
114 ibid. p.417.
115 ibid. vol.4, New Series, 1837, pp.95f.
116 ibid. p.97.
117 ibid. p.132.
118 Dawson Burns, 'Baptists and the Temperance Reform' in **The English Baptists**, ed. John Clifford, 1881, p.167.
119 Owen J. M. Gwynne, ed., **A Memorial of the 250th Anniversary of the West Midland Association 1655-1905**, Birmingham 1905, p.115.
120 **Primitive Church Magazine** vol.4, New Series, 1847, p.336.
121 ibid. p.409.
122 Dawson Burns, **Communion Wine**, 1887, p.5.
123 ibid. pp.7ff.
124 ibid. p.13.
125 ibid. p.14.
126 ibid. p.15.
127 ibid.
128 ibid. p.17.
129 ibid. p.18.
130 ibid. p.19.
131 Harrison, **op.cit.** pp.191-4.
132 **Freeman** 15 June 1888, p.404.
133 ibid. p.405.
134 ibid. 24 August 1888, p.556.
135 ibid. 25 May 1888, p.350.
136 ibid. 20 July 1888, p.476.
137 ibid. 10 August 1888, p.523.
138 ibid. 1 June 1888, p.373.
139 ibid. 17 August 1888, p.541.
140 Burns, **op.cit.** p.22.
141 **Freeman** 10 August 1888, p.523.
142 Anon., **Claremont Baptist Church (Bolton) 1869-1969**, Bolton 1969, p.6.
143 See A. M. Baines, **History of Dublin Street Baptist Church, Edinburgh (1858-1958)**, Edinburgh n.d, p.16.
144 **Freeman** 20 July 1888, p.476.
145 ibid. 13 July 1888, p.461.
146 ibid. 3 August 1888, p.509.
147 ibid. 24 August 1888, p.556.
148 ibid. 10 August 1888, p.523.
149 ibid.
150 C. Binfield, **Pastors and People: The Biography of a Baptist Church, Queen's Road, Coventry**, Coventry 1984, p.92.
151 Anon., **Tetley Street Baptist Memorial Church, Bradford 1832-1932**, Bradford 1932, pp.12f.
152 S. C. Osborne, **The First Two Hundred Years**, Hinckley 1966, p. 47.
153 Edward H. B. Williams, **Building for the Future: The Story of Baptists in**

Sparkbrook 1879-1979, Birmingham 1979, p.9.
154 Binfield, op.cit. p.92.
155 Freeman 3 January 1879, p.9.
156 ibid. 10 January 1879, p.21.
157 ibid. 17 January 1879, p.33.
158 B. and F. Bowers, 'Bloomsbury Chapel and Mercantile Morality: the case of Sir Morton Peto', Baptist Quarterly 30, No.5, 1984. pp.210ff.
159 J. Jarrom, The Lord's Supper: its institution, uses, and the obligation of Christians to regard it, being a letter to the churches of the New Connexion of General Baptists, Leicester, 1836, p.11.
160 David J. Jeremy et al, A Century of Grace, Southend 1976, p.10.
161 W.Penry Rowland Davies, Ebenezer Baptist Church,Ewyas Harold, Ewyas Harold 1962, pp.13f.
162 Osborne, op.cit. p.61.
163 Alfred C. G. Rendell, Centenary History of Baptist Church, Ashley, New Milton, 1817-1917, New Milton 1917, p.17.
164 Horton Davies, Worship and Theology in England: from Newman to Martineau, 1850-1900, Princeton, N.J., 1962, p.240.
165 Freeman 20 August 1886, p.554.
166 ibid.
167 David C. Hughes and Eric Sandford, Zion 100: A History of Zion English Baptist Church, Pentre, Pentre 1965, p.16.

Chapter Five

The Lord's Supper and Two Baptist Preachers

The second half of the nineteenth century produced two Baptists, both men of outstanding gifts, who in very different ways were to exert great influence on the life of the denomination to which they belonged. The first, Charles Haddon Spurgeon (1834-1892), lived and died within the nineteenth century. He was the last of the great Baptist Calvinists, a life-long and unswerving advocate of that Protestant creed which had so influenced the founders of the Particular Baptist churches, producing such theologically gifted men as John Gill, Andrew Fuller and Robert Hall. In his attitude to the Lord's Supper he was the last notable Baptist to betray the influence of the Calvinism which had influenced Hall at the outset of the century and which had so vividly inspired many of the eighteenth-century hymns, some of which Spurgeon had included in his hymn book. John Clifford (1836-1923) was one of those who led the Baptists from the nineteenth into the twentieth century. A son of the General Baptists, he reflected far more than did Spurgeon the ethos of the times. The changing attitudes to the Bible brought about by the critical literary and historical approach to biblical study, the vigour and optimism with which Victorians lived in and viewed the world, the socialism that waited in the wings of history as radical liberalism acted out its short but crucial role, all engaged his attention, won his approval and shaped his opinions. In his approach to the Lord's Supper he stood with those who were to the radical left of Zwingli.

Thus, in the latter part of the century, the two men represented and were eloquent spokesman of the two most widely divergent strands of Baptist eucharistic theology. What had sat uneasily side by side in the theology of Robert Hall had parted and gone along separate ways. The Calvinism with which Hall expounded the eucharist found an even more eloquent tongue in Spurgeon. The impatience with which he had dismissed baptism as a 'form' or 'ceremony' provided a vocabulary which Clifford was to take up in his description of the Lord's Supper. Charles Haddon Spurgeon was probably the most famous of all the nineteenth-century preachers, drawing five thousand twice every Sunday over a period of more than thirty years to the Metropolitan Tabernacle, a church that had been built to hold the congregations that came to hear him. His printed sermons reached an even greater audience beyond England, thousands of them being dispatched to every part of the globe each week. John Clifford, like Spurgeon, spent the whole of his ministry in one congregation, the church situated from 1877 at Westbourne Park in West London.

The contrast between the two men went further than their Calvinist and Arminian sympathies. Spurgeon received no formal education beyond that of secondary school. Yet he was a man of great intellectual gifts. He could digest the contents of a page almost at a glance and had a powerfully retentive memory for what he read. At his death his library numbered 12,000 volumes and it was said that he could put his hand on any one of them, even in the dark. Clifford spent the early years of his ministry not only engaged in the normal tasks of the pastoral ministry but also studying for various degrees at London University. His biographer, Sir James Marchant, lists his academic achievements between 1861 and 1866, during which time he graduated Bachelor of Arts, Bachelor of Science with honours in logic, moral philosophy, geology and palaeontology, Master of Arts, and Bachelor of Laws with honours in the principles of legislation. The Geological Society made him a Fellow in 1879 and Bates College in the United States of America awarded him a Doctorate of Divinity in 1883.[1] The different academic background of the two men in some small measure accounts for their reactions to the seismic shift in man's understanding of the world in which he lived, the mind with which he perceived it and the sources of religious truth by which he interpreted it. Spurgeon set his face steadfastly against what he believed to be the apostasy of the times, whilst Clifford sympathised with and sought to understand the scientific and theological questions being raised.

Of the two, Spurgeon was undoubtedly the greater preacher, his native gift of language a remarkable example of sturdy, Anglo-Saxon prose in the tradition of Bunyan and Milton. Clifford was an orator, capable of brilliance in public speaking, his words cast in a different mould from those of Spurgeon. E. A. Payne's judgment on the two men cannot be bettered: they were 'the outstanding representatives of two trends within the denomination, the one liberal, the other conservative, yet both claiming and rightly claiming that they were evangelical'.[2] They both gave some thought to the meaning of the Lord's Supper, Spurgeon through his sermons and Clifford in some of the many pamphlets for which he was responsible. Neither treated the subject systematically and at length, but both left enough for us to form a coherent picture of what they believed and the way in which their different theologies influenced them.

A) THE LORD'S SUPPER IN THE PREACHING OF CHARLES HADDON SPURGEON

Spurgeon not only sought to distance himself from the Catholic revival, he held towards the Roman Catholic Church an attitude of uncompromising antipathy. In a rare reference he acknowledged his debt to some of the spiritual writers of the Roman tradition even though he 'loathed their Romanism'.[3] His attitude probably owed more to his Calvinism than to the events of the nineteenth century. It was basic to his view of the gospel. At any time, in any circumstances, he would have been violently opposed to the Roman Catholic perception of the faith.

His main wrath, however, was reserved for the Church of England, his strictures rousing the anger of Tractarians, Broad Churchmen and Evangelicals alike. The turning point in his relationship with Anglican Evangelicals came in 1864, when he preached against baptismal regeneration which, he claimed, was taught in the Prayer Book. He adopted a position from which the Tractarians could claim him to be as much ally as enemy. His claim that the Prayer Book inculcated a doctrine of baptismal regeneration substantiated the claim of the Tractarians, namely that their emphasis was not an alien theology imposed upon Anglicanism but a true interpretation of the Catholic tradition within the Church of England. The Evangelicals read the Prayer Book differently, claiming that its teaching on baptism was in no way at variance with their own emphasis on justification by faith and that a regenerative view of baptism was not typical of Church of England teaching. It was precisely this, however, with which Spurgeon charged the Anglicans, Catholics and Evangelicals alike. Among the reasons for an increase in 'Popery' was that:

> ... you have ... this form of error known as baptismal regeneration, and commonly called Puseyism, which is not only Puseyism, but Church-of-Englandism, because it is in the Prayer Book, as plainly as words can express it - you have this baptismal regeneration preparing stepping stones to make it easy for men to go to Rome.[4]

Spurgeon had made it plain that his argument was not simply with Catholics but with the Church of England as a whole. His sermon was preached on 5 June and it eventually ran to 350,000 copies. It roused the ire of Anglican Evangelicals who, Iain Murray tells us, had only three years earlier contributed to the monies raised for building the Metropolitan Tabernacle to house the new Evangelical Goliath. Three weeks later, Spurgeon returned to the subject in his pulpit:

> I see before me now a Church which tolerates evangelical truth in her communion, but at the same time lovingly embraces Puseyism, and finds room for infidels and for men who deny the authenticity of Scripture. This is no time for us to talk about friendship with so corrupt a corporation. The godly in her midst are deceived if they think to mould her to a more gracious form.[5]

The controversy dragged on for the rest of the year. Its effects went on long afterwards and, as Murray says, in 'the remaining twenty-eight years of his life Spurgeon did not swerve from what he had taught concerning the State Church in 1864'.[6] Indeed, seven years later, in his Christmas Day sermon, he returned to the attack and was again rebuked by the Evangelical Anglicans, to whom he uncompromisingly replied:

> In view of the fearful mischief which your Church is ... doing I do not feel that it is more than the truth to say that she has apostasised from her Protestant position.[7]

His defence of what he believed to be evangelical truth was not to be directed against the Anglicans only. In 1887 the Baptist denomination

THE LORD'S SUPPER AND TWO BAPTIST PREACHERS

agonised through the trauma of the Downgrade Controversy, precipitated by charges made by Spurgeon against ministers, whom he never named, that they were guilty of departing from the truth of the gospel.

For Spurgeon the twin evils of the age were Romanism, which had entered the Church of England under the disguises of the Tractarians and Ritualists, and the new errors of biblical criticism which infected his fellow Protestants, including those of his own denomination. On both counts, he was not only an antagonist born of his own time, he was also a thoroughly consistent Calvinist. Calvinism is anti-Rome and must take its stand on the Bible as God's direct word to man. The same consistent Calvinism that set him so implacably against Romanism also preserved a theology of the Lord's Supper that was not simply a reaction against Catholicism. Where others, no less hostile if less vocal than Spurgeon, emptied their sacraments of any great significance as a result of their anti-Catholicism, he held consistently to the Calvinist roots of his view of the Lord's Supper.

Out of the thousands of sermons that Spurgeon preached, a number of those given at communion services were brought together and published in a single volume, entitled *Till He Come*, two years after his death. Some of these were preached at the Tabernacle, others in Mentone in France, where he had a holiday home which he regularly visited to rest and recuperate. Others on the same subject are found in the collected sermons of Spurgeon, entitled *The Metropolitan Tabernacle Pulpit*.

i) The Case against Catholicism

Spurgeon inevitably contrasted his own beliefs with those of Catholicism. He attacked the Catholic view of the Lord's Supper on the grounds that its ceremonial had usurped simplicity and distanced the sacrament from its beginnings in the upper room in Jerusalem; it had also, in its sacerdotal emphasis, withheld the cup from the laity, an objection that had been voiced in Protestantism since the days of the Reformation; and, lastly, that transubstantiation encouraged a magical view of the sacraments and their efficacy.

In his objection to ceremonial, Spurgeon stood squarely in the tradition of the Puritans, of whom he was an avid student. Apart from theological objections, Puritans were temperamentally opposed to the addition of visual embellishments to what they regarded as a simple and homely rite, instituted when Jesus had gathered around a table with twelve men and broken bread and shared a cup of wine. From that upper room to the grandeur of the Roman Mass was, in the eyes of the Puritans, a long journey in which truth had lost her way. Spurgeon reminded his congregation:

> Observe that Christ does not prescribe anything in the Lord's supper by way of elaborate ceremonial. There is nothing at all resembling the various intricate rules that are laid down for the celebration of the mass in the Church of Rome, or

even for the celebration of the communion in the Church of England.[8]

On another occasion he contrasted the simplicity of the original meal shared by Jesus and his disciples with the liturgy which had developed in the tradition of the church:

> It is marvellous that so plain a symbol should have been so complicated by genuflections, adornments and technical phrases. Can anyone see the slightest resemblance between the Master's sitting down with the twelve, and the mass of the Roman community?[9]

Spurgeon disliked not only the practices associated with Catholic sacramental theology but also its language which, he believed, put a barrier between the plain man, of whom he was ever a champion, and the table to which Christ had so generously invited all who believed:

> They talk of the 'chalice' and 'paten' in the strange ecclesiastical jargon that so-called 'priests' use; but I say 'cup' and 'plate'. They may be of any material and the table of any sort. A 'cloth of fair white linen' is decorous, but not needful. Let there be but a table and bread and wine, and there is all that is required.[10]

This passion for simplicity put Spurgeon on the side of those who viewed the encroachments of Tractarian influence on Baptist church architecture and furnishings with some disdain, if not alarm. It was of a piece, however, with his Puritanism and preaching. His words were never beyond the grasp of ordinary men and women and it was his concern that the Lord's table likewise should in no way be beyond their reach.

In common with the founding fathers of the Reformation, Spurgeon opposed Catholicism on the grounds that it withheld the cup from the laity in the Lord's Supper. He even disliked the term 'laity', suggesting as it did a distinction between the community and its minister. He had himself never been ordained and set little store by such distinctions. In the Lord's Supper both bread and wine were to be given to all the people of God, regardless of status or function:

> It is to be observed by eating and drinking; not by eating alone, as in the Romish church . . . It is most strange that the Papists should have taken away the cup from the 'laity' so-called, since our Lord never said to his disciples concerning the bread, 'Eat ye all of it'; but, as if he foresaw that this error would arise, he did say concerning the cup, as he presented it to his apostles, 'Drink ye all of it'.[11]

To the traditionally Protestant objections against the practice of withholding the cup, Spurgeon added a distinctively Baptist one. The Baptist emphasis upon the church as a fellowship of believers had always been hospitable to the concept of brotherhood. Clifford, a man whose religious and political convictions carried the idea of brotherhood beyond boundaries that Spurgeon would have regarded as indelibly marked out by the nature of the gospel itself, was to make the same plea for brotherhood at the Lord's table. Both men believed that the Catholics had turned the sacrament into an observance that divided men instead of drawing them together. The distinction between people and priest, the language of the liturgy, the numinous associations of the altar, all served to sunder and divide. 'Superstition has produced a sacrament where Jesus intended a fellowship', complained Spurgeon.[12] On another occasion, preaching on the text of Luke 22.14, he argued that even the idea of an altar was divisive:

> As for the table, the very emblem of fellowship in all nations - for what expresses fellowship better than surrounding a table, and eating and drinking together? - this, forsooth, must be put away, and an altar must be erected ...[13]

Baptist experience, of course, should have taught Spurgeon that the Supper was not always an emblem of fellowship to the world at large. The communion controversy earlier in the century had seen the strict Baptists arguing for a fellowship that was marked by its exclusiveness rather than comprehensiveness.

Spurgeon was at his most wounding in his rejection of the Catholic doctrine of transubstantiation, his words deeply insulting to the beliefs of Catholics in the unlikely and unhappy position of being within earshot of him:

> But as for that man-millinery show over yonder, and that 'altar' of theirs, and that bell, and the people bowing down to worship Jack-in-the-box, - for I will give it no better name, - all that is sheer idolatry.[14]

Rarely could the priesthood, the altar and the tabernacle have been more cruelly described, nor the sacramental rite of other Christians so shockingly parodied.

In more temperate tones, on another occasion, he laid the charge of magic against the Catholic interpretation of the divine presence in bread and wine:

> It is a lamentable fact that some have fancied that this simple ordinance of the Lord's Supper has a certain magical, or at least physical power about it, so that, by the mere act of eating and drinking this bread and wine, men can be made partakers of the body and blood of Christ.[15]

Here, then, was a relentless and out-spoken adversary of Catholicism both in its Roman form and as it had found a home in the Church of England. Yet here, also, was a man who argued from a consistent theological position that saved him surrendering, in the heat of battle, truths to which he himself gave consent. The vehemence of his anti-Catholicism did not force him back into a sacramental no-man's land in which the Lord's Supper was a mere shadow. What the Lord's Supper represented was in some way holy ground. The plea for simplicity was not a plea for diminished meaning:

> Here, at the communion table, we are at the centre of truth, and at the well-head of consolation. Now we enter the holy of holies, and come to the most sacred meeting-place between our souls and God.[16]

ii) The Centrality of the Atonement

Spurgeon's understanding of the atonement has to be related to his advocacy of what he believed to be the central truth of the Christian faith, the vicarious, substitutionary and atoning death of Christ. All else flowed from that. In common with all Evangelicals, Spurgeon held to the centrality of the cross. With their emphasis upon conversion over against baptism, the scriptures against tradition and preaching against sacraments, Evangelicals found in the cross the focal point of God's redeeming work on behalf of mankind. Evangelicalism 'stressed "Faith alone" as the Christian's means of salvation; salvation through Christ's atoning sacrifice, not through meritorious works or a mixture of faith and works'.[17] The scenario of salvation as it was portrayed by the Evangelicals placed the cross at the very centre:

> The centre of our holy religion is the Cross. The central thought of the whole of Christianity is Christ, and the great point in Christ's history is his crucifixion. We preach Christ; but more - we preach him crucified.[18]

The cross was at the heart of Christian faith because at the cross man found his relationship with God restored. In the tradition of Anselm and Calvin, within which Spurgeon stood, it was the cross that effected man's reconciliation with God. Justice and holiness on God's part required the payment of the incalculable debt accrued by man because of his sin. Such a debt was beyond the capacity of man to repay, thus God sent his Son, at once God and man, as God able to make an infinite offering, as man to make the offering which man alone must make. At the cross, Christ stood in man's place, bearing the divine punishment for sin and thus making possible man's forgiveness and acceptance. Such a theory of atonement requires a thorough-going doctrine of the incarnation, not because the incarnation in itself is understood as a redemptive act, but because the debt to be paid can be paid to God by God alone. Only an infinite offering can measure up to an infinite offence:

> There was no other good enough
> To pay the price of sin,

He only could unlock the gate
Of heaven, and let us in.

If, according to this theory of the cross, the incarnation itself is not redemptive, neither is the resurrection. A common criticism of the Anselmic theory has been that the resurrection plays no integral part in man's redemption since everything happens at the cross. There the work of salvation is complete. The resurrection is not the final step in the inexorable logic with which Anselm describes man's salvation. It is a postscript. Manifestly, this does not mean that in Evangelical theology resurrection is denied. Indeed, its emphasis on conversion and therefore on the encounter between the individual and his Saviour is meaningful only in terms of a Christ who is present and alive. Yet that Christ is known through the cross. The dying Saviour whose death brings forgiveness of sin makes possible union with God in the present experience of the believer. So, whilst it is true that the death of Christ was central to Spurgeon's thinking, yet it was that death which was the key to a true understanding of the incarnation, the resurrection and the union of the believer with his Lord. At the cross, sins were forgiven, the sinner justified and accepted by the Father who, his wrath and honour satisfied, out of the richness of his mercy brought the believer into fellowship with himself. What was true of Spurgeon's preaching was true also of his understanding of the Lord's Supper. The death of Jesus, at the very heart of the gospel, was the key to union with Christ and life lived in the fullness of his grace. Because the cross was the focal point of the whole gospel, the sacrament was not a place of gloom where the church's prayers turned to vapour in the chill air, it was a place where believers realized, again and again, how much God had given to them in offering up his own beloved Son upon the cross. No wonder Spurgeon cried:

> Oh, that I could have the cross painted on my eyeballs, that I could not see anything except through the medium of my Saviour's passion! Oh Jesus, set thyself as a seal upon my hand, and as a signet on mine arm, and let me wear the pledge forever where it is conspicuous before my soul's eye.[19]

It was inevitable that the central theme of Spurgeon's preaching should be the central theme of the Lord's Supper:

> It is the death of Christ which is set forth by this memorial supper. Why was that chosen? I answer, because it is the most vital of all truths. Concerning the sacrificial death of Christ there must not be tolerated any dispute in the Christian church. That must for ever stand as a settled doctrine of the gospel. The atoning death of Jesus Christ once put away, you have taken the sun out of the Church's heaven ... You have given us merely the shell and the husk if you take away this great central truth of the gospel, -

God's justice vindicated by the death of his dear Son, and, on that ground, free pardon published by the grace of God to the very chief of sinners who believe in him . . . our Lord Jesus Christ instituted this supper in order to keep this truth before men's minds, because it is the point above all others that is vital to the gospel.[20]

This atoning death Spurgeon saw represented in the bread and wine of the communion. The separateness of bread and wine he likened to the separation of body and blood that took place in the death of Jesus:

There must be in the Lord's Supper bread and wine; but bread separated from the wine, as our Lord speaks of his flesh as separated from his blood, and this was to indicate that it is as a dying Saviour that he is most precious to us. The blood separated from the flesh indicates death.[21]

The fullness of the cross in Spurgeon's preaching must be borne in mind when we come to consider his emphasis upon the role of remembrance in the supper. His call to remembrance at the Lord's table represented a summons to believers to fasten their attention upon that great act that was central to their salvation and to their present experience. Remembrance embraced their living relationship with Jesus Christ and the salvific act that had made it possible. Memorialism, for some of Spurgeon's fellow Baptists, might have represented the most acceptable alternative to Catholicism of all the Reformation options. Their Zwinglianism tended to veer off into radical suspicion of sacramentalism. Spurgeon's memorialism was coloured by his Calvinism. Where others saw remembrance as a pious spiritual exercise centred on the mental and spiritual experience of the communicant, Spurgeon saw it as a response of love to love, a grasping of Christ in the present as well as recollection of what he had done in the past. His emphasis recalled that found in the hymns of Anne Steele:

Dear Lord, while we adoring pay
Our humble Thanks to thee;
May every heart with Rapture say
The Saviour dy'd for me.[22]

The sight of the dying Saviour moved him to reach out to that Christ who had revealed himself to his disciples in the upper room on the day of the resurrection:

To remember Christ . . . is the main point of the right observance of this ordinance; - to let the memory look him in the face again, to put the finger once more into the print of the nails, and to thrust the hand again into his side; once again to adore the Saviour whose head for us was crowned with thorns, but is now coroneted with glory; - to remember him, to recall him, that is our main business as we gather round his table.[23]

The crucified Christ recalled in the supper was the living Christ who had revealed himself to his disciples. Remembering the Christ who died, the communicant was to reach out his hand and touch the Christ who was risen.

The emphasis upon remembrance was, in Spurgeon's view, a safeguard against any association between the bread and wine and the actual body and blood of Christ:

> You mock Christ if you regard this communion as anything other than the remembrance of him. What is there in that bread, what is there in that wine? There is nothing whatsoever there but bread and wine after we have invoked a blessing upon them just as there was before ... There is nothing in the whole ordinance but a help to memory ... but if you do not remember Jesus, if you have no faith in him, if you do not love him, if you do not cast yourselves wholly upon him, what business have you at his table?[24]

To come remembering, was to come with faith and love and to throw oneself wholly upon Christ. Even as he repudiated Catholic sacramentalism, Spurgeon placed the evangelical experience at the heart of communion. Remembrance was more than a commendable mental state, it was at one with faith, hope and love.

As well as renewing the devotion of the believer, the memorial of the Lord's Supper also set before him the truths by which he lived. The didactic aspect of the supper has already been encountered in other Baptist writers: in Spurgeon experience and understanding were at one:

> Where, beloved, can we find richer instruction than at the table of our Lord? He who understands the mystery of incarnation and of substitution, is a master in Scriptural theology. There is more teaching in the Saviour's body and in the Saviour's blood than in all the world besides.[25]

Spurgeon saw the constant need for this reminder of the source of salvation. He set himself against the self-sufficient who claimed to have no need for such tangible reminders. To those who placed themselves above the necessity of the supper he said:

> Happy is that Christian who can say, 'I scarcely need that memorial'. But I am not such an one; and I fear me, my brethren, that the most of us need to be reminded by that bread and wine that Jesus died; and need to be reminded, by the eating and drinking of the same, that he died for us.[26]

iii) The Presence of Christ

Spurgeon's inseparable association of the memorial of the Lord's Supper with the crucified Christ, through whom the risen Christ was known and the grace of God experienced, took him beyond the form of Zwinglianism with which many of his fellow Baptists were content. He did not hesitate to speak of the presence of Christ in the sacrament. Whilst firmly rejecting the Catholic doctrine of the eucharist that located the presence of Christ in the bread and the wine, Spurgeon remained a world away from any notion of an 'absent' Christ. He spoke freely of Christ's presence, in language similar to that employed in the eighteenth-century hymns and by Hall, Newman, Button, Jarrom and the author of the 'Sacramental Meditations'.[27] The question, 'How is Christ present?' was as difficult for him to address as for others. In his sermon on the text of Psalm 17.3, 'Thou hast visited me in the 'night', he attempted an answer:

> The priest who celebrates mass tells us that he believes in the real presence, but we reply, 'Nay, you believe in knowing Christ after the flesh, and in that sense the only real presence is in heaven; but we firmly believe in the real presence of Christ which is spiritual, and yet certain'. By spiritual we do not mean unreal; in fact, the spiritual takes the lead in real-ness to spiritual men. I believe in the true and real presence of Jesus with His people, such presence has been real to my spirit. Lord Jesus, Thou Thyself hast visited me. As surely as the Lord Jesus came really as to His flesh to Bethlehem and Calvary, so surely does He come really by His Spirit to His people in the hours of their communion with Him.[28]

The hand of Calvin is clearly on this passage of the sermon. Repudiating Luther's concept of the ubiquity of Christ's humanity, Calvin stressed the glorified nature of Christ's body. His emphasis upon God's holiness led him to distance God from man whilst, at the same time, upholding a true incarnation of God in Christ. For him, the glorified body of Jesus was not everywhere abroad in the earth, but seated at the right hand of God in heaven. The believer shared in that body through the agency of the Holy Spirit. Where Luther had stressed the descent of the divine into the human, Calvin stressed the raising of the believer through the work of the Holy Spirit. In Luther's theology, God came to be where man is, present in the 'hidden-ness' of the cross. Here, where the Godhead was most fearfully hidden (*absconditus*) he was most surely revealed (*revelatus*). In Calvin's theology, it was the Holy Spirit who raised us into the presence of God and made it possible for us to participate in Christ.

Spurgeon stood with Calvin. The two crucial features of the reformer's theology, namely the presence of the glorified Lord in heaven and the work of the Holy Spirit in bringing us into fellowship with him, are clear in the Psalm 17.3 sermon. It was this grasp of the Calvinist concept that allowed Spurgeon to speak boldly of the divine presence, even whilst rejecting Catholic doctrine. Unlike so many of his fellow Baptists, and in spite of the role he conceded to memorialism, he was not primarily a Zwinglian and certainly not to the radical side of that denominational norm. As painful as his Calvinism proved in coming to terms with theological and biblical developments within the nineteenth century, and as damaging as his conservatism was to prove for his relationships with his fellow Baptists, at this point his traditional Reformed faith enabled him to preserve something which others lost. He did not become entangled in the psychological musings of those for whom remembrance was simply a question of mental states and pious dispositions. Faith could grasp the reality behind the symbol. Communion was not a matter of thinking about Christ but of knowing him. Further, this encounter with Christ was one in which Christ himself took the initiative. He was 'the mysterious visitor' who came to the soul, even in the night, as he came to Job, to Daniel, to Saul of Tarsus, and to Peter at the end of his long night of fishing:

> To know that Jesus loves me, is one thing; but to be visited by Him in love, is more. Nor is it simply a close contemplation of Christ; for we can picture Him as exceedingly fair and majestic, and yet not have Him consciously near us. Delightful and instructive as it is to behold the likeness of Christ by meditation, yet the enjoyment of His actual presence is something more.[29]

Spurgeon's belief in the divine presence at the Lord's Supper was sometimes expressed in bold language. The sacrament was the window through which Christ was seen:

> At this table Jesus feeds us with His body and His blood. His corporeal presence we have not, but His real spiritual presence we perceive. We are like the disciples when none of them durst ask Him, 'Who art Thou?' knowing that it was the Lord. He is come. He looketh forth at these windows, - I mean this bread and wine; showing Himself through the lattices of this instructive and endearing ordinance.[30]

Preaching on Revelation 1.17,18, with its marvellous picture of the seer falling as one dead at the feet of Christ in majesty, he caught the awe and the grace of encounter with Christ. He located that encounter at the table of the Lord's Supper. It was there that believers swooned at Christ's feet as they were reminded of the misery from which they had been delivered through his death. It was there that they knew what it was to be brought to life by the touch of his right hand. To Christ they came as mendicants, friars who begged their sustenance, and from Christ they received the wealth of his love. For that touch of Christ was more than the hand of sympathy, it was the hand through which the healing power of God himself poured into the soul. Spurgeon did not shrink from powerful imagery as he spoke of the gift of Christ in the supper:

> May there stream down from the Lord's right hand, not merely His sympathy, because He is a man like ourselves, but as much of the power of *His deity* as can be gotten into man, so that we may be filled with the fulness *of God!* That is possible at this instant. The Lord's supper represents the giving of the whole body of Christ to us, to enter into us for food; surely, if we enter into its true meaning, we may expect to be revived and vitalized; for we have here more than a mere touch of the hand, it is the whole Christ that enters into us spiritually, and so comes into contact with our innermost being. I believe in 'the real presence': do not you? The *carnal* presence is another thing: *that* we do not even desire.[31]

Closely associated with the theme of Christ's presence at the sacrament was that of the union of the individual believer with Christ. Spurgeon preached the Pauline doctrine of life 'in Christ'. The crucified Christ was also the risen Christ through whom forgiveness and life in God were given. It was this Christ who dwelt in the soul of the believer and imparted the gifts of salvation. But he was a Christ who had to be received. On the part of the believer, there had to be a real reception of Christ, an opening of the doors of heart and mind. Christ was not known simply as an article of faith or a subject of meditation: he came to live in the life of the believer. This coming of Christ was through the Holy Spirit who bound believer and Christ together as one. As Calvin had emphasised the ministry of the Spirit in the ongoing sanctification of the Christian man, so Spurgeon preached a Christian life that was a union of faith and love with the crucified Christ. In the tradition both of the Catholic and the Puritan mystics, he took the language of the Song of Songs as an analogy of the union between the soul and its Saviour.[32]

This union found a focal point in the Lord's Supper. The memorial of Christ's death at the heart of the sacrament represented God's supreme gift of Christ and all the benefits he had won on the cross. The act of eating and drinking represented the believer's acceptance of those benefits. Salvation had to be received: Christ entered into the life of the believer just as bread and wine were taken into the body. Salvation came to none who stood with the detachment of a spectator. Just as there could be no communion without eating and drinking, so there could be no salvation unless Christ were received as the chief and most cherished guest of the human heart. In his sermon on 1 Corinthians 10.16,17 Spurgeon took the Pauline theme of participation in the body and blood of Christ and applied it both to the believer's surrender of faith and his sharing in the Lord's Supper. Service or suffering, each in its own way, might draw people near to Christ, but neither service nor suffering could be substitutes for the reality of Christ himself:

> ... the fellowship of the soul which receives Christ, and is received by Christ, is closer, more vital, more essential than any other. Such fellowship is eternal.[33]

The union of the soul with Christ in this fellowship was as complete as the union of the bread and wine with the body of the believer in the Lord's Supper:

> No power upon earth can henceforth take from me the piece of bread which I have just now eaten, it has gone where it will be made up into blood, and nerve, and muscle, and bone. That drop of wine has coursed through my veins, and is part and parcel of my being. So he that takes Jesus by faith to be his Saviour has chosen the good part which shall not be taken away from him.[34]

The Lord's Supper was a means by which the depth and intimacy of the soul's union with Christ might be increased. If the bread and wine were windows through which Christ might be glimpsed, they were also doors through which the believer might pass into a deeper experience of fellowship with Christ. Spurgeon longed that the communicant should not stand at the threshold of the symbol but should pass through it to that which was symbolized:

> He calls upon us to eat bread with Him; yea, to partake of Himself, by eating His flesh and drinking His blood. Oh, that we may pass beyond the outward signs into the closest intimacy with *Himself!*[35]

In his sermon, 'The Spiced Wine of My Pomegranate', based on the Song of Solomon 8.2 and John 1.16, Spurgeon again dealt with the theme of the giving of grace and its reception by faith, figured in the gift of bread and wine and the act of eating and drinking. Fellowship with Jesus was a matter of giving and receiving, of offering and acceptance:

> The Lord's supper is the divinely-ordained exhibition of communion, and therefore in it there is the breaking of bread and the pouring forth of wine, to picture the free gift of the Saviour's body and blood to us; and there is also the eating of the one and the drinking of the other, to represent the reception of these priceless gifts by us. As without bread and wine there could be no Lord's supper, so without the gracious bequests of Jesus to us there would have been no communion between Him and our souls: and as participation is necessary before the elements truly represent the meaning of the Lord's ordinance, so is it needful that we should receive His

bounties, and feed upon His person, before we can commune with Him.[36]

Believing this, Spurgeon exhorted Christians to come to the table with expectation. In his sermon on Luke 8.46, 'Real Contact With Jesus', he likened the communicant to the woman with the haemorrhage who struggled through the crowd to press the robe of Jesus in order that she might be healed. So the believer at the Lord's Supper should long to pass through the 'veil' of earthly signs in order to touch Christ himself:

> At all times when you come to the communion table, count it to have been no ordinance of grace to you unless you have gone right through the veil into Christ's own arms, or at least have touched His garment, feeling that the first object, the life and soul of the means of grace, is to touch Jesus Christ Himself . . .[37]

Eating and drinking in the Lord's Supper were not only representative of the soul's reception of Christ by faith, they also were the means by which it was nourished in its continuing life in Christ. The table was a place where spiritual food was provided for the nurture of Christian men and women:

> *Jesus has placed upon this table food* . . . He who feeds the sparrow feeds our souls . . . We could not live an hour spiritually without Him who is not only bread, but life; not only the wine which cheereth, but consolation itself. Our life hangs upon Jesus; He is our Head as well as our food. We shall never outgrow our need of natural bread, and spiritually we shall never rise out of our need of a present Christ, but the rather we shall feel a stronger craving and a more urgent passion for Him.[38]

Here, those fruits of sanctification, which Calvin, like his master Paul, had taught were the harvest of life in Christ, through the Spirit, were nurtured and encouraged to grow:

> We have enjoyed our best times when celebrating this sacred Eucharist . . . Let us, in calm meditation and inward thought, now produce from our hearts sweet fruits of love, and zeal, and hope, and patience.[39]

Spurgeon identified himself with many who, through the ages, had found spiritual nourishment at the table. It was, he said, a place that had inspired the eloquence of John Willison and Samuel Rutherford, the poems of George Herbert 'were most of them inspired by the sight of Christ in this ordinance', and the canticles of 'holy Bernard', that 'flame with devotion':

> Saints and martyrs have been nourished at this table of blessing. This hallowed ordinance, I am sure, is a spot where

hopes grow bright, and hearts grow warm, resolves become firm, and lives become fruitful, and all the clusters of our soul's fruit ripen for the Lord.[40]

So high rose Spurgeon's expectations of what was offered at the Lord's Supper that he counselled believers to come to it with joy and singing. Just as the people of Israel had sung the Hallel at the Passover so, at this Passover of the cross, Christians were to sing the praises of their Redeemer:

> Whenever we repair to the Lord's table, which represents to us the Passover, we ought not to come to it as to a funeral. Let us select solemn hymns, but not dirges. Let us sing softly, but none the less joyously. These are no burial feasts; those are not funeral cakes which lie upon this table, and yonder fair white linen cloth is no winding-sheet. 'This is My body', said Jesus, but the body so represented was no corpse; we feed upon a living Christ. The blood set forth by yonder wine is the fresh life-blood of our immortal King. We view not our Lord's body as clay-cold flesh, pierced with wounds, but as glorified at the right hand of the Father. We hold a happy festival when we break bread on the first day of the week.[41]

It is clear that Spurgeon saw the supper as something more than a representation of events which took place in the heart of the believer at other times and in other places. The table was itself a place where grace was given and Christ encountered. For Spurgeon, the Lord's Supper was rooted in a theology of grace that lay at the very heart of his religion. It was alive with the same heartbeat and characterised by the same strength. Thus he did not hesitate to encourage Christians to come to the table, believing that it was possible to see the risen Christ through these 'windows', to pass through this 'veil' into his very presence. It was that conviction that engendered a mood of joy absent from many memorialist celebrations of the sacrament. Spurgeon gave to Baptists, had they heeded him, something they sorely needed to know, that communion was truly a celebration, that he who came with pierced hands and side was the risen Christ of the upper room, and that the supper was 'none other than the gate of heaven' through which, in faith and love, believers might pass into the presence of him who was seated at the right hand of the throne of glory. It was not a place to which Spurgeon felt summoned by a 'Duty, stern daughter of the voice of God'. His evident joy and expectation meant that no Sunday passed when he did not celebrate it, whether at the Tabernacle, at his holiday retreat in Mentone, or in other journeyings. As he himself testified to the Tabernacle congregation:

> I long to get to this table again, though I have not been away from it any Sabbath for many a long day, for it has been my constant habit, wherever I have been, to get a few Christian

friends together to break bread in remembrance of Christ. When I am with you, you know that I would never be absent, on the first day of the week, from my Master's table, unless there was something that absolutely prevented.[42]

iv) The relationship of the material and the spiritual

A recurring theme in nineteenth-century Baptist eucharistic theology has been the separation of the 'ceremonial' and the 'spiritual'. As we have seen,[43] Spurgeon wished to distinguish between the Catholic understanding of presence of Christ in the sacrament, which he termed 'carnal', and the 'spiritual' presence. This did not, however, lead him in the footsteps of his more Zwinglian or radical brethren. In separating sign from thing signified they had started a hairline crack which opened into a fissure sundering soul from body and the material from the spiritual. Spurgeon did not despise the earthiness of the supper, its material symbols, its eating and drinking, pointing beyond to a 'higher' or more spiritual form of religion. Rather, he found in the sacrament a place where the material and the spiritual were joined together:

> These ordinances are the only link between the spirituality of our faith and materialism; but we must remember that God has not flung away materialism as a thing that cannot be bettered. He did curse the earth once, and it still brings forth thorns and thistles; but he does not mean it to remain under the curse always. There will come a time when there shall be a new heaven and a new earth literally; and here, where sin has triumphed, grace shall reign.[44]

Like so many of the communion hymns sung by Baptists, Spurgeon's sermons stressed the eschatalogical dimension of the Lord's Supper. The title chosen for his volume of communion sermons, *Till He Come*, emphasised the hope with which the supper was celebrated. The earth was to be renewed when all things were finally consummated in Christ. The sanctifying power of Christ was not, however, marooned in some distant future, effective only when the salvation of all things had been completed. The link between material and spiritual in the present celebration of both baptism and the Lord's Supper fostered a reverence for the world in which Christians lived here and now:

> So I thank God for the two ordinances of baptism and the Lord's supper, because they teach me that nothing is common or unclean. They sanctify the rivers to me, they sanctify my daily bread to me; they make me feel, not as if I lived, like a Brahmin, in a world where everything might pollute me, but, like a Christian, in a world where Christ has lived, and in a position in which everything may be to me 'holiness unto the Lord' if my heart is right before him.[45]

THE LORD'S SUPPER AND TWO BAPTIST PREACHERS

In another passage, Spurgeon linked together the three themes of the relationship between material and spiritual, the destiny of the material universe, and the attitude that the Christian should display to the material world by which he was surrounded:

> We are still linked with materialism; we are not yet purely spiritual, and it is no use for us to pretend that we are. Some good people sit still till they are moved, which would be an admirable form of worship if we had not got any bodies; but, as long as we have bodies, there must be some kind of linking of the spiritual with the material, let the links be as few as they may. Christ has made two; they are enough, but they are none too many, for let it be remembered that there is a time coming when the material itself is to be lifted up, and re-united with the spiritual. 'The creature itself shall also be delivered from the bondage of corruption into the glorious liberty of the children of God'. And as if to teach us not to despise the material, not to consider everything that can be touched and seen as therefore foul and beneath the consideration of spiritual minds, our Lord has given us water in which we can wash, and bread and wine the products of the earth, that, being yet earthy, we may anticipate the time when the earth shall shake off the slough which came upon her at the Fall, and, as a new earth, with her new heaven of pure blue over her, shall become a holy temple of the living God.[46]

It was a theme to which Spurgeon summoned all his powers of eloquence. Puritan that he was, he held the earth in honour. Like the sturdy prose he used to express it, his theology was rooted in reality. His sermons constantly reveal his understanding of the people who came to hear him, the sad, the toiling, the indifferent, the noble and the sinful. He refused to strip their world of the divine glory that was to be found in the simple and the commonplace. He set his face against a Catholicism that fenced off the altar in distant and numinous ceremonial, against those who, in a mistaken spirituality, took the bread and wine out of the very mouths of the children of God and against those who washed their hands of the material world.

Spurgeon's testimony to the Lord's Supper was all the more important in that he was a prince amongst the preachers of his time. It was an age in which the pulpit, in practice as well as in the architectural design of so many Nonconformist churches, overshadowed the table. The witness of Spurgeon the preacher provided a necessary redress of balance:

> I can bear my own witness that, many and many a Sabbath, when I have found but little food for my soul elsewhere, I have found it at the communion table.[47]

B) THE LORD'S SUPPER IN THE THOUGHT OF JOHN CLIFFORD

Like Spurgeon's, John Clifford's ministry was exercised in one Baptist church which provided the base for all his work. He belonged to the General Baptist wing of the denomination, Arminian in its theology and able to claim direct descent from the founding fathers, John Smyth and Thomas Helwys. The latter was responsible for the founding of the first Baptist church on English soil in Spitalfields, London, in 1612. His book, *The Mistery of Iniquity*, a copy of which he sent to James I, was a plea for religious tolerance and a challenge to the state's claim to the right to determine the religious convictions of its subjects. It led to his imprisonment in the Fleet where he died, probably around the year 1616. This emphasis upon religious tolerance was thenceforth imprinted on General Baptist beliefs. It was asserted with renewed vigour in the nineteenth century, a time in which the air rang with the cries of freedom, echoing the chants of the Parisian crowds who, in the closing years of the preceding century, had demanded Liberté, Egalité, Fraternité.

Religious freedom could find no more ardent champion than John Clifford. In all things he argued for the rights of the individual. His biographer, Sir James Marchant, placed him firmly in the tradition of John the Baptist, 'a veritable voice crying in the wilderness, eater of sacerdotal locusts and the wild honey of reform, straightener of rough paths and valiant preparer of the way of the Lord'.[48] Never narrow or sectarian in his outlook, he would, in pursuit of good preaching, visit Anglican and Catholic, as well as Nonconformist churches, on his free Sundays.[49] His advocacy of religious freedom led him, nonetheless, to oppose both Anglicanism and Romanism. He attacked the Church of England when it laid claim to privileges that he believed were denied to others. This led him to play a leading part in the educational debates of the late nineteenth and early twentieth centuries, when he passionately opposed the maintenance of the dual system in schools, believing that education should be free of all denominational constraints and dogmatic instruction. The existence of church schools, aided by public funds, was, he believed, an abuse of public money and a reinforcement of Anglican privilege. He was also fiercely opposed to any sacerdotal interpretation of the church because this was divisive and a denial of equality and brotherhood. His opposition to the Roman Catholic Church was prompted by the belief that Rome was ever the enemy of freedom and the embodiment of ecclesiastical tyranny.

His involvement in the wider life of the Christian church, however, went far beyond sectarian struggles. He strongly supported the growing co-operation between the Free Church denominations and was amongst those responsible for the setting up of the National Council of Evangelical Free Churches. Within his own denomination he was one of those who acted as Baptist Union spokesmen in the attempt to heal the rift with Spurgeon caused by the Downgrade Controversy. Whilst saddened by Spurgeon's unspecified charges and jealous of religious freedom, he was grieved by the gulf that opened between Spurgeon and his fellow Baptists. He was active in the affairs of the London Baptist Association and one of the pioneers of the Baptist World Alliance, founded in 1905. His involvement in public affairs went well beyond the boundaries of the church, for he was also a staunch supporter of the Liberal Party, the party of radicalism in his day. His influence was testified to by Lloyd George who said that there was no man in England on whose conscience he would rather ring a coin than that of John Clifford.[50] Clifford accepted, too, the challenge of the newly formed socialists. In 1908, in a speech at Forest Hill Baptist Church, he said:

> Socialism in the soul of it is divine. It is of God. The Churches ought ... to take full share in the gradual reformation and rebuilding of society, to welcome every practical extension of the Socialist principle.[51]

Clifford's denominational and political outlook contributed to the stand that he took against Catholicism and to the way he perceived the Lord's Supper. Four arguments stand out in his opposition to Catholicism. He opposed it on the grounds that he believed it to be a denial of New Testament religion which he saw as essentially one of personal response to Jesus; that sacerdotalism was, by its very nature, divisive and a denial of brotherhood; that Catholicism elevated 'church' and 'ceremonial' above 'religion' and 'discipleship'; and that all Catholicism led in the direction of Rome who was the enemy of freedom.

In his pamphlet, published in 1888, *The Ordinances of Jesus and the Sacraments of the Church*, a title that in itself offered a clear indication of the direction of his thinking, he asserted:

> Christianity ... is personal, and every act in it must be that of a conscious, responsible, and intelligent soul, going out in penitence and faith, hope and service, to and for Christ. No official order or act is to be interposed between the spirit of man and God as channels or mediums of grace.[52]

Baptism, he claimed, was itself evidence of personal choice at the very outset of the Christian life. The element of individual consent, as Clifford claimed, was inseparable from the Baptist view of baptism. The call of Christ was to be answered, faith responding to grace, invitation meeting with acceptance. Neither church nor sacraments, in the Baptist view, were the chief agents in this personal transaction between God and man. Clifford contrasted this with the Catholic view in which the church was the channel of grace and the sacraments the means by which God's saving love was communicated to man and made effective in his life. To Clifford, the church was an obstacle rather than a channel, an intrusion into the essentially personal dealings of God with the souls of men.

This view of the church set him even more fiercely against sacerdotalism. In Catholicism, grace could be channelled through church and sacraments only if the latter were administered by those who had received valid ordination at episcopal hands. To Clifford this was to place in the hands of a priestly caste a power to which no man was entitled. He saw it as a narrowing of divine grace. It divided Christians, the priestly order standing in direct relationship with God and the means of his sacramental grace, leaving other Christians dependent upon their mediatorial function. To Clifford, such a notion was not simply un-Baptist and contrary to the spirit of Nonconformity in general, it was also thoroughly un-English! Speaking at the Annual Meeting of the Council of Free Churches of London in November 1895, he said:

> Romanism and Sacerdotalism are out of accord with the genius of the Anglo-Saxon people: they are exclusive and aristocratic; they create monopolies and particularisms after the fashion of nations . . . [they] place the responsibility for the 'Church' of Christ on the priests, and turn the priesthood into a clerical 'preserve', or trades-union, to the exclusion of the people, and in defiance of the 'Crown rights of Christ Jesus'.[53]

His views had by no means mellowed sixteen years later when, in 1911, he wrote an article on 'The Attitude of Baptists to Catholicism', where he again returned to his attack upon sacerdotalism and the exclusive role of the priesthood:

> The Eastern and Western Churches are supersaturated with sacerdotalism and have created a colossal priestly order, a great official class, a clerical tyranny, shutting out God and His Son Jesus Christ from the souls of men.[54]

Clifford shared the impatience of his great Baptist predecessor, Robert Hall, when faced with divisions between Christians. Whereas Hall had attacked the theological presuppositions of his own denomination where they stood in the way of Christian fellowship at the Lord's table, Clifford turned his fury on what he saw as the erroneous and divisive theologies of others. With Clifford there was more at stake than the unity of Christ's people. He was in the forefront of those who repudiated the Catholic revival and the theology that undergirded it and, like his fellow protagonists, he allowed his anti-Catholicism to shape his own theological position.

This becomes clear in his third line of argument against the Catholics. He employed the now familiar distinction between the 'ceremonial' or 'carnal' religion of the Catholics and the 'spiritual' religion of Nonconformity. Clifford carried this line of argument to the extreme of radicalism, where it was more at home with the aspirations of late Victorianism than with the scriptures or any discernible theological tradition. In an article on the Tractarians, published in 1920, he criticized them for their emphasis on the 'church', as compared with the

Free Church emphasis on 'religion'. The Tractarian renewal of the church had, he said, been won at the price of true religion. It was:

> ... based on a false conception. It puts the 'Church' before Religion, makes Religion subsidiary to the Church, treats it entirely as a means and not an end.[55]

In contrast with that, he argued:

> The Free Church conception is that Religion is first and always first, and the Church is nothing more than the means by which Christianity is expounded and enforced, and applied in the life of the individual and of the nation.[56]

It was a strange contrast and potentially disastrous for Baptist theology. Where Spurgeon had renounced Catholicism without conceding what was of theological importance to his own beliefs, Clifford here left himself with an emasculated notion of the church. He seemed to have no perception of the church as an organic and mystical body, or of faith as a shared experience, corporately expressed in the life and worship of the church. It was little more than a servicing agency, subservient to the individuals who belonged to it, their relationship to one another owing more to the model of the countless voluntary societies to be found in Victorian society than to the New Testament image of the body of Christ. A century that began with Robert Hall making baptism less important than the individual's conscience ended with John Clifford making the church less important than his religion.

Elsewhere, Clifford contrasted the spirit with the institution:

> The Law of the Spirit of Life in Christ Jesus suffers more through the materializing of its truths and institutions than from all other causes put together.[57]

It was again an unfortunate contrast. Happier with the inner condition of the human soul, it betrayed that suspicion of historical institutions in which inner beliefs were given bodily form. It suggested that there was a citadel, concealed in the breast of the individual Christian, free of close examination, where faith remained unsullied and pure. The church, by contrast, could escape neither 'materialization' nor, indeed, the character of an institution. Of necessity, it has been an all too imperfect and earthly attempt to embody the timeless truths of the gospel in the bloody arena of human history. There could be nowhere where its life was more vulnerable to criticism or more prone to failure. For the Apostle Paul that had been its glory, for Clifford it was its shame. The contrast between spirit and institution Clifford set within the wider antithesis of matter and spirit. By 'materialism' he meant church and sacraments, understood as material and substantial realities capable of being the means of mediating grace to men and women. His choice of language, however, set his feet on a theological high-wire where he had to live dangerously, performing balancing feats that, in the history of the church, had proved fatal to others more theologically aware than he was. His practical involvement in the politics of his time and his sympathies with the socialist scenario for the future cleared him of Manichaean heresy, but his theology did seem to invite the charge in the first place. He summoned Christians to engage in a crusade:

> The battle goes on as of old between materialism and spiritualism; the flesh and the spirit; the lower, animal, and sense-bound life and the higher life of the soul . . . From Eden to this hour, the highway worn by the feet of the marching generations of the children of the Spirit, is upwards towards inwardness in religion, simplicity and spirituality in worship . . . Materialism is the one real foe of a living Christianity.[58]

It is impossible to resist the temptation of comparing Clifford's words with those of another who, like him, was a social prophet. William Temple once said, 'Christianity is the most materialist of all religions'. Spurgeon had seen the sacraments as the essential link between material and spiritual, a link that, however tenuous, transformed a Christian's perception of the physical world and engendered reverence for it. Clifford's words were an open invitation to sever that link and to open Zwingli's hairline crack between sign and thing signified, between the spiritual and the material, into an awful gaping chasm.

His fourth argument against Catholicism was that it led irresistibly in a Romeward direction. As late as 1920, his view of the Tractarian movement was that its purpose, from the very beginning, was to lead the English Church back to the arms of Rome. In his pamphlet, *Anglican Romanism and the National Character*, he recognized the effectiveness of the original Oxford group in renewing the life of the church. Of John Keble, J. H. Newman, Hurrell Froude, Hugh James Rose, E. B. Pusey and W. G. Ward, he wrote:

> Those men have remade our English Church. They were devoted, heart and soul, to the reviving of its decaying energies, the recharging of its exhausted veins with streams of fresh and palpitating life, the beautifying of its buildings, the dignifying of its services, and, above all, to the exaltation of its priests. And they have wrought great marvels. Days of laxity have given place to glowing zeal. Good works are multiplied. Generous gifts are bestowed. Rites and ceremonies are increased a hundredfold. The 'sacrament' is administered in a gloom irradiated by a glare of altar candles, and with a solemn stillness, regarded as reverence and awe.[59]

Despite the fact that he seemed unsure whether to praise or damn with faint irony, Clifford acknowledged the debt that many, even beyond the Church of England, owed to them:

> ... the original Tractarians take rank amongst the most brilliant and devout, pious and sincere, self-sacrificing and able of England's sons. Who of us has not felt the singular charm of the passionate earnestness, exalted devotion, searching teaching and fine mastery of style of Newman's *Sermons* and of his *Apologia*? What myriads have felt the magic spell of the soothing devoutness and restful lucidity of Keble's songs! How the quiet and irrepressible strength, the indomitable will, the unbroken serenity of Pusey have captured us![60]

Poison, however, was mixed with their healing preparations:

> ... the Catholic Revival was started in deception and fraud; ... [it] combined scheming and intrigue with lofty church ideals and assiduous devotion to ritual ...[61]

In Clifford's eyes the least suggestion that the Tractarians were looking Romewards would have condemned them. Given his stance on religious liberty, his political ideals, nurtured in liberalism and sympathetic to socialism, and his championship of the individual and his rights it is not to be wondered that he responded to the Roman 'threat' as he did. Events in the Roman Church since the publication of the first of the Oxford tracts would, in Clifford's eyes, only have confirmed the folly of any renewal that took the Church of England towards Rome. Not only Baptists had shuddered at the anti-liberal strictures of Pius IX's *Syllabus of Errors*, promulgated in 1864, or witnessed with dismay the ultramontanist triumph as the First Vatican Council signalled in the definition of papal infallibility. The Tractarians had, it seemed, been in pursuit of a church that, through the decades of the nineteenth century, had moved further and further away from the sort of Protestantism represented by the Evangelicals of the Anglican church and even more by the Nonconformist churches. Writing in 1911, Clifford argued that because of the loss of the Papal States in 1870 and the decline of papal power in traditionally Catholic countries:

> ... [the] forces of Roman Catholicism are now directed to the conversion of the Anglo-Saxon race. That is the goal of the policy of the Pope.[62]

Clifford's conviction that the Roman Church was intent upon the conversion of England was not the fanciful opinion of a lone Baptist eccentric. It was shared by most Nonconformists, suspected by a large section of the general public, and confirmed by those Roman Catholics who referred, indiscreetly and nostalgically, to 'Mary's dowry'.

In considering Clifford's view of the Lord's Supper, two pamphlets in particular are of importance. The first, published in 1876, was *The True Use of the Lord's Supper*, and the second, probably his most systematic attempt to expound the meaning of the Lord's Supper, was *The*

Ordinances of Jesus and the Sacraments of the Church, published in 1888. Clifford clearly rejected any sacramental connotations that might be given to the Lord's Supper and, in this, he believed he was speaking not simply for himself, nor even for his fellow Baptists, but for all Nonconformists:

> The 'Sacraments' of themselves do not bring the soul into living union with the Saviour. They cannot. They are of the earth, earthy. They reveal truth of such peerless worth, that they are its supreme symbols . . . But the 'real presence' of the Christ is the Divine answer to the penitence, trust and worship of the humble and devout soul.[63]

Elsewhere he wrote:

> Broadly speaking, we hold that Baptism and the Lord's Supper are not 'Sacraments' in the ecclesiastical sense, i.e., they are not mysteries or miracles, not causes of grace, not in themselves vehicles of grace.[64]

At least one exception to what Clifford claimed was the generally held view of the Free Churches was R. W. Dale, the gifted Congregationalist minister of the Carr's Lane church in Birmingham. Dale had argued for a real presence of Christ in the sacrament, rejecting the prevailing Zwinglianism of most of his co-religionists. Clifford took issue with Dale and accused him of being a 'Dornerist', i.e. one who believed that the sacraments were 'acts through which Christ dispenses grace mystically'.[65] Clifford also acknowledged that the Free Churches differed from the great reformer, Martin Luther. He contended that, in his doctrine of the Lord's Supper, his spirit was 'still fettered by Papal materialism'.[66] The bread and the wine were symbols, nothing more, argued Clifford. 'This is my body' had an equivalent meaning to 'The Lord God is a Sun and a Shield'.[67] The bread and wine were a 'symbolic proclamation'.[68]

Clifford's reduction of the sacraments to mere symbols placed him in a position no different from many of his fellow Baptists. His description of them, however, as 'of the earth, earthy', coupled with his passionate claim that religion was essentially inward and individualist, and his unwise polarisation of matter and spirit, placed him at the extreme wing of the radical Anabaptist position. Baptists who heeded him could only conclude that the Lord's Supper was a poor servant of the Christian life. Rather than the communicant being insufficient for what was given to him at the Lord's table, the sacrament was an inadequate expression of the depths of his religious experience:

> How can our cold symbols embody the heart-beat of the revelation of God! They are too poor and mean. They obscure it instead of illuminating it. They frustrate the purpose of Jesus and make void the gift of God, leading men to forget

that not in forms but duties, not in names but in righteousness and love does religion consist.[69]

Clifford went on to say other, more positive things about the supper, but having already described it in such dismissive language, his attempts to invest it with meaning had to contend with the strength of his own polemic. Any practice that was in danger of obscuring rather than illuminating the revelation of God, of frustrating the purpose of Jesus and making void the gift of God, could be viewed only with suspicion and alarm.

Given such inauspicious assumptions, did the Lord's Supper, in Clifford's view, serve any useful purpose? Three positive claims for the value of the Lord's Supper recur in Clifford's writings. First, he recognized that it was a means of fostering devotion in the heart of the Christian; secondly, it was a witness to the historic facts of the faith; thirdly and, for him, most significantly, it was a celebration of the central fact of love in the Christian experience.

In spite of his emphasis on the symbolism of the Lord's Supper, Clifford had to acknowledge that, in practice, the lives of Christians were nourished by it. Beside all that was denied, there stood all that was actually experienced:

> Who of us . . . has not found our heart burning within us, as we have eaten the bread and drunk the cup at the table of the Lord? How the pulse of devotion has been quickened! How much more real has Christ become to us as our Redeemer, bearing our sins in His own body on the tree; and His fulness of pardon and power more available for every-day use! The sense of sin is made more acute. We hate our mean mutilated lives. Our selfishness pains us. Our poor achievements force us to cry to God for forgiveness. Resolve is strengthened. Aspiration soars. The heart is open to all the influences for good that surround our life in such profusion.[70]

For Clifford, then, a great deal took place at the table, though all of it within the hearts and minds of those gathered about it. The bread and wine had the power to awaken a spiritual response as urgent as any stirred by the preaching of the word.

In the second place, the sacraments were 'the oldest historical monuments of Christianity'.[71] They had survived all the vicissitudes of the centuries. Their chief value was as visual symbols which had the power to stir the heart:

> . . . the Lord of all souls knew what was in man, how he was to be reached and stirred; what forces play on his inward life like the winds on the strings of an Aeolian harp, and therefore provided for his real and recurring necessities, the two ordinances which He gave to His followers.[72]

The idea that the sacraments were representations of the historic faith, Clifford took up again later:

> Baptism and the Lord's Supper, as they appear in the New Testament, embody and represent the capital facts of the Christian religion. They are historic objective monuments; 'epistles' open to the reading of all men; evangels proclaiming the life, death, and resurrection of the Messiah.[73]

The Lord's Supper presented in pictorial and symbolic form both what God had done for us and our own creaturely dependence upon his grace:

> Our communion repictures the total dependence of our souls on His gift of Himself for us and to us; His bearing our sins in His own body on the tree, so that we may have life through Him. The indestructible historical facts of Christianity are present in, and dramatically represented by, the ordinances of Jesus.[74]

The symbolic value of the sacrament lay, then, in the clear picture it presented to the eyes of the worshippers of the historic acts by which they had been redeemed. Bread and wine were 'historical monuments', recalling what God in Christ had done for mankind.

Clifford's description of the symbol as a 'monument' contrasts with Spurgeon's use of the imagery of 'veil' or 'lattice'. For Spurgeon, the reality of Christ himself lay behind the symbol; the believer could go through the veil of the sacrament to a deeper union with his Lord. For Clifford, the effectiveness of the symbol was found in the memories it stirred within the heart of the believer.

The point at which Clifford's theology of the Lord's Supper sprang most vividly to life was in his description of it as an occasion of brotherhood and a sharing in the divine love. Here it ran parallel with his own practical involvement in the awakening movements of his time that brought both those of his own denomination and the wider fellowship of Nonconformists into closer union with one another. The idea of brotherhood had occurred in his earlier pamphlet where he placed the supper firmly in the context of the church. It was an act of personal communion of the soul with its Saviour and, beyond that, a means of fostering love between Christians:

> ... [it is] a means of promoting the special grace of brotherly love, of fostering 'the communion of saints', of making the consciousness of a common Christian life a deep, intense, joy-giving and helpful experience.[75]

Here Clifford found what was, for him, the central feature of the Lord's Supper, prompting him to his most positive appraisal of its value in the life of the believer. It was Christ's purpose for his church that he himself should be:

THE LORD'S SUPPER AND TWO BAPTIST PREACHERS

> ... the Head of a great religious society, whose animating spirit is universal love, and whose goal is universal helpfulness.[76]

The communion helped to forward and deepen that love. The early church had continued to observe it as a meal of 'fellowship and affection'. It was because of the place it held in the corporate life of Christians that Clifford was able to encourage his readers to come to the Lord's table at all costs. The church was to lose no opportunity of observing the communion, though its frequency would be a matter of expediency:

> Of all services it should be holiest and welcomest. Incite, induce, allure to the Lord's table ... Nor on any account but one, let us stay away from 'Communion'. Nought but intended or unrepented sin should be suffered to bar our approach to the table of the Lord.[77]

That Clifford had here found a theme in which he could exult is evident by his return to it in the later pamphlet. Both sacraments, he said, had a social aspect, placing believers firmly in the context of the New Kingdom:

> The supper adds the momentous fact that brotherhood amongst the regenerate is the basis of the New Society, the governing principle of all its relations, and the condition of effective service to the world.[78]

The Lord's Supper quickened love within Christians and it was love that lay at the very heart of the Christian gospel. Clifford echoed Dante's celebration of that love which moves the stars:

> Love! This is the ultimate energy. This sets the whole moral world in motion! love of God and love for men, love for home and love for the City, love for the welfare of all men, which is redemption and righteousness, spiritual health, truth, and meekness, chivalrous work for the lost and oppressed, religion, and the religion of Christ.[79]

Here Clifford stood at the heart of what he believed about the Christian faith. From this ground he was able to give an unqualified endorsement of the place of the Lord's Supper in the Christian life:

> ... of all 'means of grace', I say it on the authority of the saints of God, not one increases love as does the commemoration of that matchless love that saves us.[80]

True to the prophetic tradition within which Clifford believed himself to stand, he urged love as the proper concern of the Christian's life within the world. Faith always had an ethical dimension. What was believed was inseparable from what was lived and practised. For all the misunderstanding to which Clifford's maladroit division of 'material' and 'spiritual' might have given rise, there could be no doubt about his own commitment to the world about him, nor his recognition that Christ was to be found in that world, both as its rightful Lord and as the one who stood by the side of the oppressed and the poor:

> Eating the broken bread and drinking the outpoured wine, we identify ourselves with the Man of Sorrows in the moment of His utter humiliation and surrender, and accept His unique self-sacrifice as the divine law of all our life.[81]

If the Lord's Supper was to be understood in any sense as a sacrifice, it was in the release of love through the sacrificial service of those who shared in it.[82]

C) SPURGEON AND CLIFFORD: HEIRS OF TWO TRADITIONS

By the end of the nineteenth century the two wings of Baptist church life, the Particular or Calvinist and the General or Arminian, had merged into one. They were united in the Baptist Union which, in the following century, was to provide the focal point of denominational life. Following the wounding experience of the Downgrade Controversy, Spurgeon had resigned from the Union in 1887. His departure caused great grief to his fellow Baptists but few were prepared to follow him. In the few years that remained until his death in 1892 he became an increasingly isolated figure. Clifford, on the other hand, survived well into the twentieth century and, until the day of his death, was immersed in the work of the Union and the wider work of the Free Churches. In terms of eucharistic theology, Spurgeon was the last great Calvinist, within a tradition that, at the outset of the century, had been represented by Robert Hall, followed in succeeding decades by other, less familiar, Baptists. Clifford stood far to the opposite side of the Zwinglian norm, in the tradition of the radical Anabaptist reformers. The tradition represented by Spurgeon came effectively to an end with his death, Baptists continuing to honour it but being less and less influenced by it. Clifford, on the other hand, straddled the nineteenth and twentieth centuries and was a recognized spokesman for the outlook most commonly shared amongst Baptists. A comparison of the two men is illustrative of the two traditions, the one Calvinist the other radical, that stood on either side of the Zwinglian norm throughout the second half of the nineteenth century.

Firstly, comparison must be made of the central motif in the theology of each of them. For Spurgeon, the substitutionary and atoning death of Christ upon the cross was the central truth of the Christian faith and from it all else flowed. This central truth was the key to his understanding of the Lord's Supper and the controlling factor in his interpretation of it. This meant that the sacrament stood at the heart of what he believed and was not relegated to the perimeter. It was consequently fed by all those tributaries that flowed into the main stream of Spurgeon's thought. Three in particular were clearly discernible, the Bible, Calvinism and Puritanism. Spurgeon's faith was thoroughly biblical in the sense that Bunyan's was: his thought and language were shot through with the imagery of scripture and his devotional life was richly nourished by its words. What matters more than Spurgeon's belief in the inerrancy of scripture was his unerring gift for making its wealth available to others. As a preacher he was like a man prizing open the lid of a treasure chest, allowing others to run their fingers through the mass of gold coins it contained. His view of the Bible was, however, essentially that of a Calvinist. He was committed to a theology that provided a disciplined and coherent framework to his exposition of the scriptures. Further, he had read widely and sympathetically from the Puritans and, by their deep devotion, had been immersed in a Christ-mysticism in which theology turned to prayer. All this was caught up in his doctrine of the Lord's Supper. This led to the inevitable enrichment of Spurgeon's preaching on the sacrament. It gave to it not only a biblical content but also a theological and devotional dimension that was already well-proven in the experience of the historic church. For all that he was at odds with so many of his religious contemporaries, Spurgeon remained close to the doctrinal heart of the Reformation faith and the mainstream of historic Christianity.

The central motif in Clifford's theology was his prophetic vision of a brotherhood bound together in sacrificial service under the Christ of Calvary. It is perhaps inaccurate to describe it as theology. It was more the personal *credo* of a practical man caught up in the religious movements of his time. It has been suggested that Clifford was anti-intellectual, not for any obscurantist reason, but because as a religious leader he was more at home amongst the men and movements of his day.[83] The charge of anti-intellectualism is unnecessarily severe for one who was more a religious politician than a religious thinker. He was not possessed of theological acumen, however, and, in this, was typical of a denomination that since Hall's impatient dismissal of the baptismal barrier had avoided rigorous theological discipline, regarding it more as bane than blessing. His emphasis on brotherhood as the key to understanding the Lord's Supper needed a stronger biblical and theological scaffolding to support it, if the sacrament was to become nothing more than an agape-feast.

The strength of Spurgeon's position and the comparative weakness of Clifford's becomes clear in the way that both men handled their controversy with Catholicism. Spurgeon was uncompromisingly hostile to all 'popish' teachings, displaying an aggressiveness that outstripped most of his fellow Nonconformists, including Clifford. In the heat of battle, however, he surrendered nothing of his own deeply held beliefs. He could consequently use the most daring language in his eucharistic sermons without inviting suspicion or moving an inch from his Calvinist presuppositions. Clifford, on the other hand, in the process of distancing himself as far away as possible from Catholic sacerdotalism, left himself hardly within reach of a viable eucharistic theology. His unwise polarisation of matter and spirit, in what he believed to be the interests of pure religion and undefiled, only threatened to divide that which any true theology of the incarnation must hold together in indissoluble union. His sacramental theology was a husk containing a shrunken kernel.

The importance of the two men lay in their influence, and thus the influence of the traditions they represented, upon their fellow Baptists. Spurgeon held, and has continued to hold, an honoured place amongst them because of his skills and enormous effectiveness as a preacher. He adhered to Calvinism, however, at a time when most of his fellow Baptists were turning their backs upon what they saw as the harsher features of a reformer whose word no longer spoke to the modern world in which they lived. Calvin's determinism sat ill at ease with a generation that believed itself to be on the threshold of a world marked by freedom and a growing recognition of the dignity of the human spirit. Many Baptists overcame the difficulty of remaining loyal to Spurgeon, admiring his great gifts of preaching whilst rejecting his Calvinism, by claiming that he himself was a 'great-heart' who was much 'bigger' than the narrow confines of the doctrine he professed. Of this Spurgeon was deeply resentful and rightly so. Calvinist he was and to the teaching of Calvin he remained consistently true. At this level, however, he had a decreasing influence on his fellow Baptists. In contrast, Clifford seemed to be the man of the hour, able to create confidence both in those who were Arminians like himself and those whose loyalties could be traced back to the Particular wing of the denomination. He represented Baptists as they liked to think of themselves. He stood for freedom, he was impatient of all that divided men from one another, he was a democrat opposed to all divisions of status within the church. The eucharistic theology that became typical of Baptists in the twentieth century owed far more to Clifford than to Spurgeon. Abhorrence of sacerdotalism had already led to a diminishing of their own concept of ministry. The legacy of the eighteenth century and the communion controversies of the early nineteenth had left them suspicious of theology. The temperance movement, so dear to the heart of Clifford himself, had only further diverted their attention from the attempt to wrestle with the real meaning of communion. For many, the words of their most famous preacher must have fallen on deaf ears:

> At all times when you come to the communion table, count it to have been no ordinance of grace to you unless you have gone right through the veil into Christ's own arms.

NOTES

1 Sir James Marchant, **John Clifford**, 1924, p.44.
2 Ernest A. Payne, **The Baptist Union: A Short History**, 1958, pp.107f.
3 C. H. Spurgeon, **Till He Come**, 1894 (hereafter **THC**), p.324.
4 Iain Murray, **The Forgotten Spurgeon**, 1966, p.133.
5 ibid. p.135.
6 ibid. p.139.
7 **Freeman** 6 January 1871, p.9.
8 'In Remembrance' (Sermon on 1 Corinthians 11.24,25), **The Metropolitan Tabernacle Pulpit** (hereafter **MTP**), for 1909, 55, p.62.
9 **THC**, p.313.
10 'The Double Forget-Me-Not' (Sermon on 1 Corinthians 11.24), MTP for 1908, 54, p.318.
11 'The Object of the Lord's Supper' (Sermon on 1 Corinthians 11.26) MTP for 1905, 51, p.31.
12 **THC**, p.313.
13 ibid. pp.265f.
14 'The Double Forget-Me-Not', **MTP** for 1980, 54, p.318.
15 **THC**, p.313.
16 ibid. p.148.
17 Geoffrey Best, 'Evangelicalism and the Victorians', in Anthony Symondson, ed., **The Victorian Crisis of Faith**, 1970, p.38.
18 'The Witness of the Lord's Supper' (Sermon on 1 Corinthians 11.26), **MTP** for 1913, 59, p.37.
19 'The Lord's Supper, Simple but Sublime' (Sermon on 1 Corinthians 11.25,26), **MTP** for 1909, 55, p.315. p.315.
20 'The Object of the Lord's Supper', **MTP** for 1905, 51, p.317.
21 'Meat Indeed, Drink Indeed', **MTP** for 1914, 60, p.445.
22 See above p.20-1.
23 'In Remembrance', **MTP** for 1909, 55, p.62.
24 ibid. p.72.
25 **THC**, p.222.
26 'The Lord's Supper, Simple but Sublime', **MTP** for 1909, 55, p.315.
27 **MTP** for 1908, 54, p.316.
28 **THC**, p.17.
29 ibid. p.17.
30 ibid. p.69.
31 ibid. pp.353f.
32 ibid. pp.35-113.
33 ibid. p.319.
34 ibid.
35 ibid. p.99.
36 ibid. pp.119f..
37 ibid. p.251.
38 ibid. pp.350f.
39 ibid. pp.149f.
40 ibid. p.149.
41 ibid. p.218.
42 'The Double Forget-Me-Not', **MTP** for 1908, 54, p.321.
43 see above p.176.
44 'In Remembrance', **MTP** for 1909, 55, p.70.
45 ibid), pp.70f.
46 'The Double Forget-Me-Not', **MTP** for 1908, 54, p.315.
47 'In Remembrance', **MTP** for 1909, 55, p.71.
48 Marchant, op.cit. p.94.
49 ibid. p.91.
50 A. C. Underwood, **A History of the English Baptists**, 1947, p.229.
51 Payne, **op.cit.** p.174 note.
52 op.cit. p.22.
53 **Inaugural Address to the Annual Meeting of the Free Churches of London**, 25 November 1895, p.13.
54 **Review and Expositor** 8, No.3, July 1911, p.341.
55 **Anglican Romanism and National Character**, 1920, p.15.
56 ibid.
57 **The Ordinances of Jesus and the Sacraments of the Church**, 1888, p.11.
58 ibid. p.25.
59 op.cit. p.4.
60 ibid. p.7.
61 ibid. p.11.
62 'The Attitude of Baptists to Catholicism', **Review and Expositor** 8, No.3, 1911, p.334.
63 **Ordinances of Jesus**, p.19.
64 ibid. p.4.
65 ibid.
66 ibid. p.5.
67 ibid. p.4.
68 ibid. p.18.
69 ibid. pp.7f.
70 ibid. pp.23f.
71 ibid. p.8.
72 ibid. pp.10f.
73 ibid. p.17.
74 ibid.
75 **The True Use of the Lord's Supper**, 1876, p.4.
76 ibid. p.5.
77 ibid. p.14.

78 **Ordinances of Jesus,** pp.20f.
79 ibid. p.24.
80 ibid.
81 ibid. p.20.
82 ibid. p.25.
83 Willis B. Glover, 'English Baptists at the Time of the Downgrade Controversy', **Foundations,** 1, No.3, 1958, pp.42f.

Chapter 6

A Baptist Theology of the Lord's Supper?

The Baptist churches emerged from the nineteenth century with a doctrine of the Lord's Supper that had been impoverished by theological decline and the various controversies that had surrounded belief and practice. The Calvinist legacy, inherited from the seventeenth and eighteenth centuries, evident in the communion hymns still used by Baptists in their celebration of the sacrament as well as in the theology of men such as Hall, Butler and Newman, had been gradually eroded by the Zwinglianism which Baptists, like other Dissenters, found an increasingly attractive alternative to the growing influence of Catholic doctrines of the eucharist. The incursion into Baptist beliefs of Zwinglianism, with its ambivalent attitude to the relationship between matter and spirit, encouraged a drift towards radical Anabaptist attitudes from which many earlier English Baptists had been eager to dissociate themselves. Hall's severance of any essential link between baptism and membership of the church, at the beginning of the century, and Clifford's promotion of 'religion' above 'church' at its end, undermined the ecclesial setting which had traditionally provided both context and meaning for the Lord's Supper. The drift towards a benign anarchy in the matter of ministerial presidency at the Lord's table hastened a process that discussions about the rightness or otherwise of para-church celebrations of the sacrament and a characteristically Baptist enthusiasm for 'Christian fellowship' were unable to halt. Preoccupation with the nature of the church was seen as a peculiarly Catholic pursuit or, when displayed by the Congregationalists, both in their architecture and styles of worship, an aspiration after 'churchliness' that betrayed an unmanly denial of Dissenting principles. Attention was further diverted from the meaning of the sacrament itself by the temperance-inspired advocacy of unfermented wine, the social implications of fermented wine attracting far more debate than the significance of wine as the sign of Christ's shed blood.

At the edges of the nineteenth-century communion controversies amongst Baptists, however, a deeper and more perplexing question awaited answer. It was whether, given the Baptist theological presuppositions about the nature of the church and sacraments and their relationship to faith, a coherent Baptist sacramental theology was possible or, in the eyes of some Baptists at least, even desirable.

At the outset we observed that fundamental to Baptist understanding of the church and sacraments was the priority they accorded to faith. In this, it may be argued, they were little different from other Christians. What distinguished them, however, was the way they perceived faith as marking the beginning of the Christian life. For them, faith was decision. It was an act of will. Their argument with the national church, from which they separated, was that it created members by baptizing infants incapable of understanding the faith into which they were being baptized, unable either to respond to the Christ who was known by faith alone or to take up the burden of Christian discipleship. Such momentous steps were possible only for those of sufficient maturity to make a free and conscious assent of faith. In holding that position, Baptists were implicitly rejecting the power of either church or sacrament to make Christians. Between God and the individual there was no need for any intermediary. Responsibility for proclaiming the gospel rested with the church, but responsibility for whether or not the gospel was believed and accepted rested with the individual. Closely associated with that response of faith, its theology inevitably affected by it, was the sacrament of baptism.

To understand the Baptist view of the nature of the Lord's Supper as a sacrament, or as an ordinance as it would more frequently be described, one must begin with baptism. At one and the same time, Baptists have brought baptism into intimate proximity with the moment of conversion whilst denying it any role in the making of a Christian. Indeed, it has not always been clear what exactly has been their understanding of the relationship of the two. The early General Baptists came close to making baptism an effective sign by clearly associating it with admission to the church. Their path to believer's baptism had followed an ecclesial route, their aim being to reform and renew the church by relating its initiating ordinance to the already confessed faith of those to be admitted. The Particular Baptists placed their emphasis on the death-burial-resurrection motif of baptism, without claiming that baptism itself was a death, a burial and a resurrection. Robert Hall's severance of baptism from church membership and his claim that one could, without baptism, be a 'sincere' Christian against whom no barriers to admission to the Lord's table could justifiably be raised, only further clouded the relationship between sacrament and faith. Since then, Baptists have continued to emphasise the priority of faith. In common with other Evangelicals, they have most frequently been content with the unscriptural description of Christian beginnings as 'taking the Lord Jesus Christ as one's own personal Saviour', a step that they see as owing everything to personal decision and nothing to sacramental mediation. Baptism has been viewed as an act of discipleship rather than an integral part of the process of conversion. It is submitted to as an act of obedience, following Christ's example in receiving baptism at the hands of John in the Jordan and observing his command in the final Great Commission delivered to his disciples on Olivet. Alternatively, it is viewed as an act of public witness, a highly dramatic representation of the individual's commitment in faith to Christ. The washing from sin which it signifies has already taken place in the moment of conversion, when the individual appropriated the benefits of Christ's death upon Calvary. The gift of the Spirit has also already been granted in conversion, and may perhaps be granted more fully in some future 'baptism in the Spirit', as distinguished from the baptism in water. The death-burial-resurrection motif is evidenced in the 'death' involved in the commitment of faith and the resurrection life pursued in discipleship. Admission into the church is identified with the decision of a Church Meeting and the proffering of the right hand of fellowship at a subsequent communion service. If baptism be taken as the model, then, for Baptists a sacrament is beneficial but not essential, it symbolizes a great deal but effects nothing, it is a test of obedience not a means of grace. If pressed on purely theological grounds Baptists would have had to admit that their understanding of the nature of a sacrament would apply as much to the Lord's Supper as to baptism. Yet a survey of the nineteenth century has revealed that many were not prepared to live with such bleak conclusions when it came to the former. Baptism is experienced only once, the Lord's Supper is a continuing part of the Christian's life. There were some who demonstrated their capacity for living the Christian life without the benefit of the Lord's Supper by their neglect of it on various grounds of conscience. There were others for whom its meaning lay in the fact that it was an ordinance, an institution commanded by Jesus, rather than a sacrament, or means of grace, of the church. But there were also yet others whose actual experience at the Lord's table compelled them to invest it with more meaning than their sacramental theology would properly allow and to come to it with urgent footsteps, confident that they would not leave it hungry. Of these, some undergirded their experience and expectations with a theology inherited from the Calvinist milieu out of which the Baptist separatist churches had been born and others, sometimes in addition to it as in the case of Spurgeon, by relating the truths set forth in the holy scriptures to what was received at the table.

These twin factors of scripture and tradition raise further difficulties encountered by Baptists when they resolve to seek a viable sacramental theology. Any attempt to do justice to the sacramental nature of baptism and communion has first to come to terms with the existence of Baptists as a separate denomination and the reasons for it. Baptists came into existence by a staggering rejection of what already existed. In seeking to establish baptism as a sacrament administered only to believers, they had first to pronouce null and void their own baptism as infants and then, by their re-baptism, to reconstitute the Christian church. Their step entailed a rejection of baptism as understood and practised by the greater part of Christendom and therefore an unchurching of the great majority of their fellow Christians. It was the enormity of this bequest that Hall found so intolerable and of which he rid himself by denying that baptism was in any way essential to the existence of a church. The burden, however, could not so lightly be disposed of, for its shadow continued to be cast over Baptist attitudes to scripture and tradition. The Baptists have not been alone in endeavouring to re-invent the church, setting the historical development embodied in tradition to one side and leaping the centuries in order to deal direct with the holy scriptures. This huge step is taken in the belief that the New Testament will provide a clear blueprint for the establishment of a church order and sacramental practice nearer to the first-century original. Few Baptists have, like Hall, been willing to concede that the enterprise, whilst brave and commendable, cannot succeed. In the first place, it mistakenly assumes that the seeker after New Testament truth can extricate himself not only from the traditions of the church but also from his own theological predilections and the entirely non-theological assumptions of the age in which he lives. Ironically, Christians can rarely sound so much like the children of their own generation as when they make direct and simple appeals to scripture. A church that ignores Christian history places itself in bondage to the ethos of its own time, inevitably so if there is no other perspective than that of the present. The second, more serious and more controversial assumption is, given that the contemporary church were able to divest itself of the mores of its own time, it would find in the New Testament a clear and incontrovertible pattern of church and sacramental order. Luther had the wisdom to deny that such clear directions were to be found within its pages and argued that the task of the church was to extract from it a theology of church and sacrament. Such a task cannot be separated from Christian tradition which embodies, after all, the fruits of the church's theological reflection. A scenario of church history which portrays the church as plunging into theological darkness at the close of the apostolic age, partially emerging at the Reformation, but not seeing the full light of day until the arrival of the Baptists, or the Methodists, or the restoration churches of late twentieth-century England, according to the object of one's personal loyalties, betrays an understanding of the role of the Holy Spirit that will scarcely bear examination. The practices of the generations of Christians that succeeded the apostles were not irrelevant to the interpretation of the New Testament, as Godwin and some at least of his fellow Baptists recognized in their debate with the Anglo-Catholics. Not that tradition, any more than scripture, provides a blueprint. It is itself subject to constant reformation under the Word of God, as the reformers claimed. But the truth is not to be found except through the constant dialectic of scripture and tradition. This is especially true of the Lord's Supper. The clues which the New Testament provides for theories ranging from the barest memorialism to the most materialist realism have to be weighed against the theological reflection and sacramental experience of the church down the generations. Quite simply, a church that endeavours to leap across history directly into the world of the New Testament will find insufficient material upon which to build a theology and may well decide to do without one.

Baptists varied in their attitude to history and tradition. Some, like one of the editors of the *Freeman*, were dismissive of what lay in their own Baptist history little more than twenty years earlier. Others, like Godwin, Stock and Leonard, made some, if at times desultory, attempt to relate Baptist beliefs to the early Fathers and the leading reformers. Others, like Gould, Medley and Whitley, rejected the early Fathers as so tainted by heathenism as to be perverters rather than purveyors of truth and displayed only a qualified approval of the reformers, observing that

A BAPTIST THEOLOGY OF THE LORD'S SUPPER?

on some questions they had shown themselves less than whole-hearted in their reforming zeal. Against these explicit reactions to tradition have to be set the fruits of wider theological perception that continued to enrich Baptist thinking in less observed ways. Their Calvinism kept Baptists in mainstream Protestantism and influenced their eucharistic thinking from Hall to Spurgeon. Their incorporation in their hymn books of eucharistic hymns drawn from a variety of denominational sources helped to shape their attitude to the Lord's Supper and to keep alive expectations at a devotional level that would have been discouraged by pronouncements at a theological level.

If Baptists are to have a theology of the Lord's Supper, the question of their relationship to the historic Christian tradition is a crucial one. Baptism again provides an interesting model of development. The view of baptism as either an act of obedience or of witness and nothing more was challenged in the 1950s by Neville Clark, in his book *An Approach to the Theology of the Sacraments*, and in the 1960s by George Beasley-Murray, in *Baptism in the New Testament*, and R. E. O. White in *The Biblical Doctrine of Initiation*. All three books were marked by a depth of research that drew material from a wide range of ecumenical scholarship. The result was a doctrine of baptism which, whilst true to the essence of the historic Baptist witness, had a profundity not previously encountered in Baptist circles. Through their research the Baptist understanding of baptism was made the beneficiary of insights garnered from other theological traditions and other styles of churchmanship. By the same token, Baptists now held something of enormous value that they could contribute to the wider church's understanding of itself. It is also the case that the solid work of Clark, White and Beasley-Murray provided a theology that is still in search of an adequate practical expression. Whilst not repudiating their findings, Baptists have yet to take on board their implications for church order and liturgy. The same work has yet to be done for the doctrine of the Lord's Supper. Again in the 1950s and 1960s many Baptists were influenced by the liturgical renewal and embodied a number of its insights into their Sunday worship, bringing the Lord's Supper out of the twilight and placing it at the centre of worship alongside the word, following the Reformation pattern of word and sacrament. Yet, whilst much has been done to restore the Lord's Supper to a worthy place in the worship of the church, little has been done to expound its meaning.

Where baptism is a theology in search of a practice, the Lord's Supper is a practice in search of a theology. Such a theology will not be found, however, in isolation from other Christians. The Christian eucharist is central to the faith of the majority of Christians and Baptists cannot turn their backs on theology formed out of scripture, the practice of the church from its earliest days and the experience of Christian men and women who have come to the Lord's table in faithful expectation down the generations. Some of the questions raised by that wealth of experience were central to the concerns of the Tractarians, the Ritualists and the magisterium of the Roman Catholic Church in the late nineteenth and early twentieth centuries. The reaction of Baptists then was to join many other Protestants in an ardent anti-Catholicism, in many instances going beyond their compatriots by rejecting the Reformation teaching of Luther and Calvin. Many found Zwinglianism to be a 'safe house', but others were unwilling to rest even there, going beyond it to the radical Anabaptist tradition and the liturgical iconoclasm of Carlstadt. The lesson of contemporary baptismal scholarship is that greater wealth is to be found in convergence than in polarization. Anti-Catholicism proved to be only the theological midwife of wind and emptiness.

The relationship of Baptists to their fellow Christians was starkly raised in the early nineteenth-century communion debate in which Hall and Kinghorn were the chief protagonists. Ironically, it was Kinghorn who was truest to the received Christian tradition in his insistence that only the baptized should be admitted to the Lord's Supper. His definition of baptism led him to exclude the majority of other Christians, however, on the grounds that they had received an invalid baptism. Hall, on the other hand, endeavoured to see Baptists in the context of the historic church and in their relationship to other Christians. He, no more than Kinghorn, could accept the validity of infant baptism. His conviction that other Christians were members of the true church, though unbaptized, led him to reject the historic testimony of the church and to claim the right of 'sincere', though unbaptized, Christians to be admitted to the Lord's table.

Baptists of today are in a position of greater flexibility and able to respond to the dilemma in ways that it would have been unrealistic to have expected of either Kinghorn or Hall. In the first place, it has to be acknowledged that, whereas Hall's heart was in the right place, so was Kinghorn's head. The Lord's Supper is a sacrament of the church and its integrity as a sacrament is inseparable from the integrity of the initiating ordinance of baptism. Hall held a 'high' view of the supper and a 'low' view of baptism. Many of his successors found such a sacramental dichotomy difficult to sustain and applied to the Lord's Supper the same criteria that Hall applied to baptism. If inner attitudes were more important than outward observance, if 'sincerity' was to be valued above obedience, if baptism was a sign and no more, then equally a religion of the heart was to be prized above 'ceremonies'. Sacraments play their part in the Christian life, not as optional extras, or occasional novelties, or as acts of merit, but as true signs of Christ's saving work in the conversion of the believer and in the continual nurture of his Christian life. Baptists have to stand with Kinghorn in the historic Christian tradition and maintain that Christians come to the sacramental grace of the eucharist by the sacramental path of baptism. On the other hand, they have to stand with Hall in the recognition of other people's Christian experience. Loyalty to historic tradition, however, will also require a measure of recognition of other people's baptism. A Christian baptized in infancy is not unbaptized, as both Kinghorn and Hall would have claimed. His baptism may be defective but it exists. Baptists cannot go on staring through it as if it were not there. For Baptists of the twentieth century no great risk is involved, given the changes that are taking place both in the church and in society. With the increasing de-Christianization of society the form of baptism against which John Smyth first protested, baptism indiscriminately administered to infants on the grounds of nationhood and incorporation in the national church, will be less widely sought after and more judiciously administered. Further, a great weight of theological and biblical opinion holds that 'believer's baptism' is the norm from which the church is to derive its understanding of the nature and practice of Christian baptism. The drift of baptismal theology is away from apologetic for the time-honoured practice of infant baptism towards a whole theology of baptism that will shape and determine practice as the church enters the post-Christian era of mission. In the meantime, Baptists should accept that those who are baptized in their infancy and have confirmed their baptism according to the practice of their respective churches, should be freely admitted to the communion of the Lord's table on the grounds that they are baptized believers. This is to argue for an 'open' table that is in keeping with Christian tradition. It is not the same thing as an 'open' invitation to all who sincerely love the Lord Jesus Christ regardless of whether or not they have been baptized, either in infancy or as believers. To admit the unbaptized to the Lord's table is to imply that baptism is unimportant and, thus, that communion itself is unimportant. If it be rejoined that our chief concern should be with faith, it does not follow that because faith is central sacraments are peripheral.

Recognition of the baptism of other Christians is, at the same time, an affirmation that Baptists themselves belong to the historic church. History has shown that the church did not begin all over again with the re-baptism of Smyth and his followers or the baptismal transfiguration of the Jacob-Lathrop-Jessey church. Baptists have remained a minority, a small part of that universal *continuum* of the church which has not ceased to convert sinners, sustain pilgrims and inspire saints. Recognition of the spiritual and theological wealth of the wider church has led to a renewed depth of understanding of the doctrine of baptism. It is only a similar recognition that will unlock for Baptists the wealth of the Lord's Supper. Sacramental theology, as we have seen, is inseparable from the dialectic of scripture and tradition by which it has been formed. There is no access to a scriptural theology of the sacraments that bypasses the theological tradition of the church. This is illustrated by the Baptist reaction to the Catholic revival. Faced with a revived emphasis on the presence of Christ in the sacrament, Baptists cried a transubstantial wolf, and made off in the opposite direction. Transubstantiation involved 'magic' and priest-craft and the only alternatives that they believed to be open to them were either a Zwinglianism that kept matter and spirit at a respectable distance from each other or a radicalism that mistrusted matter altogether. These were not the only alternatives, however.

Their own hymn writers, the Stennetts, provided vibrant, powerful and lovely images of the presence of Christ in the supper. The anonymous author of the 'Sacramental Meditations' showed that it was possible both to be a Baptist and to believe that God gave his people something infinitely precious at his table. Spurgeon's warm and eloquent preaching encouraged them to come in the belief that they would find Christ there. The Calvinist tradition from which they came taught that the bread and wine were the means by which the Holy Spirit raised believers into the presence of Christ where spiritually they might feed upon him. Luther took with utter seriousness the words of Jesus, 'This is my body', and taught a real eating and drinking of the body and blood of Christ that, significantly, was not dependent upon the priestly intervention of an episcopally ordained president. The further they fled from any of these alternatives the less remained to Baptists of a sacramental theology with any real content. The 'safe house' of Zwinglianism provided them, as it provided many of their Protestant contemporaries, with temporary shelter. But, for Baptists, it was less safe than it was for others. Zwinglianism's ambivalent attitude to matter and spirit, sign and thing signified, offered too many temptations for those tempted into the far country of the radicals, the *Schwärmerei*, the seekers after perfection. Affirming a faith that could dispense with baptism, identifying the Lord's Supper with the material side of religion above which men might rise in the onward and upward march of the spirit, they left themselves clutching the inedible ashes of a non-sacramental theology.

A doctrine of the Lord's Supper that has no place for the real presence of Christ, however understood, has substituted a meritorious act, a pious spiritual exercise, for the a sacrament of grace in which the Father gives his Son again to his people in the fellowship of the Spirit. We have seen that there have always been Baptists able to affirm with the apostle Paul that the cup which we bless is a participation in the blood of Christ, and the bread which we eat is a participation in the body of Christ. The question of the real presence is inescapable if the supper is to be seen as an act of God and not a rite of man, if the attention of the church is to be upon what God in Christ has done for us and not what we, in our response of faith, do for him. Baptist theology has been inhibited from grasping the issue, threatened as it has felt by the ubiquitous spectre of transubstantiation. The real presence is, however, a mystery, and Baptists have no need to flee from that mystery nor to be ashamed of the efforts that some of their forefathers made to come to terms with it. Nor can they elude it by leapfrogging across history and tradition into the pages of the New Testament. It was to those pages that the stabbing finger of Luther pointed as he defended his eucharistic doctrine against Zwingli at the Marburg Colloquy. If Baptists are to have a viable eucharistic theology then they have to retrace their footsteps along the paths they took at the Catholic revival and come again to a place where they can listen to the testimony of the wider family of the church. And, perhaps, they should listen to the testimony of their own people who used to come to the Lord's Supper singing:

> Here at thy table, Lord! we meet
> To feed on food divine:
> Thy body is the bread we eat,
> Thy precious blood the wine ...
>
> His body torn with rudest hands,
> Becomes the finest bread,
> And with the blessing he commands,
> Our noblest hopes are fed.
>
> His blood that from each opening vein,
> In purple torrents ran,
> Hath filled this cup with generous wine,
> That cheers both God and man.

BOOKS MENTIONED IN TEXT

Aldis, John, *Christian Union* (1846) 73
Booth, Abraham, *Apology for Baptists* (1778) 34,45
Bunyan, John, *Differences in Judgment about Water Baptism no Bar to Communion* (1673) 34
Clifford, John, *The Ordinances of Jesus and the Sacraments of the Church* (1888) 183,188
Clifford, John, *Anglican Romanism and the National Character*, (1920?) 186
Clifford, John, *The True Use of the Lord's Supper* (1876) 187
Cramp, J. M., *An Essay on the Obligation of Christians to Observe the Lord's Supper Every Lord's Day* 144
Daniell, J. Mortlake, *The One Church, or Sects Unscriptural* (1846) 72
Fuller, Andrew, *The Gospel Worthy of all Acceptation* (1785) 42
Godwin, Benjamin, *An Examination of the Principles and Tendencies of Dr Pusey's Sermon on the Eucharist* (1843) 91
Gould, George, *Open Communion and the Baptists of Norwich* (1860) 36
Haldane, James, *A View of the Social Worship and Ordinances Observed by the First Christians* 144
Hall, Robert, *On Terms of Communion* (1815) 45,54
Hall, Robert, *A Reply to the Rev. Joseph Kinghorn, being a further vindication of Free Communion* (1818) 45
Helwys, Thomas, *The Mistery of Iniquity* (1612) 49,182
Innes, William, *Open Communion and Christian Forbearance* (1845) 50
Kinghorn, Joseph, *Baptism a Term of Communion at the Lord's Table* (1816) 4,45
Kinghorn, Joseph, *A Defence of Baptism a Term of Communion in answer to the Rev. Robert Hall's reply* (1820) 45
Leifchild, John, *Christian Union* (1844) 71
Littledale, R. F., *The Real Presence* (1867) 102
Overbury, R. W., *A Serious Enquiry into Christian Union* (1844) 74
Spurgeon, C. H. *Till He Come* 167,180
Williams, Charles, *The Principles and Practices of Baptists* (1882) 5

JOURNALS MENTIONED IN TEXT

Baptist Magazine 8,11,15f,85,87ff,95,98,103,107ff,112f,123ff, 130,135f,140,145,174,204
Baptist Record 75
Baptist Reporter 41,75,129f
Chicago Standard 35
Christian Witness 64
Freeman 36,75,85,87ff,103f,110,114f,119,122,140, 142,146,149,151,157,159,200
General Baptist Magazine 33,89,133,138f
General Baptist Repository 132,1451f,149f
Guardian 110
Patriot 72
Primitive Church Magazine 36,55(n.91),72,74,77ff,134,151
Southend Standard 35

BIBLICAL REFERENCES

Psalm 17 v.3 174f
Song of Solomon 8. v.2 177
Daniel 2 v.24 128
Matthew 24 v.25 128
Matthew 26 v.29 99
Matthew 28 v.31 58,68
Luke 8 v.46 178
Luke 22 v.14 169
John 1 v.16 177
John 6 97,100ff
Acts 115
Acts 2 v.42 144

Acts 2 vv.46-7 140
Acts 7 v.10 128
Acts 8 v.1 140
Acts 20 v.7 144
Romans 14 49f
I Cor 1 v.15 93
I Cor 10 95
I Cor 10 vv.14-17 97,100,144,176
I Cor 11 v.24 6
I Cor 11 v.27 97,100
I Cor 15 v.50 96
Rev 1 vv.17-18 175

INDEX - PEOPLE

Alden, Edward C. 15,113
Aldis, John 66,73
Allen, James 24,27
Angus, Joseph 40,74,128f,130
Anselm 170f
Armitage, Thomas 60

Bayes, Elizabeth 37
Baynes, Bishop Robert 28
Beardsall, Francis 149ff
Beasley-Murray, George 201
Beddome, Benjamin 18f,20,22
Bernard of Clairvaux 24,178
Best, Geoffrey 84
Bickersteth, Edward 25
Bonar, Horatius 28
Booth, Abraham 34,45,56
Brock, William 36f,40
Brown, J. T. 16
Bunyan, John 34,40,165,193
Burdett, A. 72
Burns, Jabez 33f,151
Burns, Dawson 151ff
Button, William 10,54,174,197

Calvin, John 9,92,107,109,143f,
   170,174,176,178,194,202
Campbell, Dr John 64
Carey, William 42
Carlstadt, Augustine 60,202
Charles, Elizabeth 28
Clark, Neville 201
Clifford, John 6,95,131,148f,151,
   153f,164,182ff,192ff,197
Conder, James 27
Cooke, J. Hunt 16,113
Cramp, J. M. 144f
Cranmer, Thomas 94,107,144

Dale, R. W. 148,188
Daniell, J. Mortlock 72
Dante 191
Davies, Professor Horton 85,159
Doddridge, Philip 24f,144

Edginton, Ernest 159
Evans, Christmas 46f

Fawcett, John 18
Fuller, Andrew 42,124,130f,164

Gale, J. T., of Putney 110f,117
Gilchrist, J. 132
Gill, John 122,130ff,135ff,164
Glas, John 144
Godwin, Benjamin 86,91ff,
   100ff,105ff,110ff,114,200
Gould, George 36ff,109,200
Gough, T. T. 145
Grant, Dr James, of Toronto 8
Grant, J. W. 114
Green, John 151
Green, S. H. 146

Haddon, John 18
Haldane, James 144f
Hall, John Keen 131
Hall, Robert 3f,8ff,34,36,39,
   42ff,55ff,65ff,71,74,79f,90,100,104,107,1
   10,114,127,130,137,164,174,184f,192f,19
   7ff,202
Harrison, Brian 148,150,153
Heber, Bishop Reginald 24,27
Heath, J. T. 139f
Helwys, Thomas 33,49,182
Hinton, J. H. 40f,85,95ff,
   102f,104,116ff,123,128f,140
Humphrey, William 116ff

Ignatius 8,108
Innes, William 50f
Ivimey, Joseph 47,52f,55,66,
   69f,73f

James I, King of England 49,182
Jarrom, J. 10,141f,149f,158,174
Jessey, Henry 34,40
Jewel, Bishop 107
Jones, Benjamin 18

Keach, Benjamin 17
Keble, John 186f
Kinghorn, Joseph 4,36,40,42ff,
   52ff,57,61f,64ff,80,110,202

Landels, William 40
Leifchild, John 71
Leonard, H. C. 108,200
Leslie, Andrew 60
Lester, Dr (Anglican) 76
Lester, Henry (Baptist deacon) 35
Liggins, J., of Hinckley 33f
Littledale, Dr 102
Livesey, Roger 149
Lloyd George, David 183
Luther, Martin 8f,53,60,92,
   101,107,110,174,188,200,202,
   204

Mackonochie, Alexander, of St Alban's,
   Holborn 95
MacLeod, A. H. 130

INDEX

Manning, Samuel 11
Marchant, Sir James 165,182
Mary I, Queen of England 107
Matthews, Thomas W. 133
Maclaren, Alexander 6ff,87,103
McLean, Archibald 133,144
Medley, Edward 109,200
Meyer, F. B. 87
Montgomery, James 24,27
Murch, Spencer 145
Murray, Iain 166

Newman, John Henry 91,98,116, 186f
Newman, William 10,67,127ff, 174,197
Noel, Baptist Wriothesley 24, 40,71
Noel, Gerard T. 24,27
Norton, William 38f,41,74

Overbury, Robert William 74f,83

Palmer, W. 55
Parker, Dr Joseph 157
Payne, E. A. 16,165
Peto, Sir Samuel Morton 158
Pike, J. B. 17
Pike, J. Carey 17
Pius IX, Pope 84
Pollard, Frank Ward 16
Polycarp 108
Pottenger, T. 5,86
Powell, Vavasor 34
Pritchard, George 54,83
Pusey, E. B. 71,86,91ff,100, 106ff,110f,114,186f

Rawson, George 24f
Rippon, Dr John 17ff,20,22,24
Robinson, H. Wheeler 16f
Robinson, Robert 18
Rogers, Thomas 142

Room, C. 115f,119
Ryland, Dr John 18

Shirley, Walter 27
Slater, Frank 103ff
Smyth, John 33f,79,125,182,202
Socinus 60
Spurgeon, Charles Haddon 3,6,15, 18f,21ff,29,35,76,146,155,157,164ff,182f, 185f,190,192ff,199,201,204
Steane, Edward 40,71
Steele, Anne 17,19ff,26,172
Steele, William 17f
Stennett, Joseph 17ff,21,24f,204
Stennett, Samuel 18f,22ff,204
Stevens, John 55
Stevenson, W. R. 17
Stock, John 107f,200

Taylor, Dan 17,42
Temple, William 186
Thomas Thomas 127ff
Tombes, John 34,40
Toon, Peter 118
Turner, Daniel 122
Tymms, Vincent 149

Wallis, George 131
Wallis, John 133
Walters, W. 4f
Watts, Isaac 18,22ff,144
Wesley, Charles 17,22ff
Wesley, John 17,22ff,42,146
White, R. E. O. 201
Whitley, W. T. 8,109,113,200
Whiton, J. M. 113
Wilkin, S. 89
Williams, Charles 5f
Wilson, John Gavin 35
Winter, E. P. 122

Zwingli 3f,8,10f,16,60,101,107, 113,164,186,204

INDEX - PLACES AND CHURCHES
(BC = Baptist Church)

Aberdeen, King's College 44
Accrington, Cannon St BC 6

Bates College, USA 165
Beeston, Notts 139
Birmingham
    Carrs Lane BC 188
    Sparkbrook BC 157
Bolton, Claremont BC 155
Bourton-on-the-Water 18
Bradford, Tetley St BC 157

Bristol 130
    Academy 44
    Broadmead BC 36,44
Broughton, Hants 18
Burnley, Haggate BC 134

Cambridge 44,130
Canada 144
Coventry, Queen's Rd BC 35,157

Derby, Melbourne BC 132

Dundee, St Mary Magdalene 116

Egham, Surrey 38
Ewyas Harold, Ebenezer BC 158

High Wycombe, Union Chapel 74
Hinckley 33
  BC 158

Kettering, Fuller BC 132,161fn

Leeds 153
  Rawdon College 149
Leicester, Harvey Lane BC 44
London 115,124,147
  Artillery St BC 124f
  Bloomsbury Chapel 158
  Carter Lane BC 18
  Christ Church, Westminster Bridge Rd 87
  City Temple 157
  Devonshire Square BC 95
  Eagle St BC 47,74
  Forest Hill BC 183
  Hampstead 89
  Horsley Down BC 17
  Jacob-Lathrop-Jessey Church 34,203
  Marylebone 33
  Maze Pond BC, Southwark 66
  Metropolitan Tabernacle 18,35f,155,164,166f,179
  New Park St BC 18
  Pastors' College 18,35
  Prescot St BC 124f
  Putney 112
  St Alban's, Holborn 95,115
  Spitalfields 182

Stepney College 10,74,127, 126,129
Surrey Chapel 71,74
Upper Norwood BC 75f
Westbourne Park BC 164
Woodgrange BC 76
Loughborough 89

Manchester
  Oak St General BC 149
  Union Chapel 6
Melbourne BC 132
Mentone, France 147,167,179
Munster 63

New Milton, Ashley BC 159
New York, 113
Northampton, College St BC 16
Norwich, St Mary's BC 36ff,44,69,74

Oxford
  Christ Church 71,86,91
  New Road BC 86,91
  Regent's Park College 17

Pentre, Zion BC 159

Ramsgate, Cavendish Chapel 72

Scotland 144
Southend-on-Sea
  Avenue BC 34,152
  Clarence Rd BC 35

Toronto 8

Wisbech, Cambs. 141

GENERAL INDEX

Anabaptists 3,29,59f,60, 63,85, 104,188,192,197,202
Anglicans/Anglicism 1f,7,34ff, 28f,72,76,85ff,95,139,166,182
Anglo-Catholics 97,115,123,146, 200
anti-Catholic feelings 5,15,105, 110,145,167,170,184,202
architecture 85,88f,90,168,181, 197
Arminianism 10,33,41,164, 182,192,194
atonement 4,10,33,39,48,75,84, 108,111f,116,139,145,170,192

Band of Hope 153f
bankruptcy 157f

baptism 1f,6,10f,32ff,43ff,49, 53ff,68,60f,63ff,66,69,74,76, 79f,102,110,127,132f,164ff, 170,180,183,185,188,190, 197ff,201f,204
  of believers 33f,64,68,80, 132,198f
  by affusion 64,67
  by immersion 36f,46f
  (see also infant baptism)
baptismal regeneration 48,165f
Baptist Board 115,124f
Baptist Missionary Society 42,74, 129
Baptist Total Abstinence Movement 151
Baptist Union 18,40f,85,95,109, 121,129,140,146,149,182,192

INDEX

Baptist World Alliance 183

Calvinism 3,8,10f,29,34f,39, 41f,59,61,164f,167,172,193f, 201
Calvinists 34,60,92,97,122, 144,164,175,192,197,199,204
Catholic revival 2,4,11,27, 59,61,80,84ff,105,121,123, 129ff,136,160,165,184,186, 203f (see also Tractarians)
Catholics 6,8,15,57,67,84ff, 127,137ff,169,176,182 (see also Roman Catholics)
Catholicism 2,6f,11,15f,32,61,72, 76,84ff,121,123,131,140,143f, 159.166ff,172ff,181,183,185f, 193,197
Christmas 88,90
Christology 9,60,92,117
Church of England (see also Anglicans/Established Church) 1,32,35,47,71f,76,84ff,109,121, 139,146,165ff,182,186f,197
Church of Scotland 144
communion/Lord's Supper passim
  celebrant 5,86
  as celebration 12,15,145,179f, 189
  closed (strict) 2f,6,10,32ff, 121,134,160
  as commemoration 6,12ff, 112,191
  consecration 32,95,98,123
  controversy 32ff,137,160,169, 194,197,202
  as declaratory 14
  eschatological dimension 180
  frequency 2,121,143ff,191
  infrequent attendance 158ff
  institution of 4,58
  as means towards unity 71
  open 2,6,8,10,32ff,197,204
  presidency of 2,121ff,131ff, 197,204
  private 140
Congregationalists 24ff,27,64,71, 87,90,148,188,197
Council of Free Churches of London 184
cross/burial/resurrection motif 4,34,61,132,198

deacons 2,35,98,127,132,139, 155,157f,160
discipline 121ff,132,157,193
Dissent/Dissenters (see also Free Churches, Nonconformists) 10,53f,60,70f,73f,76,88,106, 110,123,135,145,197
Downgrade Controversy 167,

182,192

early church 8,16,50,54,62ff,68, 79f,91,105ff,127,143f,146,191,199f
elders 127,130,134
established church/establishment 69ff,86,131,141
eucharist passim (see communion)
Evangelical Alliance 3,70,72,74, 85,91,97,118,165f,173,187
exclusion (from table) 49,51,86, 156ff,202
excommunication 48,50,54,79, 157,160

Free Church of Scotland 24f, 27,35
Free Churches (see also Dissenters, Nonconformists) 85, 114,121,182,185,192
Friends, Society of 75 (see also Quakers)

General Baptists 10,17f,41f, 60f,65,75,89,132f,141,158, 164,182,192,198
General Baptist Home Missionary Society 150
gowns (vestments) 77,87,90,169

hymns 3,17ff,88,107,164,172, 174,179f,197,201,204f
hyper-Calvinism 42,44,74,80

incarnation 7,91ff,101,116,118, 170f,173f,194
Independents 32,53,70,74,77f
infant baptism 1,32ff,47ff,56, 58ff,64,66f,74,77,79,197,199, 202f

Kilnahan's Irish Whisky 149

laying on of hands 122,126ff, 130f,137
London Baptist Association 149,183
Lord's Prayer 87
Lord's Supper passim (and see communion)
love feast 74,99,193
Lutherans 1,47

materialism 180f,185f,188
membership (of church) 33ff, 41,51,62,69f,74,77f,132, 158,160,197f
memorialism 3ff,8,10ff,14,19, 21f,24f,29,39,94,98f,113, 119,139,144f,171ff,179f,200
Methodism/Methodists 42,74,

142,200
Midland Association of General Baptists 132
ministers/ministry passim but esp.15,89f,121ff,129,132ff, 141,194
Moravians 24f,27

New Connexion of General Baptists 10,17,42
Nonconformists/Nonconformity (see also Dissenters, Free Churches) 2f,7,42,86,88f,115f,123,128,146f,151, 154,156,159,181f,184,187f,190,193
Northamptonshire Association 72,145

ordination 86,122ff,129ff,133, 135,137,168,184,204
organs 77,89
Oxford Movement (see also Catholic revivals, Tractarians) 91,186
Oxford Tracts 95,102,187

Particular Baptists 10,17f,34, 39ff,61,132f,140,142,164,192, 194,198
Passover 11f,98,104,150, 152ff,179
Pentecost 58,62,68,140
Plymouth Brethren 24f,146
prayer/prayer meetings 71,73,84, 88,122,126ff,130,143,145ff, 158,171,193
preachers/preaching 7,15,28,65, 84,90,136,160,164,168,170ff, 175,181f,193f,198,204
Presbyterians 32,74,133f
Primitive Methodists 74
Protestantism/Protestants 1,8, 53f,57f,60ff,67,71f,84ff, 107,109f,116,118f,148,164, 166ff,187,201f,204
Puritan movement/Puritans 1,10, 167f,176,181,193

Quakers 60 (see also Friends)

real presence 32,86,107,169, 188,204
rebaptism 199,203
Reformation 3,8,16,29,52,54,

60,84,86,110,160,167,172, 193,200f
reformers, the 1,8,58f,94, 106ff,144,168,174,192,194, 200f
'Reverend' (title) 89f
Ritualists 2,84ff,100,115f, 146,160,167,201
Roman Catholics//Romanism (see also Catholics) 1f,47,57,84,135, 141,160,165,167f,182,184,187,202
sacrifice 9f,12ff,32,101,104,192f
Sandemanians 24
Scotch Baptists 133f
Scottish Baptist churches 144
'sick' communion 138ff,143,145
Socinianism 7,60
Strict Baptists 34,54,72,78f, 135,150,169
Strict Baptist Society 74

teetotalism 148ff,160
temperance movement 121,147ff, 194,197
tickets (for Lord's Supper) 35, 158
tolerance/toleration 49f,54, 67,182
Tractarians 2,59,80,84ff,105,109, 114,118f,160,165ff,184ff,201 (see also Catholic revival)
transubstantiation 7,13,91ff,97, 103,105,107ff,167,169,203f

unity (with other Christians) 43ff,51ff,65,70ff,79f,112,140,142,144,184

Vatican Council, First 2,84,90, 187

weekly celebration 121,143ff
Wesleyans 17,74
West Midland Association 145
wine, unfermented, 2,121,147ff, 160,197

Zwinglian/Zwinglianism 3ff, 10ff,14,16,26,29,59,85,98, 104,112,160,172,174f,180, 188,192,197,202ff